ROUTLEDGE LIBRARY EDITIONS: OCCULTISM

I0130852

Volume 2

THE OCCULT SOURCEBOOK

THE OCCULT SOURCEBOOK

NEVILL DRURY AND GREGORY TILLETT

Illustrated by
ELIZABETH TRAFFORD SMITH

Routledge
Taylor & Francis Group
LONDON AND NEW YORK

First published in 1978 by Routledge & Kegan Paul Ltd

This edition first published in 2020
by Routledge
2 Park Square, Milton Park, Abingdon, Oxon OX14 4RN

and by Routledge
52 Vanderbilt Avenue, New York, NY 10017

Routledge is an imprint of the Taylor & Francis Group, an informa business

British Library Cataloguing in Publication Data
A catalogue record for this book is available from the British Library

ISBN: 978-0-367-33602-8 (Set)
ISBN: 978-0-429-34389-6 (Set) (ebk)
ISBN: 978-0-367-34913-4 (Volume 2) (hbk)
ISBN: 978-0-367-34916-5 (Volume 2) (pbk)
ISBN: 978-0-429-32868-8 (Volume 2) (ebk)

Publisher's Note
The publisher has gone to great lengths to ensure the quality of this reprint but
points out that some imperfections in the original copies may be apparent.

Disclaimer
The publisher has made every effort to trace copyright holders and would welcome
correspondence from those they have been unable to trace.

THE OCCULT SOURCEBOOK

NEVILL DRURY and GREGORY TILLETT

Illustrated by Elizabeth Trafford Smith

ROUTLEDGE & KEGAN PAUL

London, Boston and Henley

First published in 1978
by Routledge & Kegan Paul Ltd
39 Store Street, London WC1E 7DD,
Broadway House, Newtown Road,
Henley-on-Thames, Oxon RG9 1EN and
9 Park Street,
Boston, Mass. 02108, USA
Reprinted in 1980
Set in 11 on 13pt Ehrhardt by
HBM Typesetting Ltd, Chorley, Lancs.
and printed in Great Britain by
Unwin Bros Ltd
The Gresham Press, Old Woking, Surrey

British Library Cataloguing in Publication Data

Drury, Nevill
The occult sourcebook,
1. Occult sciences
I. Title   II. Tillett, Gregory
138   BF1411   78-40393

ISBN 0 7100 0096 0 (c)
ISBN 0 7100 8875 2 (p)

for Colin Wilson . . . from two Outsiders

Contents

CONTENTS

Introduction

The occult is no longer what it used to be. Only a few years ago, especially around the time of the Satanic film *Rosemary's Baby*, the term 'occult' would have been reserved for obscure, demonic and vaguely diabolical practices alone. In San Francisco at this time Anton Szandor La Vey, who starred as the devil in the above film, was establishing his Satanic Church; Charles Manson was incarnating the Devil and Christ simultaneously; Bishop Pike was endeavouring to communicate with his suicide son through a medium; and witchcraft was thriving.

These days, we believe, the occult has a wider connotation. *The Exorcist* notwithstanding, the term 'occult' today includes ESP, Kirlian photography, reincarnation, palmistry, astrology, faith healing, white magic, Tarot, and even out-of-the-body experiences. The occult, too, is no longer disreputable. Scientists at Stanford investigate psychic Uri Geller; in California Professor Charles Tart carries out laboratory tests on Robert Monroe, a subject who can astral-travel at will; Arthur Koestler, previously doubtful about the powers of yogis, comes forth with a scientific rationale of the paranormal in his *Roots of Coincidence*; Colin Wilson meanwhile coins the term 'Faculty X' to describe the psychic potential of man which he believes marks the next phase of man's evolution.

In short, the occult is about man's hidden potential. Much of this, of course, relates to how he thinks and how he perceives. Many aspects of the occult dealt with in this book show how man can enlarge his consciousness.

This sourcebook was compiled with the idea in mind that many people are for the first time becoming engrossed by the possibilities underlying the occult. It seemed a reasonable idea to produce a series of articles on key areas with specially chosen references for further reading. Each of these articles, we hope, may be a 'leaping off point' to a more detailed study in those areas which the reader finds most interesting or useful. Finally we have incorporated a lengthy 'Who's Who of the occult' to provide pocket-size biographies of some of the more amazing figures who have already travelled down the mystic path. Some of these were inspired, some of them were charlatans, but all those who have been included are important in one way or another.

The occult has now moved out of the realm of superstition into the area dealing with *what man can become*. This is its relevance. It may also explain why, for many, the occult has replaced orthodox institutional religion as the pathway for man in the Age of Aquarius.

Nevill Drury and Gregory Tillett

Part

I

Source Areas

ESP

Extrasensory perception is the ability to transmit and receive information by means other than the recognized senses. People often surprise themselves by simultaneously referring to obscure thoughts in conversation, or perhaps a person acts upon an intuition about an unforeseeable course of action which later proves to be correct. Another will dream of, or foresee, an event before it occurs or perhaps is able to receive 'mental impressions' from a friend while concentrating. All of these occurrences could be cited as examples of extrasensory perception, which is normally divided into three areas: *clairvoyance*, the extrasensory perception of events; *telepathy*, the direct 'transmission' of ideas; and *precognition*, the perception of future events.

Although such phenomena have always had a mystic tinge about them, and have been regarded traditionally as the faculties of soothsayers and oracles, the serious, scientific study of ESP occurrences is less than a century old. In Victorian times, ESP was considered to be a possible 'sixth sense' and was researched by a number of important scientists, including Sir William Crookes, Sir Oliver Lodge and Alfred Wallace. In 1882 the famous Society for Psychical Research was founded at Cambridge University with Henry Sidgwick as its first president.

It has to be admitted, that like a number of spiritualist and occult phenomena, for every possible genuine occurrence there are countless falsifications and the SPR got off to a bad start. In July 1882 Sidgwick prematurely announced that he had found conclusive evidence for ESP in a clergyman, Reverend Creery, his five daughters, and their servant. Later, embarrassingly, it was discovered that they had been using a code to trick the researchers.

Another such case followed hard on its heels: that of Messrs Smith and Blackburn. Smith would hold Blackburn's hands, and concentrate, and seem to read his thoughts as Blackburn imagined them. Sidgwick and two

3

of his colleagues, Edmund Gurney and Frederic Myers, with whom he was later to share fame as a spiritualist researcher, investigated the case. Myers derived a test whereby he would make a detailed picture and show it to Blackburn who would in turn attempt to 'transmit' it into the mind of Smith, behind whom he stood. Smith, who was shrouded in a blanket, was able to reproduce the pictures fairly accurately, and Myers and his colleagues had to admit they were convinced. Accordingly, the SPR recorded the case in its annals as genuine. Years later, in 1908, Blackburn made the sensational admission that he had cheated during the sessions. He had hurriedly copied the drawing onto a cigarette paper and concealed it inside a propelling pencil which he managed to pass to his partner unseen. Since Smith had been concealed beneath a blanket for secrecy purposes, he was able to rummage for the picture in the pencil. There was sufficient light for him to reproduce a reasonable 'telepathic' copy.

The test conditions in the early investigations were very poor, and the SPR decided to try to improve and regulate its experimental procedures. From this time onwards, research into ESP took the form of experimental testing whereby subjects had to attempt to record above-chance odds in telepathic guessing sessions.

In England, G. N. M. Tyrrell constructed a device made up of five boxes each containing a light bulb. The circuitry was designed so that a certain bulb would light up when the lid of its box was lifted. Basically, the experiment tested possible telepathic communication between the subject and the experimenter, who decided which light would come on, on each occasion. One of Tyrrell's subjects, a Miss Johnson, gained some high scores using this device. However, a colleague of Tyrrell's, G. W. Fisk, claimed that the experiment could only be valid if the selection of the lights was completely random. He said, quite rightly, that a person would tend not to choose a box which has just 'lit up'. In the case of random numbers, however, a given number will follow itself about half the time. When Tyrrell introduced a 'randomizer' into his device, Miss Johnson scored at only the normal chance rate.

Meanwhile in the 1930s serious research into ESP was well under way in the United States under the auspices of Dr Joseph Rhine and his wife Louisa at Duke University. Earlier experiments had been carried out by Professor John Coover at Stanford and Professor William McDougall at Harvard, but Rhine's work was to be the most far-reaching. In 1932 he had some good results while using Zener cards with thirty-two subjects in a clairvoyance experiment. The cards had been designed by a colleague, K. E. Zener, and incorporated five distinct symbols: a square, a circle, a cross, three wavy lines and a star. Rhine's subjects scored 207 successes out of 800 tries while chance would have expected only 160. The odds against were in excess of a million to one.

Rhine gradually sifted out his most gifted subjects and continued to test them with Zener card experiments, which were basically experimentally controlled card-guessing sessions. He soon began to discover that his subjects performed best under certain conditions and in his book *Extra-Sensory Perception* (1934) he stressed that for best results, subjects should be open-minded, be allowed an informal atmosphere rather than a restrictive one, and should be neither extravagantly praised nor discouraged in their results. Rhine also found that subjects tended to improve after the first hundred test runs, and that married people or friends often demonstrated a better 'psychic' rapport.

Rhine's work at Duke gained considerable attention in the 1930s and several sceptical psychologists, including W. S. Cox at Princeton and J. H. Heinlein at Johns Hopkins, were unable to duplicate Rhine's findings. After Rhine's cards were produced commercially in the United States, some critics also argued that it was easy to see through the cards or detect the imprint on the back surface of each card. Rhine insisted, however, that his results had been derived using thick opaque cards, and that subjects had not been allowed to touch the cards in any way.

Another psychologist of the period, J. L. Kennedy, suggested in 1938 that future ESP experiments should attempt to minimize all sensory cues between experimenters – whether visual, auditory or 'subliminal' – and should eliminate all types of preferences or non-randomness. He also considered that at least two people should keep records of scores and results.

In 1940 the Duke researchers published a book entitled *Extra-Sensory Perception After Sixty Years*. Professor Rhine and his colleagues considered a test held in October 1938 and February 1939 to be one of their best ESP trials because of its 'advances in experimental precaution'. There were two experimenters, J. L. Woodruff and J. G. Pratt, together with the subject. Pratt acted as 'observer'. Meanwhile, Woodruff sat at one end of a table and a screen 18″ high separated him from the subject who was seated at the other end. The screen had a one-way aperture which allowed the experimenter to observe a pointer held in the subject's hand. The subject had to guess the top card in the experimenter's hand by pointing with a pencil to one of five optional ESP symbols on his side of the screen.

Since the experimenter's pack consisted of twenty-five cards, this was the number of trials in each series. The 'observer' carefully recorded the symbol sequences by himself as an extra check. Woodruff and Pratt held over 2,000 runs of twenty-five trials in this manner.

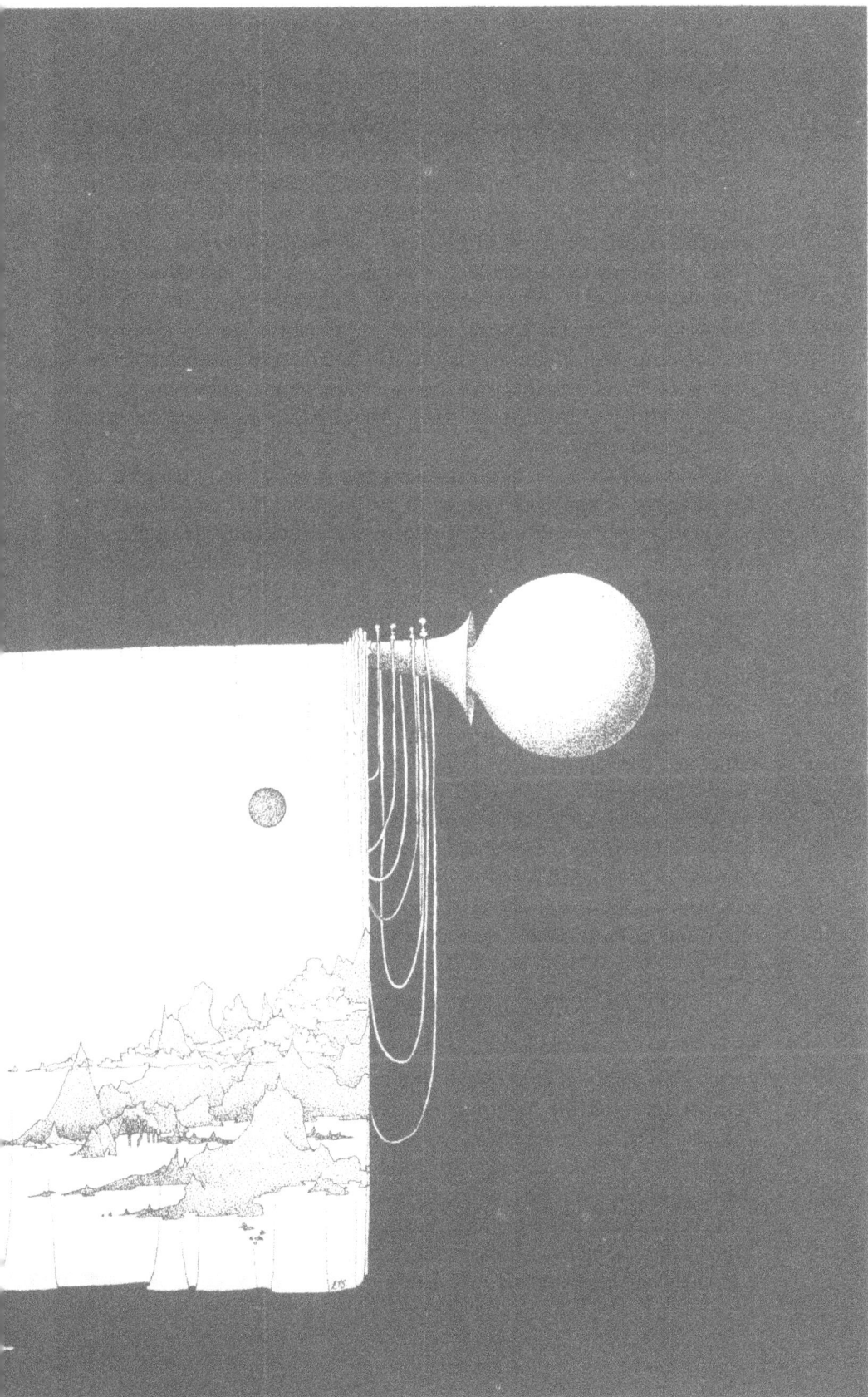

The result was not dramatic in an obvious sense. Thirty-two subjects scored 12,489 successful hits out of 60,000 when they could have expected 12,000 by chance alone. Nevertheless, the odds against the additional 489 hits occurring by chance were more than a million to one. One of Rhine's staunchest critics, Professor C. E. M. Hansel, has admitted that there are 'clear indications that something other than guesswork or experimental error was involved in this experiment and also that its effects were by no means negligible in the case of at least one subject' (*ESP: A Scientific Evaluation*, p. 89). However, Hansel felt that the experiment could be invalidated unless the cards were shuffled between runs, and we only have Pratt's word for it that this was done. Hansel thus believes that the case is not conclusive (p. 103).

In England, Dr S. G. Soal, a leading parapsychologist, attempted to duplicate the Rhine experiments, at first without success. However, Soal noticed that two of his subjects achieved significantly above-chance scores for both the card ahead and the one behind. One of these subjects, Basil Shackleton, was tested for ESP by Soal and Mrs K. M. Goldney between 1941 and 1943. Shackleton had to guess the identity of cards with drawings of certain animals on them. He sat in one room while the experimenter sat in another, calling out when Shackleton should guess. They could not see each other. Meanwhile, the experimenter would show a random number to another person in his room (the 'agent') who would glance at a corresponding card. The test was to see whether Shackleton could telepathically predict which card would come next.

On one occasion, Shackleton managed to obtain scores of the '+1' type, that is, he guessed one card ahead. In 3,789 trials he was successful 1,101 times when he should have scored only 776 by chance. In fact, he managed to achieve high scores on several occasions, and the tests were regarded by Rhine and by Professor Hutchinson of Yale as among the best ever made.

NEW DEVELOPMENTS IN ESP

Most of the pioneering ESP research was based on documented card-guessing sessions and correspondingly, most of the criticisms that arose were an attack on the 'tightness' of the laboratory testing procedures. Professor Hansel, for example, was especially critical of the fact that a number of the Duke experiments *could* be fabricated by trickery and cheating, without inferring, of course, that they necessarily were.

In recent years, however, ESP research has taken on wider horizons. The Apollo 14 moon astronauts undertook an ESP experiment with colleagues on the earth and produced an above-chance test result, and

Dr Eugene Konecci of NASA told an international astronautical conference in Paris in 1963 that the United States was now pursuing ESP research more seriously since it was apparent that the Russians were investigating it as a means of communication in outer space.

In their book *Psychic Discoveries Behind The Iron Curtain*, Sheila Ostrander and Lynn Schroeder described Russian attempts to 'catch the tracks of telepathy as it arrived in the brain'. Dr Lutsia Pavlova of the University of Leningrad, and Dr Genady Sergeyev, a well-known mathematician, harnessed one of their best telepathic subjects, Karl Nikolaiev, in an electroencephelograph apparatus. His respiration, heartbeat, eye movements and brain wave patterns were all recorded. Meanwhile, his friend, Yuri Kamensky, a biophysicist, was to attempt to communicate telepathically with him from Moscow. Kamensky began to concentrate and, three seconds later, Nikolaiev's brain waves changed drastically on the monitoring devices at Leningrad University! (p. 22) Dr Pavlova says that following further EEG documentation of both subjects, it is clear that when telepathic rapport is achieved 'the brain activation quickly becomes specific and switches to the rear, afferent regions of the brain' (p. 23). This focusing of force field waves has also been noted in the EEG registration of another remarkable subject, Nelya Mikhailova, who is able telepathically to order objects to move, and under laboratory conditions also willed the white and the yolk of an egg to separate. Dr Sergeyev says that while most people generate three or four times more electrical voltage in the back of their brains than in the front, Mrs Mikhailova generates *fifty times* the amount! He has concluded that measuring the voltage there is thus a good indicator of ESP potential.

Interesting EEG research has also been done in the West by the Maimonodes dream-state researchers in New York. Basically, the testing has been for psi-phenomena in the dream-state. Researchers Montague Ullman, Stanley Krippner and Alan Vaughan wanted to establish whether, under laboratory conditions, a psychic person could influence by will the images occurring in the dreams of another person, perhaps situated miles away.

Rapid eye movements (REM) indicate when a person is dreaming, so the Maimonodes team argued that the best period of dream recall would be just after this phase of sleep. Meanwhile, they selected certain images for telepathic transmission and these included detailed and distinctive paintings by Henri Rousseau, Salvador Dali, Marc Chagall and other artists.

A subject would try to 'beam' the picture to a given recipient who was being monitored under laboratory conditions elsewhere, and who would be wakened after the REM period of sleep for dream recall. A panel of judges would scrutinize the imagery content of the dream and decide on objective criteria as to whether there was sufficient parallel to warrant claiming an above-chance 'psychic transmission'. Their results were generally quite impressive. One example involved the English para-psychologist Malcolm Bessent and the rock group, the Grateful Dead. In early 1971 the group gave six concerts in Port Chester, New York. During these sessions large-scale slides were thrown up on the screen and the rock group asked the audience to try mentally to transmit their content into the dreams of Bessent who was located forty-five miles away at the Maimonodes Dream Laboratory in Brooklyn.

Bessent was to go to sleep at 11.30 during the second concert. The target slide was a picture called the *Seven Spinal Chakras* by Scralian, which shows a man in the lotus position practising yogic meditation. The seven chakras, or spiritual centres of the nervous column, are depicted as bright orbs of energy in the painting. Forty-Five miles away, Malcolm Bessent dreamed the following:

> I was very interested in . . . using natural energy . . . I was talking
> to this guy who said he'd invented a way of using solar energy and he
> showed me this box . . . to catch the light from the sun which was all
> we needed to generate and store the energy . . . I was thinking about
> rocket ships . . . I'm remembering a dream I had about an energy
> box . . . and a spinal column. . . .

The dream is suggestive, and there are certain overlaps, particularly if we remember that the mind operates symbolically. The human frame in yogic terms, is indeed a box for storing energy, and the spinal column is the vital causeway up which the Kundalini energy is raised.

At this stage, the experiments in dream telepathy are still being refined, but the work of the Maimonodes team has been praised by leading psychologists Sir Cyril Burt and Dr John Beloff.

What is most important in all the new research, both in the USSR and in the West, is that there is a new positive attitude among scientists to researching ESP, which did not exist on a large scale even a few years ago. And the new direction attempts to take ESP away from the spiritualist fringe into an area of systematic knowledge, so that it may complement what is already known about the functioning and potential of the brain.

SOURCEBOOKS

J. B. RHINE ET AL.: *Extra-Sensory Perception After Sixty Years*, Bruce Humphries, Houston, first published 1940, new edn 1966.

A classic account of all the major pioneering experiments conducted at Duke University, compiled by Rhine, J. G. Pratt and other members of the Parapsychological Laboratory. It is especially useful for its critical comments on testing procedures.

C. E. M. HANSEL: *ESP: A Scientific Evaluation*, MacGibbon & Kee, London and Scribners, New York, 1966.

An important work criticizing the early experimental methods of testing for ESP, but nevertheless, presenting a good coverage of the subject up to around 1960. Hansel tends to be pessimistic about the chances of proving ESP under laboratory conditions. His book contains some details of the work of Professor Leonard Vasiliev at Leningrad, but none of the more important later developments of Dr Pavlova and Dr Sergeyev. He continues to be the staunchest critic of ESP research.

SHEILA OSTRANDER and LYNN SCHROEDER: *Psychic Discoveries Behind The Iron Curtain*, Bantam Books, New York, 1971 and Abacus, London, 1973.

An exciting, journalistic account of new developments for ESP testing in the Eastern bloc countries including full accounts of the abilities of Mrs Nelya Mikhailova and Wolf Messing, a telepathic subject who impressed Freud and Einstein, and also details of the Nikolaiev-Kamensky tests.

MONTAGUE ULLMANN, STANLEY KRIPPNER and ALAN VAUGHAN: *Dream Telepathy*, Turnstone Books, London, 1973.

The first full account of the Maimonodes dream-testing research, with documented descriptions of telepathic dream-recall occurrences.

Meditation and Biofeedback

In recent years there has been increased interest in Yoga, Zen Buddhism and Maharaji Mahesh's Transcendental Meditation exercises. It seems that the direction has been from activity in the outer world back toward the inner world of meditation and contemplation.

Basically, meditation involves the practice of enhancing the quality of inner peace, through what may be termed 'alert relaxation'. A person meditating is not drowsy, but his thought train changes so that instead of observing all the details of external reality, he is more involved with the source of thought itself, and the underlying one-ness of manifestation.

Meditation is a key practice in the Zen sects, and in Raja Yoga. In the West it also plays a significant part in magical practice and Roman Catholicism, especially the Cistercian and Carthusian traditions. William Johnston, a Western theologian with a specialized interest in Eastern mysticism, has pointed out that just as Zen uses paradoxical *koans*, or tales that force the meditator to transcend rational thinking, and just as yogis use the mandala in meditation, Christianity also has certain related practices. He believes that meditation resembles Christian 'contemplation', and notes that recently a Zen practitioner demonstrated to a group of Christians that the cross could be used as a type of koan symbol.

It seems clear, then, that meditation itself is a mental process not necessarily bound to any particular religious or mystical school. Edward Maupin has described it as 'deep passivity, combined with awareness'. In yoga and other Eastern meditative disciplines, the practitioner sits cross-legged, often in the 'full lotus' position so that the right foot rests on the left thigh, and the left foot rests on the right thigh. In yoga, the meditator is allowed to close his eyes, but Zen, which is more oriented to the 'here and now' requires that the eyes are open. The gaze is cast downwards about a metre in front of the knees.

Until recently, it was difficult to assess what types of mental activity were occurring in yogis and mystics as they meditated. However, analytical science has now enabled specific tabulation of their brain wave activity under laboratory conditions. Basically, the meditators have been wired to an EEG machine and all brain wave functions have been meticulously recorded.

The existence of brain waves was first established by a German scientist named Hans Berger, shortly after World War I. Berger attached two electrodes to the scalp of a young mental patient, and with the help of an indicator, noted that there was an electronic response. Berger considered that there were two main types of brain wave patterns; alpha, connected with passivity, and beta, associated with concentration and problem-solving. It has since been found that there are four main types of brain wave activity:

(1) *Alpha:* This has a frequency around 8–12 cycles per second and produces a focusing on inner states of awareness, including mystical consciousness. Most people who close their eyes produce some alpha waves, but it is harder to produce with the eyes open. High level alpha activity indicates a state of deep concentration.

(2) *Beta:* This occurs in alert, waking consciousness, and measures around 13 cycles per second. Whereas *alpha* relates to the inner world of thought, *beta*, is more a part of the external world of action.

(3) *Theta:* This is linked to the mental state of drowsiness, and the condition immediately preceding sleep. It measures around 4–7 cycles per second.

(4) *Delta:* Delta rhythms are produced in deep sleep and measure 0–4 cycles per second.

Experiments have been conducted in Japan and in the United States to identify which of these brain wave patterns occurred during meditation. Drs Akira Kasamatsu and Tomio Hirai of Tokyo University, employed the services of forty-eight Zen Buddhist monks and recorded their EEGs during meditation. Some of the 'masters' produced alpha waves after only 50 seconds and the electrodes did not appear to interfere with the meditation. It was noted that if a clicking noise was made, this blocked the production of alpha waves for 3–5 seconds, by interfering with the concentration. (This was not the case in another study, made of Raja yogis, who were totally oblivious of any movement or noise in the environment.) Kasamatsu and Hirai noted that their Zen subjects sometimes passed from the alpha state into theta. By contrast, in the Raja Yoga study of Anand, Chhina and Singh (1961) the meditators produced persistent alpha waves, which were heightened during *samadhi* (deep concentration).

In 1958 Dr Joe Kamiya of the University of Chicago was researching the brain wave activity registered during the sleep state and, in particular, the spasmodic traces of alpha. He wired a subject up to record his EEGs and asked him to guess the state of mind he was in. At first the subject guessed correctly at only the normal rate of 50 per cent but by the fourth day he guessed his mental activity correctly 400 times in a row! This was an amazing discovery because it showed that a person could, with practice, learn to identify his mental state. Kamiya later discovered also that it was possible for a person to learn to sustain a given state, such as alpha, and the modern technique of biofeedback was about to be born. The next step was to concoct a machine which would transmit the presence of alpha waves as measured by the EEG into an audible sound which could be heard by the meditator, thus showing his progress. The biofeedback device thus developed as an aid to maintaining a positive and contemplative state of mind.

Further devices have since been invented which allow a person to recognize all of his brain wave activity, and in some cases the signal is a light rather than an audible tone. Biofeedback has become especially popular in the United States, where it has been hailed in some circles as a 'short cut to mystical enlightenment'.

Several commentators, including William Johnston, have been keen to point out that while contemplative states contain alpha, alpha in itself does not equate with mystical consciousness per se. In fact, theta waves may be just as important. Many artists and writers gain inspiration from the theta dream state, and it is generally associated with creativity. Marvin Karlins and Lewis Andrews have also pointed out that each of the mental states has its place and the pursuit of alpha for its own sake is not necessarily a good idea. Some subjects have found the transition from beta to alpha 'a source of anxiety and apprehension', not the state of well-being and passivity that is usually claimed, and they go on to say that 'some alpha experiences are strictly a function of the subject's expectations.'

Nevertheless, biofeedback has undoubtedly put mystical states of consciousness on the scientific map. We can now charter meditation and be surer of its positive effects. Through EEG recordings we can tell how deep a state of contemplation is, and through biofeedback, ordinary urban people, who may not have had the opportunity of joining a Zen monastery can now regulate their meditative development by means of an indicator machine.

SOURCEBOOKS

MARVIN KARLINS and LEWIS ANDREWS: *Biofeedback*, Garnstone Press, London, 1973.

A lucid, popular account of the history and background of biofeedback and the study of altered states of awareness. The authors also consider the relationship of biofeedback training to ESP ability and mind over matter. Their book contains an excellent, annotated bibliography.

CHARLES TART (ed.): *Altered States of Consciousness*, John Wiley, New York, 1969.

Already a virtual classic in its field, Tart's book is one of the most complete anthologies of key articles in the area of documented states of consciousness. Included are accounts by Drs Kasamatsu and Tomio; Anand, Chhina and Singh; Dr Joe Kamiya; and Edward Maupin. There are also important related articles on the hallucinogens, hypnosis and dreaming.

WILLIAM JOHNSTON: *Silent Music: The Science of Meditation*, Collins, London, 1974.

A readable account of meditation practice and altered states of consciousness by a Christian theologian who nevertheless has extensive personal knowledge of Zen training. Johnston believes that meditation and biofeedback techniques may revolutionize religions generally, and ground them more solidly in experience.

Dreams

Throughout history, man has regarded the dream state as something awesome and mysterious, in which strange supernatural omens could be revealed, or perhaps new courses of action and behaviour demonstrated. In the Bible we find the account of Joseph, who dreamed that one day his whole family would bow to him. His dream did not show the members of his family in the literal sense, but used the language of symbols: 'Behold, I have dreamed a dream more; and behold the sun and the moon, and the eleven stars made obeisance before me. . . .' In this instance, Joseph's dream followed the mythological symbolism of representing his father as the sun, his mother as the moon and his brothers as companion stars.

A quite different culture, that of the Iroquois Indians, also paid special attention to the symbolism of dreams. An early Jesuit missionary among the Iroquois, Father Fremin, wrote that they had substituted the dream for a divinity; in other words, they had made dreams their god. In 1642 a Huron man (the Hurons were one of the Iroquois tribes) dreamed that a non-Huron Iroquois had captured him and burned him alive. When he awoke, a council of chiefs was held to discuss the portents of the dream. The chiefs decided that the events of the dream must not come to pass, so several Indians procured firebrands and tried to trap the dreamer and burn him to death. Realizing the extreme danger he was in, the Indian grabbed a small dog and paraded around with it over his shoulders, begging that it be sacrificed instead of him. Finally, the dog was clubbed to death and roasted in flames, as an offering to the demon of war 'begging him to accept this semblance instead of the reality of the dream . . .'.

Dreams have indeed exercised a special fascination in both ancient times and in the present. The Egyptian pharaohs believed that dreams were messages from the gods, and Hippocrates, the 'father of Medicine' wrote a lengthy treatise on dreams. The classical Chinese Taoists were interested in speculating on whether dreams were more real than everyday life, and many native societies, including the Fiji islanders, believed dreams represented the wanderings of the soul. In modern times Frederich Kekule, the organic chemist, pondered on the structure of the benzene molecule, and then had a dream which revealed its formation, and included the symbolism of a snake eating its tail, which is also a symbol from alchemical mythology. One of the most famous predictive dreams is Abraham Lincoln's dream of his own assassination, and another dreamer, J. W. Dunne, formulated the philosophy of 'serial time' on the basis of his dreams. He had developed the particular faculty of predictive dreaming, and on one occasion dreamed that the *Flying Scotsman* steam train would crash near Forth Bridge several months before it did, in April 1914. Dunne speculated that the universe consisted of parallel bands or spectra of events and that events occurred at one level before another. In this way, he thought, the dreamer or claivoyant may have access to a plane of reality before the events 'manifested' in the everyday world. Dreams thus revealed a different dimension of causality.

How have dreams influenced the occult and what special role do they play? Apart from their elusive and mysterious quality, dreams are also regarded by modern-day occultists as significant for two major reasons. First, Jung's analysis of dreams has provided us with several important concepts – like the Collective Unconscious and the theory of Archetypes – which are the basis of modern magical thinking. Second, the dream may be used as part of a technique for 'astral travelling'.

While it is true that Freud first showed that dreams relate to the *dreamer*, rather than being portents from external deities, Jung discovered that the religious side of dreaming could be explained by potent, mystical energies deep in the psyche itself. Originally, Freud had thought that dreams were most relevant to a person's *conscious* thoughts. He soon discovered, however, that when a patient was encouraged to discuss his dreams, he would uncover *unconscious* elements as well. These often revealed neuroses and, thus, if the patient could recognize the symptoms, he could benefit therapeutically from the analysis of his dreams.

Freud tended to analyse dreams from the viewpoint of their having certain motifs whose meaning was constant. The following is a typically Freudian dream analysis, and is made by a particularly fervent follower of Freud, Angel Garma, Spanish psychoanalyst:

Dream : 'A Lion was pursuing me and I wanted to escape. I was shut up in a room and I could not find the door to get out. I felt terribly anxious. . . .'
Garma's explanation : 'Dreams such as this are frequent in women who have not yet started a normal heterosexual life. An unmarried woman often has the above dream. The lion, like wild animals, monsters, or

abnormal or bad people, represent a sexually excited man pursuing her. She cannot escape because of her own desires . . . ' (p. 115).

Another, more questionable analysis was the following:

Dream: '*My father tells me that if I do not pass my B.A. examination I shall not be able to marry George. . . .*'

Explanation: 'A woman dreamed this shortly before her marriage. She doubted her instinctual capacity, which appears as anxiety about her B.A. exam. The father is her super-ego, or psycho-analyst, telling her that she cannot marry unless her genital response is normal' (p. 118).

Whereas Freud and his school have tended to uncover sexual motifs in dreams, Jung was anxious to discover why certain symbols rather than others had occurred in the dream. For example, the key in a lock, the wielding of a heavy stick or the battering ram, may all occur in dreams as sexual motifs. Jung writes: 'The real task is to understand why the key has been preferred to the stick or the stick to the ram. And sometimes this might even lead one to discover that it is not the sexual act at all that is represented but some quite different psychological point' (*Man and His Symbols*, p. 13).

Jung further made the vital discovery that not all contents of a dream relate to *personal* memories or neuroses, and this is extremely relevant to magical theory. 'There are many symbols', he wrote, 'that are not individual but collective in their nature and origin . . .'. These were images that Jung called the Archetypes of the Collective Unconscious, and in effect they represent a body of mythological images which recur throughout the psychic history of mankind, in all his creative functions: in art, in music, in legends, in poetry. Jung believed that because man had experienced certain 'constants' in his environment, like the sun, the moon, the stars, the ocean, changes of season etc. he began to formulate these as basic images in his psyche. However, they were not impressed upon man in an abstract way, but as deities of nature so that all these forces of nature became gods. Jung claimed as a result of thousands of analyses of dreams from this level of the mind that what was revealed was the myth or symbol, the *archetype* rather than the process or event itself. The mind tended to formulate these experiences in an anthropomorphic way.

The sun is an especially significant archetype and has long been an object of veneration because of its eternal nature, and because it is the source of *life* and *light*. Sun gods are found in many religions – Apollo Helios in Greece; Ohrmazd in ancient Persia, Osiris in ancient Egypt and Christ in our own culture. Invariably they represent life, rebirth, light and purity. What Jung is saying is that they are relevant to our psyches because they represent symbols of inner harmony and integration and Jung believed one of the main functions of the psychoanalysis of dreams, was to come to terms with what dreams were trying to say. In other words, one has to recognize both the personal and archetypal contents and try to learn the lesson of their symbolism.

Most practitioners of modern magic accept the Jungian view that the gods of mythology, which may be revealed in dreams or in visions, trances and ritual, represent inner processes which are normally subconscious. By using the Tree of Life, *which relates these gods as symbols of the mind*, the magician comes to know and integrate the more transcendental processes of his mind.

The second major function of dreams in the occult, as mentioned above, is their use as a method of astral projection (or out-of-the-body experience). Celia Green has noted in her book *Lucid Dreams* that we can now separate, as a special category, those dreams where the dreamer *knows* he is dreaming. He finds himself conscious within the dream, and sometimes able to direct his dream and his actions within it. When this occurs, the dreamer may experience the very remarkable process of finding himself 'outside his body'. It is as if he has entered a new time–space location which is populated not by the objects of the real world but rather of his thoughts, his imaginings and perhaps the symbols of his unconscious mind.

The magician recognizes in this phenomenon an extraordinary new dimension of life and being. He finds new access to his creative energies and sources of inspiration; he finds himself in weird and surreal mythological landscapes; he discovers that he can move without the limitations of his physical body, *to any location where he wills himself to go*.

Because of this strange application of the dream state, the psychical researcher Sylvan Muldoon decided to formulate an exercise of dreaming which meant that one willed oneself to dream a certain way. The person had to try to retain his consciousness in the dream state, and could *will* certain images to appear in a certain sequence by 'programming' his dream. Out-of-the-body experiences are related to dreams of flying and floating and so Muldoon suggested that if a person willed himself to dream these sequences he could find himself astral travelling into new dimensions of the mind.

Dreams are thus valuable not only for an analysis of sexual, and other, neuroses, but they may also be used as a technique for acquiring magical consciousness. The dream, on the one hand, is a sequence of visual events which demands to be understood. But it is also the realm of ideas and thought processes which allows the magician to impose his will and to use the dream to increase the range of his perception.

SOURCEBOOKS

(Preference is given here to books on dreams and related areas which are relevant to the occult.)

RAYMOND DE BECKER: *The Meaning of Dreams*, Castle Books, New York.
   A useful treatment of both the historical sources for dream divination and prophecy and also different frameworks of explanation. De Becker, who has also written an important work on homosexuality, was a pupil of Carl Jung.

CARL JUNG: *Man and His Symbols*, Dell, New York, 1968.

CARL JUNG: *The Archetypes and the Collective Unconscious*, Routledge & Kegan Paul, London, 1959.
   These are both classic works of Jungian psychology, but are especially interesting for their relevance to inner psychical processes. Jung relates the archetypes to all forms of creativity. The first of the above-mentioned works also contains articles by M. L. von Franz Joseph, Joseph Henderson, Jolande Jacobi and Aniela Jaffe, all of whom are distinguished analysts in the Jungian school.

ANGEL GARMA: *The Psychoanalysis of Dreams*, Pall Mall, London, 1966.
   An interesting volume on dream analysis from the Freudian viewpoint with a large section on genital symbolism in dreams. The book contains some fascinating illustrations from both classical and modern sources, which are included for their symbolic content.

GAY GAER LUCE and JULIUS SEGAL: *Sleep*; Heinemann, London, 1967.
   Gay Luce is a prize-winning popular writer on scientific themes, and she prepared a review of sleep research for the National Institute of Mental Health in America. Dr Segal is a psychologist and also works for the Institute. This book is one of the best general accounts of sleep and dreaming and contains sections on both the bodily mechanisms of sleep and also the meaning of dream symbolism.

CELIA GREEN: *Lucid Dreams*, Hamish Hamilton, London, 1968.
   The companion volume to *Out-of-the-Body Experiences* by the Director of the Institute of Psychophysical Research in Oxford. Special attention is given to the accounts by the astral projectionist Oliver Fox, but the work is a valuable and scholarly comparative source.

SYLVAN MULDOON and HEREWARD CARRINGTON: *The Projection of the Astral Body*, Rider, London, 3rd impression 1971.
   Muldoon developed a special technique of using dreams to initiate out-of-the-body experiences, and this book contains a full account of both his 'floating' imagery sequences and his favourite controlled dream, which was to will himself to rise upwards in an elevator, then leave it at the 'top floor'.

Reincarnation

Reincarnation, or the belief that the human soul or consciousness continues to be reborn through a series of lifetimes, is one of the most widespread religious beliefs.

Its most prominent representation is in Hinduism and Buddhism. In the *Bhagavad Gita* we find a dialogue between Krishna, the noble and wise spiritual mentor, and his disciple Arjuna. Krishna explains that it is only the spiritually illumined who know of their former incarnations: 'Both I and thou have passed through many births. Mine are known to me, but thou knowest not of thine. . . . I incarnate from age to age for the preservation of the just, the destruction of the wicked and the establishment of righteousness. . . .' Krishna also goes on to say that according to our deeds in one life, so we find ourselves incarnating into a family appropriate to our spiritual attainment: 'The man whose devotion has been broken off by death goeth to the regions of the righteous, where he dwells for an immensity of years and is then born again on earth in a pure and fortunate family; or even in a family of those who are spiritually illuminated. . . .'

The Tibetan Buddhists believe that the highest Lamas continue to be reborn as spiritual leaders of their community. When a Dalai Lama has died, it becomes necessary to search through the kingdom to find the valid successor. In his book *Meditation, the Inward Art*, Bradford Smith describes how this was done:

When the previous Dalai Lama died, wise men had gone forth to seek the new holy one, and had found a little boy who recognized things that had belonged to his predecessor and could pick them out unerringly from among similar objects. . . . [This is an example, he continues] of the universal religious impulse and of the way man seeks to represent the cycle of death and rebirth that runs through all of nature. In Tibetan Buddhism, with its firm faith in the rebirth of the soul, not only of Dalai Lamas but of all, and of a progress based upon behaviour during past lives, this impulse is dramatically present . . .

It seems certain that the ancient Egyptian followers of Amen-Ra, who also believed in reincarnation, derived their belief from observing nature. It was clear to them that the sun sank or 'died', each evening in the West, and was 'reborn' with each dawn. The sun was also a vital symbol of life, and so the Egyptian who threw in his lot with the sun god could be assured of continuing and everlasting well-being. He too would follow the cycles of birth and rebirth.

Perhaps as a result of the Egyptian influence in ancient Greece, a number of prominent philosophers continued the idea of reincarnation. Pythagoras (582–507 BC) believed that he had once been a man named Aethalides and later Euphorbus, slain at the siege of Troy. Mercury, the messenger of the gods, had granted him the special faculty of being able to remember his previous lives. Socrates and Plato also believed that the soul passed through many lifetimes.

Reincarnation continues to be a popular idea today, and many people feel instinctively drawn to it as a more realistic after-death belief than the Last Judgement. A few years ago a London Sunday newspaper, read mostly by English working people, asked its readers whether they believed in: heaven and hell, reincarnation, or simply did not know. The editor was very surprised that a considerably greater number of readers believed in reincarnation than in heaven and hell.

Reincarnation is after all, a rather appealing belief. It offers all of us a chance to continue our lives beyond the apparent finality of death, and it is something tangible. Heavens and hells are somewhat remote by comparison, and less easy to visualize than another life in the world we know.

In 1956, in both Britain and the United States, popular interest in reincarnation gained special impetus from the publication of *The Search for Bridey Murphy*. A Colorado businessman named Morey Bernstein had hypnotized a young woman, Virginia Tighe, into a past existence. Under hypnosis, Mrs Tighe became an Irish girl named Bridey Murphy. She remembered that she was the daughter of an Irish barrister, and that she had lived between the years 1798 and 1864. She was able to recall minute details of her incarnation in Cork and it appeared that there was a strong case for linking the two personalities. It was subsequently discovered, however, that Virginia Tighe had grown up in a house resembling Bridey's; one of her neighbours had the name of Bridie Murphy (only a slightly different spelling), and that there was a parallel in the backgrounds of the two people.

More impressive cases have, however, reared their heads from time to time. Some of the most impressive come from the files of British researcher, Arnall Bloxham, who with his wife Dulcie, uses retrogressive hypnosis to uncover previous incarnations. The Bloxham's first case was Ann Ockenden, a girl who easily entered a state of trance. During a two-hour hypnotic session in 1956, she remembered vivid previous existences in prehistoric times. Another of the Bloxham's sitters entered an incarnation as a British gunner during the Napoleonic War. He described the sea battle, and then during the session, screamed agonizingly when he was wounded seriously in the leg. Bloxham's tape contained so much detailed historical data that it was shown to Lord Mountbatten, who played it to a number of experts on naval history.

Some of the most stringently tested cases have been those investigated by Dr Ian Stevenson. Stevenson is the Chairman of the Department of Neurology and Psychiatry at the Medical School, University of West Virginia. His 1961 essay on selected reincarnation cases won the William James prize, and Stevenson's documented case histories have earned him world-wide respect in his field. His preference, from the analytical point of view, is for reincarnation cases involving small children, who could not have learned of other social contexts.

Among his best cited evidence are the cases of Shanti Devi and Eduardo Esplugus-Cabrera.

Shanti Devi, who was born in Delhi in 1926, began from the age of three to recall and detail incidents from a previous life at Muttra, eighty miles away. She told her parents that she had been called Lugdi, and had died giving birth to a son. Her husband's name had been Kedar Nath Chaubey. When she was nine, and after Shanti continued to press her claims, her parents wrote to a relative of the dead woman, and were surprised when a letter returned confirming all that Shanti had claimed.

Shanti went subsequently to Muttra, and was able to recognize relatives of Kedar Nath Chaubey in a large crowd. She correctly led a carriage through the streets of the town to her old house, which she recognized even though it had been painted a different colour. Shanti was able correctly to answer questions relating to the arrangement of rooms and objects in the house, and also correctly claimed that a sum of money had been buried beneath the floor in her father-in-law's house.

Shanti Devi remains one of Stevenson's best cases. In all, Shanti made twenty-four substantiated statements about her earlier life, and there were no instances of error.

23

Cuban Eduardo Esplugus-Cabrera was only four when he told his parents of a previous life in Havana. He gave the name of a number of relatives and described his mother in detail. She had a 'clear complexion, black hair, and made hats . . .'. Eduardo said that in his previous life he had been known as Pancho. Stevenson says that the parents were sure Eduardo had not visited the location of his 'earlier existence'. The boy was unfamiliar with the route to the house when taken there, but identified the specific house immediately. Eduardo did not recognize the inhabitants of the dwelling but enquiries were made concerning the previous occupants. A family whose names had been given by Eduardo, did indeed live in that house, and had moved out shortly after the death of Pancho. All data given by Eduardo proved to be correct, except for his father's Christian name.

Stevenson began his researches as a sceptic, and was keen to test a number of hypotheses of explanation rather than assume reincarnation. He considered possibilities like fraud, 'racial memory', and extrasensory perception as alternative frameworks, but he has nevertheless come to believe that reincarnation is the most likely answer. Noted medical authority Dr Elisabeth Kubler-Ross has also stated recently that she regards reincarnation as a 'fact'.

Cases such as those mentioned above could never be said to prove the universality of reincarnation, but they suggest that it may occur in some cases. Together with the out-of-the-body documentation of Dr Robert Crookall and Celia Green, such cases suggest that the faculty of consciousness (and memory) may not be dependent on the physical organism, and may in fact survive bodily death.

SOURCEBOOKS

JOSEPH HEAD and S. L. CRANSTON: *Reincarnation in World Thought*, Julian Press, New York, 1967, reissued by Causeway Books, New York, 1970.
Possibly the most complete study of reincarnation beliefs ever compiled, this book is a complementary volume to the authors' earlier and shorter, *Reincarnation, an East-West Anthology*. Reincarnation references in Hinduism, Jainism, Buddhism, Taoism, Judaism, Christianity and Islam are detailed from textual sources. The views of prominent writers, philosophers and scientists on the subject of rebirth are also provided.
IAN STEVENSON: *The Evidence for Survival from Claimed Memories of Former Incarnations*, Peto Publications, 16 Kingswood Road, Tadworth, Surrey, England, 1961.
IAN STEVENSON: *Twenty Cases Suggestive of Reincarnation*, American Society for Psychical Research, New York, 1966.
The first of these is Stevenson's William James Memorial Essay, and it provides a concise summary of some of the main cases for analysis together

with an assessment of different hypotheses for explaining reincarnation occurrences. Stevenson went on to a more penetrating analysis of cases from India, Ceylon, Brazil, Alaska, and Lebanon in his second book which remains one of the most authoritative in the field.

MARTIN EBON (ed.): *Reincarnation in the Twentieth Century*, Signet Books, New York, 1970.

Ebon is a member of the New School for Social Research and has previously edited volumes on ESP, hauntings and prophecy. This volume is a general account of some of the more famous cases, including the Shanti Devi and Bridey Murphy incidents. One of the book's most valuable features is an account by Lee Markham of Buddhist organizations which document reincarnation cases and try to explain physical abnormalities in terms of previous karma.

Case Studies

MOREY BERNSTEIN: *The Search for Bridey Murphy*, Doubleday, New York, 1956.

DULCIE BLOXHAM: *Who Was Ann Ockenden?*, Neville Spearman, London, 1958.

ARTHUR GUIRDHAM. *The Cathars and Reincarnations*, Neville Spearman, London, 1970.

The author believes he lived formerly at the time of the Cathars, a medieval heretical sect in France, dating from around the middle of the thirteenth century. British occult author Colin Wilson regards it as one of the best documented reincarnation accounts.

The Origins of Magic

The origins of magic lie at the very beginnings of human history when man first appeared and was faced with a strange, often hostile, environment and a mysterious, almost inexplicable, existence. Vast forces moved around him, upon which he was totally dependent, and yet which were completely outside his control – the sun, the moon, the forces of nature, the movement of the animals, the growth of the plants. And in his own life man was faced with mysterious, powerful forces – birth, death, sickness, hunger. It was in search of an explanation for, and the ability to exercise some control over these powers, that man developed magic. What he couldn't control physically – the movement of the seasons, the fertility of the herds – he tried to manipulate symbolically in rituals. He developed myths to explain what things were, and how they came to be. And in the course of these explorations he also stumbled onto some rudiments of science, and thereby began astronomy (at first as astrology), chemistry and medicine (in herbalism, and later alchemy) and other disciplines. Most importantly, he began to explore his own nature, developing an elementary psychology. Indeed, one author has described magic as 'a system of archaic psychology'.

As his adaptation to and control of the environment increased, and his dependence on the forces of nature lessened, magic became more speculative, and less concerned with the everyday needs of survival. Great controversy has raged over the differences between magic and religion, yet it seems certain that in the beginning there was no distinction, and that it was only with the passage of time and the increasing specialization of activities within human communities that distinctions developed. A religious system developed to provide a mythology for the general populace, while magic remained the domain of a few, to whom the rest turned in times of need.

As science and technology relieved the more urgent needs of man, and made the hostile world less hostile, magic turned inward to become a science of mind, and developed away from the search for control of the physical environment. In the West this development led to the emergence of an 'intellectual' magic, while in other non-Western societies the original, so-called primitive, tradition has continued.

We consider many of these developments in subsequent chapters.

SOURCEBOOKS

C. A. BURLAND: *The Magical Arts*, Arthur Barker, London, 1966.
  By one of the greatest authorities in this area, the best basic introduction to the origins of magic.

E. O. JAMES: *Prehistoric Religion*, Thames & Hudson, London, 1957.
  Contains important material on prehistorical magic. Although rather detailed and academic this is an important sourcebook.

ERNEST DE MARTINO: *Magic Primitive and Modern*, Bay Books, Sydney, 1972.
  An excellent basic survey, focusing on non-Western societies and the origins of magic.

JAMES FRAZER: *The Golden Bough* (in various editions, from the 22-volume set to various small paperback abridgments).
  The classic work in this area, this was the first serious attempt to correlate and analyse material on magic and religion. Frazer was, unfortunately, getting material at second, third or fourth hand (he never left England) and accordingly many of his theories are based upon incorrect evidence.

RICHARD CAVENDISH: *The Black Arts*, Routledge & Kegan Paul, London, 1967.
  For the origins and development of more traditional magic, this is a valuable sourcebook.

Supernatural and Occult Beings

All religions and mythologies describe a vast array of supernatural beings that guide man, trick him, offer him enlightenment or occult secrets. Joseph Smith, the founder of Mormonism has described how the angel Moroni appeared in a blazing vision and showed him certain sacred tablets. Madame Blavatsky, the famous Theosophist, used to claim to her followers that she had constant mystical rapport with certain spiritual 'Masters' including one Koot Hoomi who lived in a mysterious region of the Himalayas. MacGregor Mathers, co-founder of the Order of the Golden Dawn similarly claimed that he had contacted beings he called 'Secret Chiefs' and Aleister Crowley believed that he received an occult revelation from Aiwass, a mysterious Egyptian entity. Of course, if we look further back into Christianity, Judaism and other religions we find accounts of angels appearing to the prophets, and other types of strange entities such as the Kerubim of the 'Book of Revelations'.

The world of the occult is one in which the entire universe is filled with mysterious personages and beings. Some of these the occultist can beseech for help in his quest for greater knowledge. Others – some of which he may meet on the astral planes – are horrendous and frightening and to be avoided at all costs.

The ancient Gnostics, whose magical universe was rather similar to that of modern magicians, have described some of these beings. One of them was Paraplex, 'a ruler with a woman's shape whose hair reacheth down to her feet under whose authority stand five and twenty archdemons which rule over a multitude of other demons. It is those demons which enter into men and seduce them, raging and cursing and slandering; it is they which carry off hence and in ravishment, the souls and dispatch them through their dark smoke. . . .' The Gnostics, in a way rather similar to the medieval hell-fire Christians, conceived of grotesque Hells, and in particular twelve dungeons of 'Outer Darkness'.

28

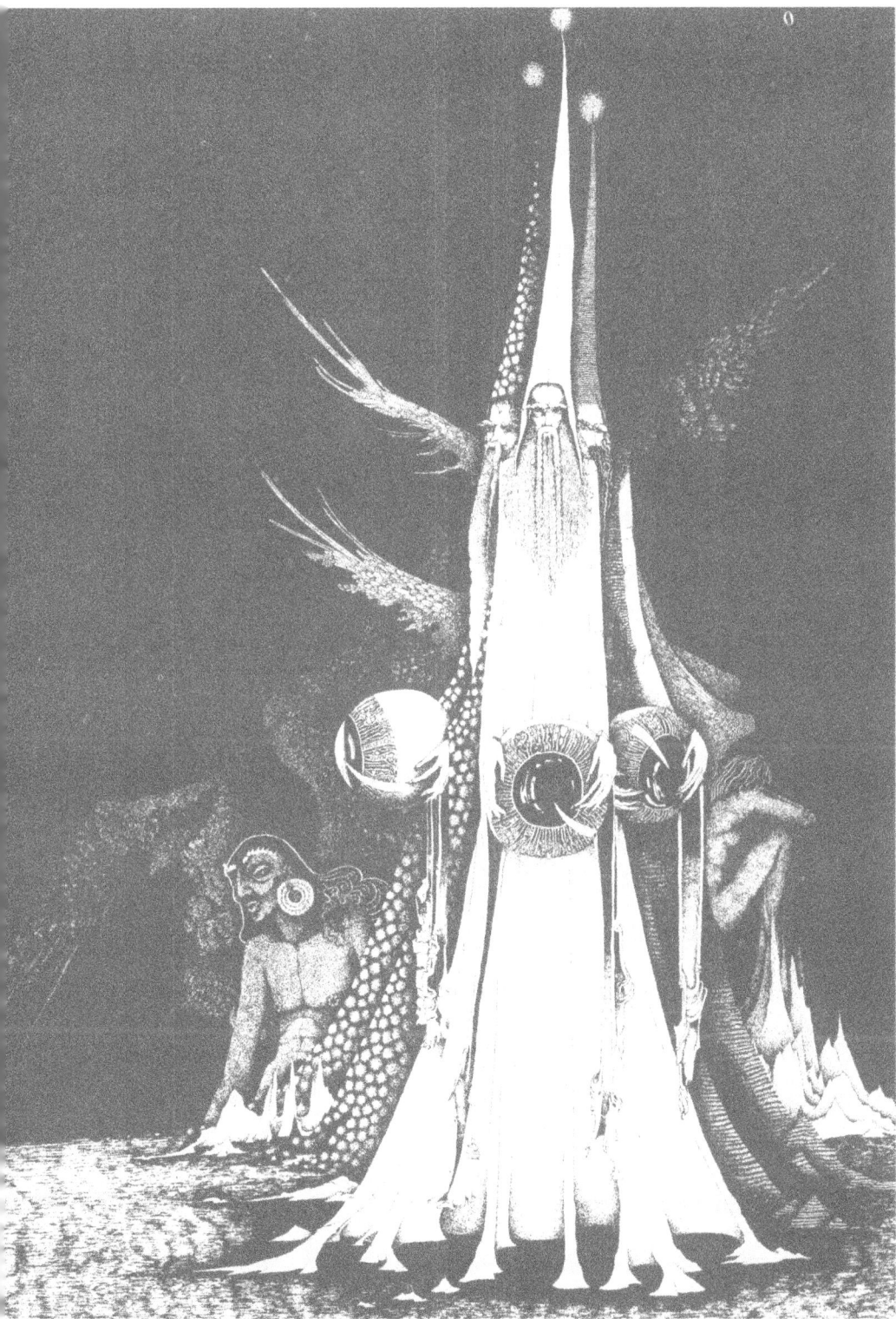

These accounts of strange, supernatural beings are not confined to the West. The Tibetan Buddhists believe that when a person dies he is confronted by a vast array of entities which are really a reflection of the good and evil tendencies inherent in a person's mind. One of the so-called 'wrathful deities' is an awesome being known as The Great Glorious Buddha-Heruka, said to appear on the eighth day after death:

> Dark brown of colour it had three heads, six hands and four feet firmly postured, the right face being white, the left red, the central dark brown; the body emitting flames of radiance, the nine eyes widely opened in a terrifying gaze; the eyebrows quivering like lightning. . . .

Of course, not all such supernatural encounters are horrific or demonic. We recall St John's apocalyptic revelation:

> And in the midst of the seven candlesticks [I saw] one like unto the Son of man, clothed with a garment down to the foot, and girt with a golden girdle.
> His head and his hairs were white like wool, as white as snow; and his eyes were as a flame of fire. And his feet like unto fine brass, as if they burned in a furnace; and his voice as the sound of many waters . . . (Revelations I: 13–15).

Magicians and occultists believe that they have access to the far reaches of the mind, and they hold, like Carl Jung, that these beings are a reflection of different levels of consciousness. A person who has opened his mind to its spiritual, regenerative side will have visions of God, or Christ, or Buddha; a person besieged with doubts, worries, hatred or greed will perhaps be tormented by devils essentially of his own making.

The practice of magic, at least in its ritual form, is to invoke and evoke supernatural beings representative of the whole of the manifested universe. A white magician invokes angels and other spiritual beings because he believes that they will bestow knowledge and grace upon him; a black magician is seeking to enhance the more hedonistic, animal side of his nature, and he thus evokes elementals and familiar spirits of a lower order than himself. In a sense he is moving in a counter-evolutionary way, for he is seeking to revitalize all his basically animal drives and instincts.

In the Qabalah, the basis of modern magic, each of the ten levels of consciousness on the Tree of Life has an archangel associated with it, and also angels and planetary ascriptions. The names of these beings, which are the most exalted individual entities for each level, are as follows:

1   Metatron   — Primum Mobile (beginnings of the Cosmos)
2   Raziel   — The Zodiac
3   Tzaphquiel — Saturn
4   Tzadquiel   — Jupiter
5   Kamael   — Mars
6   Raphael   — The Sun
7   Haniel   — Venus
8   Michael   — Mercury
9   Gabriel   — The Moon
10 Sandalphon — Earth (four elements)

According to occultist Franz Bardon, there are also spirit beings for every degree of the planetary zodiac. For example, Ecdulon, a spirit of the zodiac sign Aries, 'can initiate the magician into the magic of love. If desired by the magician, he can change hostility into friendship and secure for the magician the favour of very important persons . . .'. But there are other supernatural beings in the magical universe. Sometimes they are human, but not always!

Ancient myths and legends refer to several fabulous beasts, that were often 'combination animals'. For example, the *mantichora* was a Persian beast with a lion's body and a human head. It could shoot poisonous barbs from its tail, and had a voice like a trumpet. The *Hydra*, against which Hercules pitted his strength, was a dragon with seven or nine heads. Each of the heads was immortal and if any were cut off, new ones would spring up in their place. The beast called a *Hippocampus* was half-horse and half-fish, and drew Poseidon's chariot, and the *Harpies* were aggressive vultures with female heads and breasts. Meanwhile the *Chimera*, a creature described by Homer, was a combination of a lion, a serpent and a goat.

Such fanciful creatures are regarded by most of us as figments of the imagination, but for the magician venturing onto the astral planes, it is quite a different matter. Such beings can confront him as if they are real, since he is really journeying into the 'mythological' areas of the mind.

One of the most positive and far-reaching contributions of the magician Aleister Crowley was to relate the Tree of Life levels of consciousness to the gods of different religions. He also correlated the Tarot paths on the Tree with other mythological visions, such as those of imaginary animals.

For example, according to Crowley Path 25 of the Tree, represented by the Tarot card *Temperance*, is a location where one might see a centaur or a hippogriff. A centaur, of course, is the famous half-man, half-horse and is none other than Sagittarius who fires his arrow upwards towards the sun. The centaur occurs here because the card Temperance leads to a mystical vision of the sun and sun-gods, when used for meditative purposes. The hippogriff is a variation of a griffin and this creature was sacred to the sun-god Apollo.

We can see, then, that magic regards all supernatural entities as being at least in one sense, real. Even if they are only figments of the creative imagination, they *are* real at that level. And as the magician expands his consciousness and moves further into the mind, he has to learn to expect almost anything!

SOURCEBOOKS

ALEISTER CROWLEY: *The Qabalah of Aleister Crowley*, Weiser, New York, 1973.
Contains Crowley's book *777* which includes full and detailed tables correlating the Tree of Life levels of consciousness with the deities of Greek, Roman, Egyptian and Indian religion. Also full listings of supernatural animals located on the Tree of Life.

JORGE LUIS BORGES: *The Book of Imaginary Beings*, Avon, New York, 1970 and Penguin, Harmondsworth, 1973.

RICHARD BARBER and ANNE RICHES: *A Dictionary of Fabulous Beasts*, Walker, New York, 1971.
Both rather similar in treatment, but both invaluable handbook guides for tracking down imaginary beasts of legend and folklore. The Barber/Riches volume is well illustrated with black and white line drawings.

GUSTAV DAVIDSON: *A Dictionary of Angels*, Free Press, New York, 1971.
The most complete reference book on angels with full alphabetical listings.

FRANZ BARDON: *The Practice of Magical Evocation*, Rudolf Pravica, Graz, Austria, 1967.
A detailed account of the planetary and other spirits that populate the magical universe, and the ritual means for contacting them. Full descriptions are given of the spirits for each of the signs of the zodiac.

W. Y. EVANS-WENTZ (ed.): *The Tibetan Book of the Dead*, Oxford University Press, New York, 1960.

G.R.S. MEAD (ed.): *Pistis Sophia*, Watkins, London, 4th impression 1963.
Two volumes among many dealing with after-death worlds and the supernatural beings that inhabit them. The first Tibetan, the second Gnostic.

Ritual Magic

From the very beginning of his awareness of magic and religion man has employed ritual as a means of expressing his involvement with the powers of the universe, and as a means of gaining contact with those powers, and causing them to manifest to him. The earliest evidence of religion in human history is that of the ancient cave dwellers who left remains of their rituals, essentially cults of the dead, the hunt, and the great mother. Ritual implements have been uncovered dating back to the very beginnings of man – statues of the earth mother; skeletons painted in red ochre to symbolize the blood of new life, and buried in a foetal position within the womb of the earth; paintings of man disguised as an animal, performing rituals designed to ensure the success of the hunt; evidence of offerings being made to the earth to ensure the fertility of the plants which provided man with some of his food.

As he became increasingly less dependent on the hunt and the nomadic life of his early ancestors so man developed a different approach to magic and ritual. Early man had been surrounded by a world of frightening phenomena which he was largely powerless to control – flood, famine, darkness, death, sickness, fire, all the forces of the natural environment on which his precarious existence was so much dependent had to be symbolized and controlled ritually, for actual control was beyond his limited technology. When he became a cultivator of crops, his interest became even more centred on the cycles of nature, on which he was dependent for the success of his harvest. He was intimately involved in the cycle of life and death and rebirth which is at the very heart of the cultivator – the seeds which contain the germ of life, yet appear dead, and are planted in the soil to burst forth with life, the heavens which give rain and sunshine, the earth which gives warmth and nourishment.

As his technology improved, man became less dependent upon nature for his basic survival, and his approach to religion changed. But it remained a ritual involvement; there was only a limited amount of expressly theoretical teaching, for the masses could not read, nor did they have the time to devote to speculative religion. In the rituals, however, which communicated the teachings which could not be put into words, but were contained in experiences, they could both participate and learn.

Gradually, with the separation of magic and religion, and the establishment of the church as the most powerful influence on the culture, ritual magic largely disappeared; certainly, it existed in small enclaves and amongst individuals, but the church was most diligent in her persecution of those who participated in practices outside her scheme of belief. Amongst such groups as the alchemists, the Rosicrucians and, later, the Freemasons, some of the traditions of ritual magic were continued. Within the church herself the old methods of teaching by ritual involvement were continued – for those who could neither read nor write, and had insufficient education to understand the basic concepts of the faith, let alone the sublime mysteries contained within the Catholic religion, the dramas of the Sacraments and the annual cycle of the church year continued to communicate the doctrines of the Christian religion.

But at the same time there existed other traditions – some specifically non-Christian, some within the Christian tradition – which employed ritual for magical purposes. Various groups developed to perpetuate particular traditions of ritual magic, and, with the declining power of the Church, these occasionally emerged into the open. Unlike the traditions of ritual magic in the distant past, these were specifically for the educated and the learned, who sought power, knowledge and experience through the techniques of ritual magic. Freemasons, Rosicrucians, alchemists, Templars – a whole range of traditions developed, and numerous individuals worked alone in the practice. Names like Paracelsus, John Dee and others recall that the traditions continued, albeit often hidden from the world.

It was not until the nineteenth century that the traditions of ritual magic really emerged again. In 1801 Francis Barrett published *The Magus* (an almost unreadable and extremely complex volume) and thereby began what has proved to be a long line of works on this subject. His influence was small, compared to that of Eliphas Lévi, whose book *The Dogma and Ritual of High Magic* was published in 1856, and who has achieved a largely undeserved reputation as a great authority on the subject. The latter half of the nineteenth century saw also the development of the Hermetic Order of the Golden Dawn which, more than any other group, has profoundly influenced the course of ritual magic and made it known to the general public. Deriving from this Order, a number of other groups (The Order of the Cubic Stone, the Fraternity of the Inner Light and others) have emerged to perpetuate, in varying forms, the traditions of magic. Today, these traditions are continued by a variety of occult groups, and by individual ritual magicians who work alone in the pursuit of this ancient path. Many of the schools which once followed the magical tradition have now ceased to do so, although continuing to exist in an altered form; foremost amongst this group are the Freemasons who, although once a genuine school of ritual occultism, now de-emphasize this aspect of their work.

Ritual magic is that approach to magic which employs ritual, symbols and ceremonial as a means of representing and communicating with forces underlying the universe and man. Ritual is a process of dramatizing what is being expressed, so that the whole man – body, emotions and mind – are employed in causing a total experience. Ritual makes use of all the senses – sight, hearing, smell, taste, touch – and uses all the methods of drama and all the techniques of religion. Ritual magic centres on symbols, those keys to the subconscious by which it is possible to communicate concepts and ideals beyond words or intellectual understanding. The aim of ritual magic is a transcendental experience – an experience beyond the limitations of the mind, an experience of the reality of being, of the realms of what might be called the 'superconscious', but an experience in a controlled, balanced and integrated way. Ritual magic thus aims at the same end as many other techniques – that of the mystic and that of the drug taker. But unlike the mystic, the ritual magician works through action rather than through contemplation, through the externalization of inner realities, rather than through introspection. And unlike the drug taker, the ritual magician strives for a consciously controlled and directed journey inwards, relying not upon synthetic or chemical experience, but upon the utilization of the natural faculties which he possesses, but rarely uses. All the equipment of magic, all its ceremony and ritual, all the words and symbols are designed to focus and to direct the will of the magician, and to 'turn him on' to inner realities. The ultimate end of ritual magic is not the causing of spectacular and apparently supernatural effects, but the transformation of the individual from a limited mortal, into what can only be described as a 'superman', fully alive and totally free.

There are, as Eliphas Lévi noted, three basic laws of ritual magic:

(1) *the law of will* – the power of man's will is a real power which, when correctly stimulated and harnessed, is as potent as any physical force; but this will is quite different to the vague, ill-defined 'wishing' with which most people confuse it. The will must be cultivated, disciplined and controlled.

35

(2) *the law of astral light* – all things consist of one basic substance which is known by various names, but which, once understood, can be used by the magician and moulded by his will.

(3) *the law of correspondence* – this is the ancient doctrine of the microcosm and the macrocosm, according to which 'that which is above is like that which is below'; man is a model of the universe, and the universe is a greater expression of those same principles embodied in man. A knowledge of these correspondences between man and the universe enables the magician to summon up within himself any of the powers of the universe.

But, although principles can be codified and expounded, the only real teaching of ritual magic comes from individual experience, and involves disciplined self-development and the laborious transformation of the self.

SOURCEBOOKS

Not because his books embody any greatly practical or important information, but because they are historically important, the works of Éliphas Lévi are key sources:

Transcendental Magic : Its Doctrine and Ritual (reprinted, Rider, London, 1962).

History of Magic (reprinted, Rider, London, 1968).

The Key of the Mysteries (reprinted, Rider, London, 1968).

More important and more practical information is given in the writings of contemporary ritual magicians:

W. E. BUTLER: *Magic, Its Ritual, Purpose and Power*, Aquarian Press, London, 1952.

W. E. BUTLER: *The Magician, His Training and Work*, Aquarian Press, London, 1959.

Excellent introductions to the nature and principles of ritual magic, without the usual jargon and unnecessarily complicated phraseology.

W. GRAY: *Magical Ritual Methods*, Helios, Cheltenham, 1969.

W. GRAY: *The Inner Traditions of Magic*, Aquarian, London, 1971.

Practical studies of the subject by a practising ritual magician who offers very valuable hints to the student.

W. B. CROW: *A History of Magic, Witchcraft and the Occult*, Aquarian, London, 1968.

For coverage of the history of magic in general, with valuable material on ritual magical traditions.

FRANCIS KING: *Ritual Magic in England*, Spearman, London, 1970.

The classic study on the traditions of Western magic in Britain, this covers the period of the Golden Dawn.

J. H. BRENNAN: *Astral Doorways*, Aquarian, London, 1971.

J. H. BRENNAN: *Experimental Magic*, Aquarian, London, 1972.

Two very practical introductory books, with valuable material for the student on the basic theory and practice of magic.

ISRAEL REGARDIE: *The Middle Pillar*, Llewellyn, St Paul, Minnesota, 1970.
ISRAEL REGARDIE: *The Tree of Life: A Study of Magic*, Weiser, New York, 1971.
More advanced studies, contemporary classics in the field.

Regardie successfully integrates the basic teachings of ritual magic and the occult with the principles of analytical psychology; his own background derives from the Stella Matutina and Aleister Crowley.

Ritual Consciousness

A ritual, in effect, is an act of imitation. In primitive societies, native shamans mirror in their actions the movements of the animals, birds and fish that they wish to ensnare. When rain is required, a ceremony may be conducted in which the fall of rain upon the earth is symbolized by a fluttering movement of the arms of the performers, or the pouring of liquids upon the ground or some similar, appropriate action.

In the world of the occult, rituals similarly play a paramount role. Just as rituals of fertility beseech the gods to shower abundance, so too can rituals incorporate the opposite intentions. There are, for example, certain occult rituals which practise a type of scapegoating effect. In Francis Barrett's famous compendium *The Magus* published in 1801 we see that certain witch rituals transferred illness and pain to an unfortunately victimized creature:

> Take the eyes of a frog, which must be extracted before sunrise, and
> bind them to the breasts of a woman who be ill. Then let the frog
> go blind into the water again and as he goes so will the woman be
> rid of her pains. . . .

Removing the eyes of the frog clearly asserted man's will over the frog since it could no longer leap to freedom. The breasts, with their life-giving milk, were regarded as symbolic of health, and the casting of the frog into the purifying waters was clearly a ritual act of cleansing the body of evil and pain.

Often in ritual, the *contact* between the ritual object and the person who will benefit is crucial. A rather similar ritual to the above states that one cure for fever was for a naked woman to take the heart of any animal and bind it to the patient. The disease would then depart. In this instance the fever is equated with the death of the sacrificed animal. The heart is its very life force, and this is virtually exchanged for the perilous illness . . . at the animal's expense!

Witchcraft and primitive magic frequently dwelt on the afflictions imposed by nature upon man, or by enemies or hostile gods. Man was subject to a barrage of external forces – wind, fire, drought, flood, storms – and his rituals were a form of protection. The only way man knew of protecting himself was by imitating the gods whose forces raged all around him.

In ancient Egypt, which saw the rise of one of the most profound early cosmologies, it became clear that one of the most enduring phenomena in the observable universe was the sun. No one had ever seen it go out. No one had ever seen it fail to rise with the new dawn each day. It was appropriate then, that the sun became a symbol of the Egyptian's destiny, for by imitating its motion, and by identifying and following the sun god, a man could find new life. It is from the Egyptians that we have the earliest representation of resurrection as a doctrine, although this was mirrored by other religious groups in a reincarnation teaching. In some instances the two went side by side.

Osiris, the god slain by his brother Set and miraculously reborn, symbolized resurrection. After death his followers would travel down the river of the Underworld to the Elysian fields, passing on the way through dungeons representing the hours of the night. In the fields they would be sustained ritually by eating barley cakes and by drinking ale, symbolic of the body and life of Osiris himself. On the other hand the followers of Amen-Ra had noted that the sun constantly reappeared daily, and they assumed, again in an act of ritual identification, that man too, in the company of the sun god, must be perpetually reborn. In their after-death belief it was said that man travelled in the train of the sun god, and took part in the continuing battle of (sun)light over darkness.

We see in the above, the beginnings of rituals *designed to transform man himself*. Egyptian mythology had a major influence on the ritual magic practices of the Hermetic Order of the Golden Dawn (see pages 48–51). The aim of this Order, which practised white or beneficial magic rather than black or destructive magic, was to use ritual to illuminate the mind.

Israel Regardie writes in his *Tree of Life*:

There are hierarchies of consciousness which are celestial and there are those which are terrestrial; some divine, other demonic, and still others including the highest Gods and Universal Essences . . . the whole Universe is permeated by One Life, and that Life in manifestation is represented by hosts of mighty Gods, divine beings, cosmic spirits or intelligences . . . (p. 57).

39

Unlike primitive societies, modern occult groups tend to regard the gods as symbols of the positive and negative energies of the mind. White magic thus entails enhancing the spiritual side of man's nature, whereas black magic or satanism tends to arouse the sexual or animal side of man.

In the Golden Dawn the rituals were designed to provide the initiate with the feeling that he was travelling among the gods. These, of course, were represented by members of the Order dressed in appropriate mythological regalia. However, for many the rituals were emotionally and intellectually inspiring. The poet W. B. Yeats, who at one time headed the Golden Dawn, and who won the Nobel Prize for literature in 1923, found ritual particularly illuminating: 'There is traced within the evil triangle the rescuing symbol of the Golden Cross united to the Rose of seven times seven petals...' he wrote, in describing one of the key rituals. For him, with his poetic imagination inflamed by ritual, each petal seemed to be transformed 'into the likeness of Living Beings of extraordinary beauty...'. When turning to the pillars of Horus in the ritual it seemed that each one had become a 'column of confused shapes, divinities ... of the wind, who in a whirling dance of more than human vehemence, rose playing upon pipes and cymbals ...'.

According to modern occultism, the gods are alive in the minds of us all, and it is up to us to open the channels of inspiration. In this way, white magic is very similar to Kundalini Yoga for it too demonstrates the opening of channels of energy and illumination.

In ritual magic it is essential that all the senses should be heightened, and so the ritual itself has to appeal to all of them, in unison. It does this as follows:

Sight All of the ritual clothing and symbolic colours focus the consciousness in a certain way. For example the colours of life are gold and yellow, in imitation of the sun. Red is the colour of aggression, symbolizing blood spilt in war.

Sound Magic draws upon a vast repertoire of chants, mantras and invocations which have a powerful effect on the mind and the creative imagination.

Taste This may take the form of a sacrament like wine, or in some instances, like the Mysteries of Eleusis, a hallucinatory drink.

Smell Incense and perfumes are frequently used to provide a sensory atmosphere suitable for the ritual.

Touch Throughout the ritual the initiate has contact with sacred objects. Perhaps it is the glass from which he drinks the life-giving fluid, or the sword with which he holds at bay the demons (of his mind) who are hostile to his task of enlarging consciousness.

We see from the above that ritual magic especially is designed to allow man to transcend himself. He does this by using symbols and mythology to help himself imagine that once again he walks among the gods, and in fact, has become one himself. In so doing he gains access to Cosmic Consciousness.

SOURCEBOOKS

For medieval magical and witchcraft rituals see the following:

A. E. WAITE: *The Book of Ceremonial Magic*, University Books, New York, 1961.

IDRIES SHAH: *The Secret Lore of Magic*, Abacus, London, 1972.

The above include important primary references such as selections from The Key of Solomon the King, the Almadel, the Grimorium Verum, the Grimoire of Honorius, and details of occult spells and evocations. Shah's book contains an interesting section on conjurations of spirits and demons with the appropriate hours and times for magical practices.

For complete facsimile translations of key ritual works see:

S. L. MACGREGOR MATHERS (ed.): *The Sacred Magic of Abra-Melin the Mage*, De Laurence, Chicago, 1938, 3rd impression 1948.

S. L. MACGREGOR MATHERS (ed.): *The Greater Key of Solomon*, De Laurence, Chicago, 1914.

L. W. DE LAURANCE (ed.): *The Lesser Key of Solomon: Goetia, the Book of Evil Spirits*, De Laurence, Chicago, 1916.

The above works are available through Wehman Publishers, Hackensack, New Jersey, and represent key manuscripts relating to descriptions of spirits and their ritual conjuration. Of the three, the first is considered by modern occultists to be the most important, and it was held by Aleister Crowley to be one of the most powerful works of ceremonial magic, hampered only by the fact that the rituals took a total of six months to perform! All in all, however, the Abremelin rituals (allegedly written in 1468) allowed the magician the services of 316 spirit advisors. The rituals were also said to allow one to communicate with one's own Holy Guardian Angel, or higher spiritual self.

Two important works relating to the spells and rituals of witchcraft and satanism respectively are:

PETER HAINING: *The Warlock's Book*, University Books, New York, n.d. and

ANTON SZANDOR LA VEY: *The Satanic Rituals*, Avon, New York, 1972.

Haining's book contains sections on sexual magical rituals and love potions, the Black Sabbat and witchcraft rituals, based on the Sloane, Harleian and Lansdowne MSS in the British Museum. Attention is also given to the hallucinogens employed by witches, including henbane, thornapple and mandrake. La Vey's work, which describes satanic rituals performed in the author's San Francisco Church of Satan, represents the companion volume to *The Satanic Bible* (Avon, 1969). Some of the rituals are in Enochian, the angelic language first transcribed by Dr John Dee, Elizabeth I's astrologer.

Among the most relevant sourcebooks dealing with contemporary magical ritual are the following:

ISRAEL REGARDIE: *The Golden Dawn*, Aries, Chicago 1937–41. Reissued in one volume, Llewellyn, St Paul, Minnesota, 1974.

R. G. TORRENS: *The Secret Rituals of the Golden Dawn*, Aquarian Press, Wellingborough, Northants, 1972.

ALEISTER CROWLEY: *Book Four*, Sangreal Foundation, Dallas, Texas, 1972.

FRANZ BARDON: *The Practice of Magical Evocation*, Pravica, Graz-Puntigam, Austria, 1967.

Regardie, at one time Aleister Crowley's personal secretary, first discarded the tradition of secrecy in the Golden Dawn and Stella Matutina occult societies by publishing their rituals in full. His compilation represents the most significant single magical source of modern Kabbalistic ritual. Torren's shorter version, which purports to come from an alternative manuscript source, omits the important mystical rituals which lead to the experience of spiritual rebirth in the Kabbalistic level of consciousness known as Tiphareth. However in some respects it is more accessible than Regardie's larger work. Crowley's *Book Four* details all of the magical implements that were used in the Golden Dawn and in his own Argentinum Astrum Society (the Order of the Silver Star), and also explains the symbolism of the magical triangle (evocation) and circle (invocation). Franz Bardon's works, while outside the Golden Dawn ritual tradition, are highly respected and carry their own signs of authenticity. Like Crowley's book, Bardon details the magical 'weapons' and then proceeds with a number of remarkable descriptions of the elemental spirits, for example:

'*Mentfil* . . . a mighty king of gnomes in the kingdom under the earth . . . This ruler can inform the magician about all medicinal herbs . . . Apart from this, Mentfil is a master in alchemical work and reveals to the magician how the prima materia can be transformed into the philosopher's stone . . .' etc.

All in all, Bardon includes ritual sigil diagrams for all the spirits of the 360° of the Zodiac.

The mythological sources of modern ritual magic are examined in:

ISRAEL REGARDIE: *The Tree of Life*, Rider, London, 1932; Weiser, New York, 1971.

This book describes the comparative pantheons of deities which have been included in modern magic, and also describes the *Tattvas* or Hindu symbols of the elements, used in meditation and trance magic.

For anthropological frameworks the following may be useful:

GUY SWANSON: *The Birth of the Gods*, University of Michigan, 1964.

A. F. C. WALLACE: *Religion, An Anthropological View*, Random House, New York, 1966.

VICTOR TURNER: *The Ritual Process*, Aldine Press, Chicago, 1969; Penguin Books, Harmondsworth, 1974.

Magical Equipment

Popular fiction, films and television – from *Rosemary's Baby* to the whole series of *Dracula* films and Dennis Wheatley novels – have made the public familiar with the traditional equipment of the magician and the witch, often in a highly dramatic and not altogether accurate manner. Traditionally, magicians worked in a room set aside and consecrated for the purpose (*temple*, or *lodge*), within a defined area usually marked on the floor (magical *circle*), upon an *altar*, wearing *robes* specially prepared for the occasion, and using specific *tools* (typically, a *chalice, pentacle, sword, wand*). Additionally they burnt *incense* in a *thurible*, sometimes used *daggers* and *Staffs*, and usually worked by the light of *candles*. All this equipment was traditionally prepared very carefully, in the strictest traditions, by the magician himself, and solemnly consecrated for work. The old *grimoires* (books of magical rituals) include elaborate directions for the making and use of magical equipment, although most of their instructions are beyond the abilities of contemporary magicians (e.g. to make a sword, iron had to be mined by the magician, who refined and smelted it, and beat it into the sword), who have limited time and money to devote to their art. If the magician is unable to make his equipment, then he should at least search carefully for the best possible, and be prepared to pay high prices for the right things; all equipment is traditionally consecrated during a special ritual, and thereafter kept from all common usage, and away from other people. Certainly, it is never used for any purpose other than magical work, or its potency will be lost. The equipment should always be kept clean, wrapped in silk, and treated with reverence; the psychological power of the objects derives from this devotion with which they are treated.

(1) *The Temple* (lodge, chapel, oratory, shrine, laboratory) – this should be a room in which only magical working is carried out, and to which

outsiders have no access. After being scrupulously cleansed it is consecrated for use and the ritual objects are placed within it. Traditionally it should lie east–west. At the door are two *pillars*, symbolizing the doorway to the inner world, through which the magician passes when entering his temple. In the centre is the *altar*, surrounded by the *circle* within which the magician works. In some workings, the altar is placed in the east, symbolic direction of the rising sun. At each of the four *cardinal points* (north, south, east, west) are placed objects or symbols representing the four elements (earth, air, fire, water) and the four archangels (Michael, Gabriel, Auriel, Raphael).

(2) *The Circle* represents the actual working space of the magician, and he should never step outside it during a ritual. Traditionally, to do so was believed to place him in terrible danger since the powers which he had summoned would destroy him if he left the protection of the circle. The circle was usually traced in chalk on the floor, or laid out in pieces of material, with symbols inscribed around its circumference.

(3) *The Altar* was usually a double cube, black on the bottom (symbolizing earth) and white on the top half (spirit); only magical equipment was ever placed upon the altar, which usually had one or more white cloths upon it, and in some cases a perpetual *lamp* burning, symbolizing the divine presence. All magical working was done within the circle upon the altar.

(4) *The Robes* included the outer and inner robes, sandals and, in some traditions, a stole and a head-dress. The inner robe was usually a monastic-style garment in white (although some traditions employ black to symbolize, not darkness, but the unregenerated man), with a hood. The outer garment varied in colour and was usually a sleeveless cloak-style coat. While sandals were generally worn, some traditions advocate that the feet should be bare. The stole symbolized the power of the magician, and was simply a strip of material, usually decorated with symbols, hanging around his neck, down to his knees.

Head-dresses varied in form from elaborate ones looking like Bishops' mitres, to Egyptian styles, or simply skull caps. They were worn usually because tradition (deriving from the Old Testament) taught that man's head should be covered when approaching the divine.

(5) *The Tools* – each of these represented a natural element, the cup (water), the pentacle or plate (earth), the sword (air) and the wand (fire). Additionally, candles burnt upon the altar, and sometimes other vessels were used (for example, for storing oil or water). Traditionally, the tools should be of metal, engraved with sacred symbols, and specially consecrated for the work.

(6) *Incense* was burned both to purify the air and drive away evil spirits, and also to give a pleasant atmosphere and attract good spirits. A thurible (incense container on a chain) was used to hold burning charcoal, upon which granulated gum was placed (usually derived from Arabia, taken from trees, and usually olibanum and benzoin mixed together). Sometimes additional herbs were added (e.g. rosemary, cinnamon) to increase the fragrance, or drugs added to affect the mind. Incense sticks and cones tend to be unacceptable because they derive from virtually unknown origins, and may contain all manner of odd substances. Pure gum, with sandalwood dust, and natural herbs, spices and oils are best, and should be blessed when placed upon the charcoal.

Obviously, the equipment was modified according to the needs of the magician and the ritual he was performing. Egyptian-style equipment would not be used in a ceremony invoking Roman gods, nor would statues of Buddha stay in a room devoted to the Christian tradition. The magician had to be an interior decorator in part, co-ordinating and integrating his material resources to create the most conducive atmosphere for his work. He did not collect odds and ends, but was a specialist craftsman.

With the contemporary revival of interest in magic, a large-scale business had been established in the selling of allegedly genuine magical equipment – robes, tools, incenses, oils. This is completely contrary to the traditions of magic, and great care should be exercised in purchasing any object for magical use. The burning of mail-order incense and oils is especially unhealthy; their constituents remain unknown, their makers of dubious intent and their effects unpredictable.

SOURCEBOOKS

GARETH KNIGHT: *The Practice of Ritual Magic*, Helios, Cheltenham, 1967.
    An excellent small handbook on the essentials of ritual magic and the equipment it uses.
W. G. GRAY: *Magical Ritual Methods*, Helios, Cheltenham, 1969.
W. G. GRAY: *The Inner Traditions of Magic*, Aquarian, London, 1970.
    Both of these books contain detailed studies of the symbolism and meaning of ritual implements.
ALEISTER CROWLEY: *Book 4*, Sangreal, Dallas, 1969.
    Most of this work is devoted to an analysis of magical equipment which, although written from Crowley's rather specialist position, is valuable.
DAVID CONWAY: *Magic: An Occult Primer*, Mayflower, London, 1974.
    An interesting practical approach to magic, containing considerable material on magical equipment, rituals and herbs.

W. B. CROW: *The Occult Properties of Herbs*, Aquarian, London, 1969.
   A concise handbook by a great authority on the biology of the occult.
ERIC MAPLE: *The Magic of Perfume*, Aquarian, London, 1973.
   A study of aromatics and their esoteric significance.

The Golden Dawn

The present occult revival owes much of its direction to the important
Hermetic Order of the Golden Dawn (1888) which first gathered together
the workings of a fully developed magical system. A number of important
writers all belonged to the Order – MacGregor Mathers, translator of the
Zohar; A. E. Waite, an authority on the Qabalah, the Rosicrucians and the
Holy Grail legends; W. B. Yeats, the poet; and the fantasy novelists
Arthur Machen and Algernon Blackwood. So too did Aleister Crowley,
famous and perhaps unjustly maligned as 'The Great Beast'. In any occult
bookshop today one will see Waite's Tarot deck in a position of prominence, and perhaps Crowley's spectacular, visionary cards also. Most
contemporary occult groups practising magic as a type of Western Yoga,
acknowledge their debt to the Golden Dawn.

The rituals of the Order were based originally on five masonic grades
discovered in the papers of a deceased English Rosicrucian. Dr Wynn
Westcott, a London coroner and Freemason, asked Samuel (later
'MacGregor') Mathers to expand the material so that it could form the
basis of instruction for a new occult society. This group would nevertheless claim an ancient lineage and would compete, in a sense, with the
esoteric section of the Theosophical Society, which had become rather
obscurely fashionable in London in the 1880s.

The rituals themselves were not merely artificial or theatrical. They
were intended to symbolize certain stages of enlightenment or mystical
consciousness upon a certain cosmic pathway called the Tree of Life. The
Tree of Life in itself is a key motif in the Qabalah, or Jewish mystery
tradition, and represents ten levels of consciousness between man and
Godhead.

Beginning from the lowest levels upon the Tree there are four major
levels of consciousness, representing in simple terminology: our perception of the environment (*Malkuth*); the sexual instincts (*Yesod*); the

rational intellect (*Hod*); and the capacity for love and emotion(*Netzach*). Mathers and Westcott aligned these and an initial Neophyte grade with the five Rosicrucian rituals, and these later became the Golden Dawn rituals per se.

The next level of consciousness upon the Tree (and it has to be remembered that the aim of white magic is to trace the mystical stages back to Godhead) was called *Tiphareth*, and this represented the mystical level of the god-man. It was in itself a very profound spiritual experience in which the magician felt the power of the God energy living within him, and experienced 'rebirth'. Mathers and Westcott devised a type of 'occult society within a society' now, designating this level, and the next two stages upon the Tree, *the Second Order*. Its existence was kept a secret for the beginners in the Golden Dawn grades. It was also given the grandiose title of the Rosae Rubae et Aurea Crucis (the Red Rose and the Cross of Gold), linking the Order with the Rosicrucians. Westcott, Mathers and another member, Woodford, appointed themselves as figureheads of this exalted level of consciousness. Above them, on the Tree, remained three levels of consciousness, the Trinity, consisting of *Kether*, the Crown; *Hokmah*, Wisdom; and *Binah*, Understanding. Mathers, in particular, insisted before members of lower rank that he had sole access to these lofty realms of inspiration.

The first Golden Dawn Temple, that of Isis-Urania, was opened in London in 1888, and by 1896 there were Temples of Osiris in Weston-Super-Mare, Horus in Bradford, Amen-Ra in Edinburgh and Ahathoor in Paris. We can see from the names of these temples that apart from the Rosicrucian symbolism of the mystical grade of Tiphareth, the predominating influence was that of ancient Egypt. The Egyptian gods had been well illustrated in mural motifs and papyri, and provided an elaborate pantheon of gods symbolizing the occult potential of man. It was appropriate that they should have been revived at this time.

Mathers, who assumed increasing importance in the Order, eventually sealed its doom by his essentially autocratic manner. He was fond of chastising members like Annie Horniman, who criticized him for withdrawing into a state of élitist isolation. Mathers spent much of his time translating important occult texts, like the *Magic of Abramelin*, and he expected his colleagues to finance and maintain his sojourns in the British Museum and the Bibliothèque de l'Arsenal in Paris.

Finally Mather's claim to exclusive occult authority wore thin and schisms formed within the Order. Florence Farr mobilized her 'Sphere Group' around an astral Egyptian entity, and Dr Felkin formed the breakaway Stella Matutina around certain Sons of Fire who dwelt in the

Arabian desert. With the death of Mathers in 1918, the original Golden Dawn fragmented completely, although Felkin's group continued to exert an influence which is still felt today in the form of the Fraternity of the Inner Light and its derivatives.

There were certain occult knowledge lectures which the Golden Dawn members had to master and these in themselves brought together a lot of information on magic, the tarot, alchemy and astrology that is still of vital interest today.

The grade of *Malkuth* included details of alchemy and the elemental spirits of earth, air, water and fire. Also included were the symbolic connections between the gods of different religions and the ten basic levels of consciousness upon the Tree of Life. (Aleister Crowley, who left the Order in 1904, compiled a detailed list of 'correspondences' in his book *777*, recently republished in the volume *The Qabalah of Aleister Crowley* (Weiser, New York, 1974).)

At the stage of Yesod, the practitioners learnt the division of the soul or consciousness into *Neschamah*, the animal instincts.

In *Hod*, they learnt in detail the connections between the twenty-two major cards of the Tarot and the levels of consciousness on the Tree, and in *Netzach*, the sacred names of the Gods.

All of the magicians took part in rituals appropriate to their grade, and these were intended to impress upon the performers, a sense of awe and mystery (see pp. 38–42). Between 1937 and 1941 Israel Regardie published the full rituals of the Stella Matutina, as they derived from the Golden Dawn. R. G. Torrens's more condensed *The Secret Rituals of the Golden Dawn* presents a slight variation on these. Many contemporary occult groups in both the United States and Britain still base their grades on the Golden Dawn pattern, and ripples of influence continue also to find their way into the occult music and literature of the counterculture.

SOURCEBOOKS

ISRAEL REGARDIE: *The Golden Dawn* (reissued in one volume), Llewellyn, St Paul, Minnesota, 1974.

R. G. TORRENS: *The Secret Rituals of the Golden Dawn*, Aquarian Books, Wellingborough, Northants, 1972.

The above contain authentic transcripts of the Golden Dawn rituals. Regardie's however is more meaningful because it also includes the important 'Knowledge Lectures' of the grades, and also a section on the rebirth grade of *Tiphareth*, which actually belonged to the so-called Second Order above the Golden Dawn.

For a historical account of the Golden Dawn and its derivative offshoots, the following are recommended:

FRANCIS KING: *Ritual Magic in England,* Spearman, London, 1970.

ELLIC HOWE: *The Magicians of the Golden Dawn,* Routledge & Kegan Paul, London, 1972.

King's book contains valuable details on occult groups like the Astrum Argentinum, the OTO (a sexual magic group), the Cromlech Temple and the Fraternity of the Inner Light. Howe's work created something of a sensation when it was published because it showed very clearly that Dr Wynn Westcott, one of the founders of the Golden Dawn, fabricated a correspondence with a fictitious German Rosicrucian named Anna Sprengel, in order to claim links with an 'ancient Western tradition', in Europe. Israel Regardie has criticized Howe because he feels that he is undermining the authenticity of the Order. Nevertheless, Howe's work remains the definitive historical account of the Society. It is evident that historical factors are incidental to the value of the Golden Dawn system of magic as a means of consciousness development.

W. E. BUTLER: *The Magician, his Training and Work,* Aquarian, London, 1959.

W. E. BUTLER: *Apprenticed to Magic,* Aquarian, London, 1962.

ISRAEL REGARDIE: *The Middle Pillar,* Llewellyn, St Paul, Minnesota, 1974.

ISRAEL REGARDIE: *The Art of True Healing,* Helios, Cheltenham, 1966.

WILLIAM G. GRAY: *The Ladder of Lights,* Helios, Cheltenham, 1968.

The above represent contemporary occult guidebooks, formulated within the Golden Dawn tradition. Butler and Regardie, in particular, demonstrate the occult use of colours in meditation, the use of mantras and visualization, and the relationship of the Tree of Life to the body of man. Regardie's *Middle Pillar,* which describes mental exercises based upon the central column of the Tree of Life, demonstrates a process of altering consciousness just as the yogis do. The *Ladder of Lights* written by a protégé of Regardie's, describes the climbing-back-to-Godhead process, and details the cosmic–mythological imagery of the mind.

Magical Cosmology

Cosmology is the study of the universe as an orderly whole, and for the mystic and the magician the cosmos is indeed an awesome and vast ongoing process.

Since earliest times, man has sought to rationalize his place in his environment. In Paleolithic times he realized that he must do battle with the elements to survive, and he conceived of gods in the wind and in the floods and storms. He imitated the animals he hunted to trick them into his lair, and perhaps he considered that by a similar method of imitation – in ritual or in special offerings – he could similarly ensnare the gods, or at least appease them in their wrath. Throughout recorded history man has structured his universe. There have been regional gods – of mountains, streams and the earth – and there have been ineffable, transcendent gods far beyond the sky.

Samuel MacGregor Mathers, one of the founders of the Order of the Golden Dawn (see pp. 48–50) was especially interested in cosmology and the study of ancient systems of mystical thought. He translated the medieval *Zohar*, the central books of the Qabalah, and other rare grimoires and magical writings. He was responsible too for writing some of the beautiful rituals of the higher Rosicrucian grades beyond the Golden Dawn, which were given only to advanced occultists. In writing these he assembled in a type of collage the sacred hymns, prayers and occult cosmologies of a number of ancient sources. Basically, he drew on those mystical religions which *structured the universe*. Magic basically asserts that man's psyche is the microcosm of the entire universe, and therefore the old religions which produced hierarchies of gods, are also useful symbolic frameworks for the expansion of consciousness.

Mathers believed, as all occultists do, that gods and deities are symbols of both the personality and aspiration. The gods of ancient Greece often seemed very human in their exploits; they were jealous and proud. Set, in

Egyptian mythology, successfully lured his brother Osiris to climb into a coffin, and he later scattered his body in pieces all over Egypt.

Is this the way, we ask, that gods should act? A careful analysis of comparative mythology shows that gods embody both negative and positive qualities, and it is up to us to emulate or neglect their example.

Mathers, in the Golden Dawn, was using the meditative structure called the *Tree of Life* (see pp. 57–60) as his magical focus because it enabled a detailed comparison of the gods of several major ancient religions to be made.

Magic seeks to enlarge the consciousness step by step, in a particular way. For the magician to meditate upon the figure Mercury from the Roman pantheon, for example, would enhance the sense of lucidity and rational intellect. Luna and Diana, on the other hand, were changeable, emotive and instinctual, and symbolized quite a different facet of the personality! Mathers decided that since he was dealing with the Western mind, he should take Western gods. And since he wished that his magical procedures should be step by step, in grades, he had to choose cosmologies in which the gods, or levels of consciousness, were *distinct*.

The cosmologies chosen as the basis of western magic were: The Egyptian, the Greek, and a special Neoplatonic mystical system called 'Chaldean' which grew up around AD 300. These he correlated with the Qabalah, which is described in a separate section of this book.

THE EGYPTIAN COSMOLOGY

The ancient Egyptians conceived of their world as being surrounded by a chain of mountains. The sun rose each day through a hole in the East, and sank each night in the West. The sun, whether he was Ra or Osiris or Khenti Amenti, was personified as a deity who travelled through the hours of both day and night, so that half his time was spent traversing the sky by day and the other half, in battling the forces of the under world – the twelve hours or 'dungeons' of night. The underworld was in fact a rather frightening place. Wallace Budge writes: 'In all the books of the otherworld we find pits of fire, abysses of darkness, murderous knives, streams of boiling water, foul stenches, fiery serpents, hideous animal-headed monsters and creatures, and cruel death-dealing beings of various shapes . . .' (*The Egyptian Heaven and Hell*, p. 88).

The Egyptians noted to their satisfaction that the sun always rose with the new dawn, and so the sun became a symbol of the triumph of light over darkness and of good over evil. The sun god entered and passed through the regions of the underworld (which was called the *Tuat*) by means of sacred words of power called *hekau*, and these had been originally given by Thoth, the god of wisdom.

Two of the most important Egyptian sacred books were the *Am Tuat*, compiled by the priests of Amen Ra at Thebes, and the *Book of Gates*, an Osirian work dating from the Middle Kingdom (c. 2000 BC). The latter is supplemented by the *Egyptian Book of the Dead*.

The Egyptian cosmologies stressed the rebirth of the sun worshipper – in reincarnation and by resurrection. In the first case, the follower of the sun god entered his boat after death and rode with him through the underworld to be reborn with him each day. In the second case, the deceased person travelled down to Osiris' Kingdom in the Elysian fields where the great god and his forty-two companion deities were in residence. To get there, the deceased person had to know the sacred names of power in the underworld, and the names of the forty-two gods of the fields. The essence of the person (his heart) would be weighed against truth (a feather) by Anubis in the Hall of Judgment, and Thoth would give his verdict. The deceased, if pure, would be allowed to stay in the Elysian fields. Meanwhile, a monster called Am-nut – a combination of crocodile, lion and hippopotamus – waited to devour the condemned . . . !

Application in magic

Modern white magic similarly offers its practitioners 'rebirth' or initiation. In the Qabalistic rituals, the 'sun-god' level of consciousness is represented by Tiphareth. The rituals of Tiphareth, the most important of all, were strongly influenced by the myths of Osiris, and the magician was dressed in ritual robes so that he could imagine he was Osiris reborn. Also, in modern magic, there is a strong emphasis on names of power. These are usually the sacred names of God in Hebrew, but the so-called Ritual of the Hexagram, which can be used as a type of exorcism, has a strong Egyptian content. It has to be remembered that the sacred name (invocation or 'spell') reflects the universal belief in the power of sound. In the Bible we are told: 'In the Beginning was the Word', and the same was true of the ancient Egyptians. In Hinduism and Yoga, we find a similar emphasis on sacred mantras which may be used in meditation, almost, as it were, to take the yogi back to the essence of creation.

While the Egyptian religion has had most influence on modern magic, largely because of the diversity of its god images which are useful for ritual, the Greek and Chaldean religions were also important.

GREEK COSMOLOGY

One of the main concepts which influenced modern magic was the idea, developed by the Greeks, of an underworld which one could explore. The initiates of the Orphic mysteries were told that the body was like a tomb. On death (or in ecstasy) the spirit went into the heavenly regions and was then reborn until it eventually emerged as a pure spirit living in an Olympian heaven far beyond the sky. (It was only in the early cosmology that Olympus was a mountain.) As with the Egyptian religion, the mysteries of Eleusis also dealt with the cycles of nature which were linked symbolically with the fate of man. The lessons of Eleusis were centred upon Persephone and Demeter, symbolizing the corn and 'Mother Earth'. Initiates were told the legend of Persephone's abduction into the underworld at the hands of Aidoneus (Hades). Demeter, her mother and goddess of the harvest, sat in mourning and the crops failed, so Zeus sent Hermes into the Underworld to give Persephone the seed of life (a pomegranate). This allowed Persephone to spend half her time in the world of the living, but for the other half she was obliged to continue as queen of the Underworld. The Greeks (at Eleusis) were thus instructed that *life comes out of death*, and that rebirth is the natural order of things.

Application in magic

Modern magic regards the Tree of Life diagram as a symbol of the mind and its potential. In most people this potential is unrealized so that the energies of the psyche are largely *unconscious*. The Underworld thus becomes an excellent symbol for man's unconscious thought processes. It is interesting to note that the first path on the Tree of Life is that of the twenty-second Tarot card, *The World*, which shows Persephone dancing in a wreath of wheat. Just as she was taken down through the earth, the lowest sphere on the Tree, *Malkuth*, (normal consciousness), is represented by the four elements, Persephone, as a symbol of the wheat grain, is undoubtedly an earth deity. We see here the idea that mythology represents the symbols of the mind. Other references may be found in Plato's myth of Er (in *The Republic*) and the Roman *Aeneid* of Vergil, which both deal with journeys in the Underworld.

CHALDEAN COSMOLOGY

This was the least important classical influence in the Golden Dawn magical society but represented a vestige of Persian religion and Mithraism. The so-called *Chaldean Oracles* were the work of three Neoplatonic

55

philosophers: Julian the Chaldean; Julian the Magician (his son); and Iamblichus, who wrote the book *Concerning the Mysteries*.

The Chaldean system was similar to the Tree of Life. Its cosmology incorporated a trinity consisting of *Mystes*, the Primordial Fire; the *Great Mother*; and their *Divine Son*. There was also a fourth deity, the *Daughter*, whom the Chaldeans called Hecate, and she was said to be the goddess of nature and the moon. Like Diane, she was pure and virginal, but she also had an unpredictable, stormy side to her nature; her hair consisted of 'snakes that terrified with fire'.

According to the Chaldean system, a person's body was intrinsically impure, and the spirit had to be untainted if it had any hope of finding its way back to its divine source. The initiate learned that he had to perform special rituals to rid himself of the impurity of Hyle (earth), otherwise Hecate's demons would be unleashed upon him in revenge. Nevertheless, like the Egyptians, and also the Gnostics, who were contemporaries of Iamblichus, there was special emphasis on *magical formulae*. Illumination was said to result from gnosis, divine knowledge. A person who knew the names of the cosmic rulers could call them forth and be uplifted by them.

Application in Magic

Possibly from the Chaldean system more than any other source, modern magicians acquired the idea that one could invoke the gods in ritual for specific spiritual illumination. A number of Persian/Mithraic passages, of considerable poetic beauty, were used in the magical ritual of *Taphthatharath*, which was supposed to conjure a spirit of *Hod* (Intellect) into visible appearance.

SOURCEBOOK

For all the above traditions, see N. Drury: *The Path of the Chameleon*, Spearman, London, 1973.

The Qabalah

Probably more than any other mystical philosophy, the Qabalah has exerted a profound influence on the occult. Like most forms of mysticism it describes the levels of consciousness and being between man and Godhead, but it is not for this reason that it has become the basis of modern magic. The Qabalah employs a complex symbol called the Tree of Life as its central motif, and it is because this Tree is such a pragmatic framework on which to base rituals and meditations that the Qabalah is relevant today.

In the Qabalistic tradition – and the world QBLH means an oral or secret tradition – the whole of the manifested universe is said to have originated in Ain Soph, the hidden and infinite God-Energy which is without qualities or attributes. The Qabalists believed that as soon as one tried to ascribe qualities to Ain Soph, the sense of infinity and limitlessness would be lost.

The Tree of Life in effect describes a type of crystallization process by which the *Infinite* gradually becomes *Finite*. And the latter is the world as we see it all around us. For the Qabalist, though, there are intermediary stages of being or mind, or energy or consciousness – call it what you will. The Ain Soph thus reveals aspects of its divinity to man and on the Tree of Life these are represented symbolically by ten major stages called *sephiroth*. In modern magical usage, whereby magic becomes rather similar to yoga, the *sephiroth* are best regarded as levels of consciousness. The magician begins with his present level of 'earth consciousness' and tries to retrace the sacred steps back to Godhead. The ten levels are designated as follows:

KETHER	*The Crown* or peak of Creation
HOKMAH	*Wisdom* (The Father)
BINAH	*Understanding* (The Mother)

HESED	Mercy
GEBURAH	Severity or Strength
TIPHARETH	Beauty and Harmony (The Son)
NETZACH	Victory
HOD	Splendour
YESOD	The Foundation
MALKUTH	Kingdom or Earth (The Daughter)

One distinction which becomes immediately obvious is that some of the sephiroth have 'personal' attributes – the Father, Mother, Son and Daughter – while others mention only abstract attributes, e.g. Mercy. In fact, a closer analysis, particularly of the way in which the Tree has been incorporated into magic, shows that this is not really so. The magician takes considerable notice of the gods and goddesses of different world religions and he endeavours to compare and correlate them in terms of the attributes, sacred qualities and aspirations which they personify. He considers the gods to be symbols of *what he himself may become*, and regards their mythology as a type of symbolic energy process deep in the spiritual areas of his mind. This is what Jung was implying in his theory of the Archetypes of the Collective Unconscious, but for the magician it is a pragmatic reality. He knows the gods are inherent in his mind and he devises rituals and meditations *as aids for encountering them*.

Returning to the Tree, it becomes apparent that each of the sephiroth levels of consciousness play an important harmonizing role.

The Crown, *Kether* resides at the top of the Tree. It is a level which transcends duality and in this sense resembles the Buddhist state, *Nirvana*, or infinite bliss. The next levels, *Hokmah* and *Binah* have sexual ascriptions, being the Great Father and Mother respectively. Together with *Kether* these form the Qabalistic Trinity. Hokmah is the outward dynamic creative force, and Binah is the womb of creation from which all is born. As such, she is the mother of us all.

It is interesting to note that the Qabalists regarded their mystery teaching in part as a commentary on Genesis, and the remaining seven levels on the Tree were said to be the Seven Days of Creation. These seven also have mythological counterparts, and in fact to all extents and purposes, the Seven Days represent the total mystical Universe. The reason for this is that man was separated from Godhead by the Fall, and the gulf between the Trinity and the rest of the Tree is described as the Abyss. Magicians claim it is possible to cross the Abyss, but at this level of being, all notion of ego and self disappear. The finite transforms to the infinite.

In mythology, the levels represented by *Hesed* and *Geburah* refer to the Father of the world as we know it. Often, like Zeus, he is said to reside high up upon a mountain reaching into the infinite sky, and it is appropriate that Zeus' home was on lofty Olympus. Hesed represents the father-god in his merciful form and Geburah represents him at war. The Greeks called this form Aries, and the Romans, Mars. According to the Qabalah the universe is composed of a dynamic conflict between life and death – building up and breaking down. Hesed maintains peace and order in the cosmos, Geburah breaks things down once their use is past.

Below them, we come to Tiphareth, which resides in the centre of the Tree. As can be seen from its location. it is midway between man and Godhead, and thus represents the god-man or messiah. The aim of all spiritual philosophies is to allow man to become the child of the gods, and so Tiphareth is the *Son*. In different religions and mythologies, we find that Osiris, Apollo, Dionysus and Christ have a strikingly similar role as symbols of *new life*. Usually these figures are also sun gods, since the sun is always reborn from the 'death' of night time, with each dawn.

The main aim of the Hermetic Order of the Golden Dawn, was to prepare its practitioners for the mystical experience of Tiphareth, and their rituals incorporated both Egyptian and Christian symbols.

Descending now on the Tree, we come to *Netzach*, which represents love, art and the emotions. Opposite, we find *Hod* which counterbalances, with rational intellect and reason. Then we come to *Yesod* which in a sense represents the lower areas of the mind, if we realize that the Tree is in effect a symbolic diagram representing the mind-potential of man. In Yesod, which equates in psychology with the lower unconscious we find the basic sexual drives. The Qabalists referred to it as the *Nephesch* or animal soul, and mythologically it is represented by the moon. Just as the moon *reflects* the sun (true illumination), lunar worship tends to arouse the animal instincts rather than the spiritual ones. Witchcraft, in particular, with its lunar Sabbats, incorporated the worship of the Goat (beast) and the witches rode to Sabbats on their brooms (a symbol of the male phallus). Witchcraft was and is a sexual religion.

The final sephirah is *Malkuth*, which represents our present consciousness. Our task is to find our way back into the occult areas of the mind, which are in fact the source of all inspiration and knowledge.

In fairness to the classical Qabalists, it has to be admitted that the summary given above presents a modern, occult view of the Qabalah rather than an historical one. Judaism, of course, was monotheistic, and hence it was not appropriate to talk of 'the gods' so much as 'the One God'. However, it is probably true that the distinction between polytheism and monotheism is overplayed academically when in reality it tends to be a symbolic division. Wallis Budge has mentioned that even in ancient Egypt, all the gods were said to come from *one* – Ra – although for practical purposes, the gods were represented as separate beings in their own right.

Magicians and occultists use the Qabalah and the Tree of Life as a framework on which to pin the symbols of all Western (and Eastern) religions. They have thus expanded its use beyond its original Judaic confines. In recent times also (since the lifetime of Eliphas Lévi a century ago) a connection has also been made between the major arcana of the Tarot, and the ten levels on the Tree. The Sephirah are the levels of consciousness as such, and the Tarot cards are the 'doorways' or 'paths' which lead to them. The Qabalah has thus become an intricate and profound 'modernized' cosmology. Its use is to allow man to harmonize all his mind processes and eventually to rediscover the spiritual illumination which lies within.

SOURCEBOOKS

Classical translations of the Qabalah

H. SPERLING and M. SIMON: *The Zohar*, Soncino Press, London, 1970.
  This is the most accessible complete translation of the medieval *Zohar*, the first Qabalistic treatises ensuing from the essentially oral tradition. It is thought that they are the work of Moses de Leon and date from around AD 1280, although the origins of the Qabalah as such are several centuries BC.
MACGREGOR MATHERS: *The Kabbalah Unveiled*, Redway, London, 1888; reprinted in several editions by Routledge & Kegan Paul, London.
  It is considerably embarrassing to modern Hebrew scholars that much of the recent interest in the Qabalah has come from occultists, and that it was MacGregor Mathers, co-founder of the Golden Dawn, who translated the Latin version of the Zohar into English. The book is a translation of the work *Kabbala Denudata*, by the medieval scholar Knorr Von Rosenroth.

Academic sources

GERSHOM G. SCHOLEM: *Major Trends in Jewish Mysticism*, Schocken Books, New York, 1961.
  Scholem is regarded as the major living authority on the Qabalah, and although he is the author of several books on the subject, this one, which includes a full treatment of the major Qabalistic schools of thought, is one of his best.

A. E. WAITE: *The Holy Kabbalah*, University Books, New York, 1960.

Aleister Crowley used to refer to this writer as 'dead-Waite', referring to the heaviness of his style, and unfortunately this is true of most of Waite's scholarly works. Scholem has acknowledged Waite's contribution, however, and this was all the more remarkable when we consider that Waite was not fluent in Hebrew itself. This book is regarded as one of Waite's best. Apart from outlining the classical sources of the Qabalah, it also considers the related alchemical literature of the Middle Ages, and the ways in which the Qabalah influenced magic, astrology, Freemasonry and the tarot.

CHRISTIAN GINSBURG: *The Kabbalah*, Routledge & Kegan Paul, London, 1956 (1st edn 1863).

ADOLPHE FRANCK: *The Kabbalah*, University Books, New York, 1967 (1st edn 1843).

Two of the classic treatments of the Qabalah, both over a century old, Ginsburg's book tends to be rather dry in its treatment, while Franck's is simplistic, and has been overshadowed by more recent writers.

CARLO SUARES: *The Cipher of Genesis*, Bantam Books, New York, 1973.

One of the functions of the Qabalah was a symbolic commentary on Genesis, and this volume is the best treatment of the magical codes of the Old Testament.

LEO SCHAYA: *The Universal Meaning of the Kabbalah*, University Books, New York; Allen & Unwin, London, 1971.

Z'EV BE SHIMON HALEVI; *Adam and the Kabbalistic Tree*, Rider, London, 1974.

These two recent books provide an excellent coverage of the cosmic side of the Qabalah. Schaya describes the 'heavenly' sephiroth and mantras admirably and several Jewish authorities have commended it as a lucid text. Halevi's volume, a successor to his less impressive *Tree of Life* relates the Qabalah to a study of Jung's psychology and theory of Archetypes.

CHARLES PONCE: *Kabbalah*, Garnstone Press, London, 1974.

Extremely easy to read, and superbly decorated with medieval etchings from the works of Jacob Boehme, this book is a valuable recent addition to the Qabalistic literature. Poncé also relates the Qabalah to Yoga and other Eastern philosophies.

Books on the Qabalah written by occultists

GARETH KNIGHT: *A Practical Guide to Qabalistic Symbolism* (two vols) Helios, Cheltenham, England, 1965.

Divided into Part I, dealing with the sephiroth or spheres on the Tree of Life, and Part II, dealing with the Tarot Paths, this work is possibly the best modern treatment from the occult viewpoint. All of the sephiroth are discussed in detail, and the full symbolism of the Tarot is given. His work on the Qabalah is, however, based on Dion Fortune's earlier volume *The Mystical Qabalah* (Benn, London, 1957) which is also recommended.

ISRAEL REGARDIE: *The Garden of Pomegranates*, Thorsons, London: Llewellyn, Minnesota, 1970.

Written by the former secretary to Aleister Crowley and one of the most resourceful living authorities, this book is a reliable summary of the modern application of the Qabalah. It is supplemented by his *Tree of Life* (Weiser, New York, 1971) which provides one of the best studies of the connection between mythology and modern magic.

WILLIAM STIRLING: *The Canon*, Garnstone, London, 1974 (first edn 1897).

Deals primarily with the symbolic, mystic relationship between numbers and words in the Qabalah.

FRATER ACHAD: *Q.B.L.*, Weiser, New York, 1972.

The key work by Aleister Crowley's 'magical heir' Frater Achad (Charles Stansfeld Jones). Achad is noted for his spurious attempt to reallocate the Tarot trumps on the Tree of Life and for his total adoration of his occult master. There are a number of references to the 'New Aeon' which Achad thought was heralded by Crowley.

The Tarot

One of the most interesting and popular of all occult practices is the use of the Tarot cards. Most people know them as ancestors of the standard playing cards, and they are perhaps best known for their use in fortune-telling. They have also appeared as symbols in modern plays and musicals, and as large, colourful posters. Tarot cards are popularly held to have been handed down by the gypsies, and there is a certain veneer of superstition surrounding them. However, most of the legends concerning the Tarot cards are false. They were certainly not invented by the gypsies of medieval Europe since they are known to have been present in Italy a century before the gypsies arrived. Nor did the Tarot originate in ancient Egypt. This legend is part of the eighteenth- and nineteenth-century romance of 'lost cultures'. People looked back to a golden age which had possessed a secret, esoteric wisdom and they transposed into all sorts of fictitious or symbolic locations like initiation chambers in the Great Pyramid, or Atlantis and the lost Lemuria.

Antoine Court de Gebelin (1725–84), a French theologian and student of mythology, was responsible for some of the early, fanciful tales about the Tarot. In his book *Le Monde Primitif*, Gebelin surmised, without any proof, that the Tarot was part of the Egyptian Book of Thoth - the book of divine wisdom – and that the cards symbolized in a pictorial form the arcane knowledge of the initiates of ancient Egypt. Particularly important was the number 7 – there are twenty-two major Tarot cards: $3 \times 7 +$ 'The Fool', zero. Each of the four suits was composed of 2×7 cards. Gebelin also claimed that the word *Tarot* was derived from the Egyptian phrase meaning 'royal road of life', and he anticipated that the cards were an important occult tool for the transformation of man.

Gebelin's speculation was continued by Alliette, a Parisian wig maker or professor of mathematics – according to different accounts. Alliette, who wrote under the pseudonym Etteilla (his own name reversed), declared that the Tarot originated 171 years after the Deluge and was produced by seventeen magicians. From his room in the Hotel de Crillon he used to offer pronouncements on the divinatory use of the Tarot including the fate of his fellow men in the French Revolution.

The next major theorist of the Tarot, and one who has perhaps influenced modern occultism more than any other, was Eliphas Lévi. Lévi, was a priest of the Catholic Church, a graphic artist and a political satirist. He was fascinated by the Qabalah with its ten levels of consciousness, and he made the brilliant discovery that the twenty-two Major Tarot Trumps correlated symbolically, *as the paths leading to these stages of consciousness.* Likewise with the Tree of Life, there are 22 links between the 10 spheres or 'sephiroth'. The Tarot, therefore, was an important representation of the images of mystical consciousness.

Lévi's work was extended by Gerard Encausse ('Papus'), who similarly wrote commentaries on the relation between the Tarot and the Qabalah, and in particular, the twenty-two letters of the Hebrew alphabet.

Lévi also exercised a strong measure of influence on the Order of the Golden Dawn. A. E. Waite, whose Rider Pack is well known, translated a number of Lévi's books including the *Histoire de la Magie* into English, and regarded him as the most significant magus of his age. Aleister Crowley even considered himself to be Lévi's reincarnation, and drew on Lévi's correlations in formulating his own work on the Tarot, *The Book of Thoth.*

The Golden Dawn magicians used the Tarot cards as pathways into the mind, rather than as a means of divination, and the former is undoubtedly its most significant means of application. Each of the cards could be visualized as a doorway, through which the magician could imaginatively pass. He would then have symbolic and mystical visions related to the imagery of the Tree of Life.

The most commonly agreed-upon correlation of the Tarot cards with the Hebrew Letters (that followed by A. E. Waite and Paul Foster Case) is as follows:

0	The Fool	—	Aleph
1	The Magician	—	Beth
2	The High Priestess	—	Gimel
3	The Empress	—	Daleth
4	The Emperor	—	Heh
5	The Hierophant	—	Vau
6	The Lovers	—	Zain
7	The Chariot	—	Cheth

8	Strength	—	Teth
9	The Hermit	—	Yod
10	The Wheel of Fortune	—	Kaph
11	Justice	—	Lamed
12	The Hanged Man	—	Mem
13	Death	—	Nun
14	Temperance	—	Samekh
15	The Devil	—	Ayin
16	The Tower	—	Peh
17	The Star	—	Tzaddi
18	The Moon	—	Qoph
19	The Sun	—	Resh
20	Judgement	—	Shin
21	The World	—	Tau

The modern occultist, therefore, uses the Major arcana of the Tarot as his doorway to greater consciousness (the other 56 cards, which are divided into 4 suits: wands and swords (masculine), and cups and pentacles (feminine) – are of less significance). Each of the Major Trumps relates to a certain portion of the psyche, symbolized by the Tree of Life. The Tree is a living, vibrant thing, and each *sephirah* flows into another. The magician too, must flow along the tides of consciousness.

Rather in the same manner as Jung's Archetypes of the Unconscious the Tarot images constitute a type of mythology of the mind. The magician meets the gods in his visions for they are in fact embodiments of different facets of his personality: his warring aspect for example being represented by Mars (*The Chariot*) and his more intuitive emotional side, by Venus (*The Star*). The Tarot card meditations *help the occultist to balance his personality*.

The following are the brief meanings of the Tarot cards as incorporated in the Golden Dawn teaching (from S. L. MacGregor Mathers, *The Tarot*).

1 *The Juggler or Magician* Before a table covered with the appliances of his art stands the figure of a juggler, one hand upraised holding a wand (in some packs, a cup), the other pointing downwards. He wears a cap of maintenance like that of the kings, whose wide brim forms a sort of aureole round his head. His body and arms form the shape of the Hebrew letter Aleph, to which this card corresponds. He symbolizes *Will*.

2 *The High Priestess, or Female Pope* A woman crowned with a high mitre or tiara (her head encircled by a veil), a stole (or a solar cross)

upon her breast, and the Book of Science open in her hand. She represents *Science, Wisdom* or *Knowledge*

3 *The Empress* A winged and crowned woman seated upon a throne, having in one hand a sceptre bearing a globe surmounted by a cross, while she rests the other upon a shield with an eagle blazoned therein on whose breast is the cross. She is the Symbol of *Action*, the result of the union of Science and Will.

4 *The Emperor* He is crowned (and, leaning against a throne, his legs form a cross, while beside him, beneath his left hand, is a shield blazoned with an eagle). In his right hand he bears a sceptre similar to that of the Empress. His body and arms form a triangle, of which his head is the apex, so that the whole figure represents a triangle above a cross. He represents *Realisation*.

5 *The Hierophant or Pope* He is crowned with the papal tiara, and seated between the two pillars of Hermes and Solomon, with his right hand he makes the sign of esoterism, and with his left he leans upon a staff surmounted by a triple cross. (Before him kneel two ministers). *He is the symbol of Mercy and Beneficence.*

6 *The Lovers* This is usually described as representing Man between Vice and Virtue, while a winged genius threatens Vice with his dart. But I am rather inclined to the opinion that it represents the Qabalistical Microprosopus between Binah and Malkuth (see my *Kabbalah Unveiled*), while the figure about shows the Influence descending from Kether. It is usually considered to mean *Proof* or *Trial*; but I am inclined to suggest *Wise* Disposition as its significa-tion.

7 *The Chariot* This is a most complicated and important symbol, which has been restored by Eliphas Lévi. It represents a Conqueror crowned and bearing a sceptre, riding in a cubical chariot, surmounted by four columns and a canopy, and drawn by two horses, one of which looks straight forward, while the other turns his head towards him. (Two wheels are shown in the complete single-headed figure.) It represents *Triumph*, and *Victory* of Justice and Judgment.

8 *Justice* A woman crowned and seated on a throne (between two columns), holding in her right hand an upright sword, and in her left the scales. She symbolizes *Equilibrium* and *Justice*.

9 *The Hermit* An old and bearded man wrapped in a mantle, and with his head covered with a cowl, bearing in his right hand the lantern of occult science, while in his left he holds his magic wand half hidden beneath his cloak. He is *Prudence*.

10 *The Wheel of Fortune* A wheel of seven spokes (the two halves of the double-headed cards make it eight spokes, which is incorrect) revolving (between two uprights). On the ascending side is an animal ascending, and on the descending side is a sort of monkey descending; both forms are bound to the wheel. Above it is the form of an angel (or a sphinx in some) holding a sword in one hand and a crown in the other. This very complicated symbol is much disfigured, and has been well restored by Lévi. It symbolizes *Fortune*, good or bad.

11 *Strength or Fortitude* A woman crowned with crown and cap of maintenance, who calmly, and without effort, closes the jaws of a furious lion. She represents *Strength*.

12 *The Hanged Man* This extraordinary symbol is almost unintelligible in the double-headed cards. Properly, it represents a man hung head downwards from a sort of gibbet by one foot (his hands are bound behind his back in such a manner that his body forms a triangle with the point downwards), and his legs a cross above it. (Two sacks or weights are attached to his armpits.) He symbolises *Sacrifice*.

13 *Death* A skeleton armed with a scythe (wherewith he mows down heads in a meadow like grass). He signifies *Transformation*, or *Change*.

14 *Temperance* An angel with the sign of the Sun on her brow pouring liquid from one vessel into another. She represents *Combination*.

15 *The Devil* A horned and winged demon with eagle's claws (standing on an altar to which two smaller devils are bound by a collar and cord). In his left hand he bears a flame-headed sceptre. He is the image of *Fate* or *Fatality*, good or evil.

16 *The Lightning-struck Tower* A Tower whose upper part is like a crown, struck by a lightning-flash. (Two men fall headlong from it, one of whom is in such an attitude as to form a Hebrew letter Ayin.) Sparks and debris are falling. It shows *Ruin, Disruption*.

17 *The Star* A nude female figure pours water upon the earth from two vases. In the heavens above her shines the Blazing Star of the

Magi (surrounded by seven others), trees and plants grow beneath her magic influence (and on one the butterfly of Psyche alights). She is the star of *Hope*.

18 *The Moon* The moon shining in the heavens, drops of dew falling, a wolf and a dog howling at the Moon, and halted at the foot of two towers, a path which loses itself in the horizon (and is sprinkled with drops of blood), a crayfish emblematic of the sign Cancer, ruled over by the Moon, crawls through water in the foreground towards the land. It symbolizes *Twilight, Deception*, and *Error*.

19 *The Sun* The Sun sending down his rays upon two children who suggest the sign Gemini. (Behind them is a low wall.) It signifies *Earthly Happiness*.

20 *The Last Judgment* An Angel in the heavens blowing a trumpet, to which a standard with a cross thereon is attached. The Dead rise from their tombs. It signifies *Renewal, Result*.

o *The Foolish Man* A man with a fool's cap, dressed like a jester, with a stick and bundle over his shoulder. Before him is the butterfly of pleasure luring him on (while in some packs a tiger, in others a dog, attacks him from behind). It signifies *Folly, Expiation*.

21 *The Universe* Within a flowery wreath is a female figure nude save for a light scarf. She represents Nature and the Divine Presence therein. In each hand she should bear a wand. At the four Angles of the card are the four cherubic animals of the Apocalypse. Above, the Eagle and the Man; below the Lion and the Bull. It represents *Completion, Reward*.

SOURCEBOOKS

PAUL F. CASE: *The Tarot*, Macoy, New York, 1947.

A. E. WAITE: *The Pictorial Key to the Tarot*, Rider, London, 1910. Reprinted several times.

Possibly the best accounts of the symbolism of the Tarot as it relates to magic and the Tree of Life. Waite at one time headed the Golden Dawn in England, and Case was his opposite number in the New York group, the Builders of the Adytum. Both writers employed female graphic artists to portray the cards, Waite drawing on the official symbolism of his Order. The designs in the Case book, drawn by Jessie Burns Parke, are more professional and in a practical sense, more useful than those of Pamela Coleman Smith in the Waite-Rider pack. The latter are sometimes depicted in rather garish colour which obscures the detail and also hinders the perception of the subtlety of the cards. Both versions however follow a similar sequence, and have been employed by later commentators like Eden Gray and Dr Louis Martello.

GARETH KNIGHT: *A Practical Guide to Qabalistic Symbolism* (vols I and 2, the second being explicitly on the Tarot), Helios, Cheltenham, England, 1965.

Knight provides a detailed description of the mythological imagery associated with each of the Tarot Paths, and the magical effects on consciousness. He also adds helpful comparative notes on each of the major Tarot packs, and comments on their respective strengths and weaknesses. His book is illustrated, however, by the Grimaud pack which consists of simplistic wood-cut designs and is of little or no use for visualization purposes.

ALEISTER CROWLEY: *The Book of Thoth*, Weiser, New York, 1971.

This book was Crowley's last major work, and it has been reprinted with mostly black and white illustrations of his spectacular Tarot pack. The cards themselves, which were painted by Lady Frieda Harris, have been re-issued in colour by Llewellyn, Minnesota.

Crowley's book is not a good guide for the beginner since it includes elements biased strongly in favour of Crowley's own personal philosophy, e.g. in accordance with his formulation of a technique of sexual magic (in which he was the Great Beast 666, and his partner the Whore of Babylon) Crowley's representation of the card strength is called Lust and depicts his scarlet woman. Crowley also adopts the unorthodox procedure of placing *The Emperor* in the position of *The Star*, and vice versa.

However, his cards are undoubtedly the most exciting pack visually and seem to contain a great deal of psychic energy. Their only rival from the graphic point of view is the modern Palladini Pack known also as the Aquarian Pack. This is in the Art Nouveau style and is extremely beautiful. It is however inaccurate in some of its colour treatments, a notable example being the confused colouring of *The High Priestess* and *The Empress*.

STUART R. KAPLAN: *Tarot Classic*, Grosset & Dunlap, New York, 1972; Robert Hale, London, 1974.

A good general history of the Tarot, with several pages of representations of different packs, notably the Venetian Tarot, the Mantegna Tarocchi, the Italian Minchiate cards, the Marseilles Pack, the Burdel Tarot, the Grand Etteilla Pack, and the Waite Pack, among others. Kaplan's survey of the Major Arcana is fairly superficial, but his book covers the full development of the Tarot. Considerable attention is given to the theories of Court de Gebelin, who considered the Tarot to be of Egyptian origin.

ALFRED DOUGLAS: *The Tarot*, Penguin Books, Harmondsworth, 1973.

Douglas favours the hypothesis that the Tarot conceals a mystical doctrine essentially in line with the Gnostic-Cathar-Albigensian world-view, and that because of this symbolism was heretical and remained a secret, underground tradition. A useful text, marred only by rather simplistic textual illustrations.

The Tattvas

The Tattvas were one of the most notable Eastern elements in the ritual magic of the Golden Dawn, an all the more remarkable inclusion when we consider that this Order was based solidly on the occult inspiration of Western mythology.

Nevertheless, the Tattvas were adopted from their original Hindu context as appropriate symbols of the elements. There are five basic symbols in the series:

Tejas, a red equilateral triangle   = FIRE
Apas, a silver crescent   = WATER
Vayu, a blue circle   = AIR
Prithivi, a yellow square   = EARTH
Akasa, an indigo egg   = SPIRIT

W. E. Butler has alluded to the Tattvas as tides operating in the magnetic sphere of the Earth so that 'The Element of Akasa is strongest at sunrise, then it merges into the element of Vayu. This in turn merges into Tejas, and this into Apas, and finally Apas merges into Prithivi. . . .'

However, the major function of these symbols is as doorways into the visionary recesses of the mind. The symbols may be used in isolation or with one superimposed upon the other. In a sense they act as a directive to the unconscious. The symbols become catalysts for releasing certain imagery, so that a magician who meditated on the red symbol Tejas, would begin to experience visions associated with the element fire. If he meditated upon Apas, representing water, he could expect visions of water and these may entail fantasy beings of Western mythology, for example, water spirits or mermaids.

The method used by the magician is as follows. Having prepared a series of pictorial representations on white cardboard, he stares at the symbol until its after-image beings to appear. He then retains the latter in his mind as an image and meditates fixedly upon it. The next step is to imagine that the after-image has become a doorway through which one may pass. If the meditator is able to project his consciousness in this way, he then experiences visions appropriate to the element which he has selected. He is able to withdraw from the vision, rather in the manner of Hesse's magic theatre described in *Steppenwolf*, by returning through the doorway by which he entered.

The technique of using the Tattvas as 'astral doorways' is not intended as an escapist diversion, but instead is supposed to show the practitioner that certain active energies are operative in his unconscious mind. These are rendered into a human form by the structuring processes of the mind itself and appear in visions as gnomes, elves, fairies, nature-spirits and so on. In its most profound form such meditation could lead to visions of angels and archangels because these too have a symbolic relationship with the elements. For example, Michael is the archangel of Fire, Raphael of Air, Uriel of Earth and Gabriel of Water. The vision takes the form whereby the magician is able to address the spirit beings and request certain information from them. In practical terms, he is addressing the repository of his unconscious mind, and bringing to the fore valuable, symbolic insights which may have been forever lost. It was also intended in the Golden Dawn that a magician could harmonize his personality by encountering those spirits which could counterbalance his weaknesses. A person with an 'airy', dreamy approach to life would benefit from a meeting with the goblins of the earth, for example, and a person with a somewhat 'watery' disposition could perhaps fortify his personality with fire!

The following account of a short Tattvic vision recorded by Mrs Mathers in the Golden Dawn, provides an example of the form the experience can take. Her focusing symbol had been the Crescent of Water combined with the Indigo Egg of Spirit:

a wide expanse of water with many reflections of bright light and occasionally glimpses of rainbow colours appearing. When divine and other names were pronounced, elementals of the mermaid and merman type [would] appear, but few of the other elemental forms. These water forms were extremely changeable, one moment appearing as solid mermaids and mermen, the next melting into foam.

Raising myself by means of the highest symbols I had been taught, and vibrating the names of Water, I rose until the water vanished, and instead I beheld a mighty world or globe, with its dimensions and divisions of Gods, Angels, Elementals and demons . . . the whole Universe of Water . . . I called on HCOMA and there appeared standing before me a mighty Archangel, with four wings, robed in glistening white and crowned. In one hand, the right, he held a species of trident, and in the left a Cup filled to the brim with an essence which he poured down below on either side. . . . (*Note*: HCOMA, pronounced He-Co-Mah is a special magical word for water, based on the so-called Enochian language which was used extensively in the Golden Dawn.)

SOURCEBOOKS

ISRAEL REGARDIE (ed.): *The Golden Dawn*, first published 1937–41, Aries Press, Chicago; new edition in one volume, Llewellyn, Minnesota, 1974.
    Volume 4 of the Golden Dawn material contains extensive notes on the Tattvas and the Enochian tablets, which derive from Dr John Dee, the Elizabethan astrologer. This is the best single source on the Tattvas, although J. H. Brennan's *Astral Doorways* (Aquarian Press, London, 1972) and W. E. Butler's *The Magician, his Training and Work* (Aquarian, London, 1959) are also useful books.
    For illustrations of elemental spirits see Geoffrey Hodson: *The Kingdom of the Gods*, Theosophical Publishing House, Adyar, Madras, India, 1952, and Arthur Rackham's and Edmund Dulac's illustrations to Shakespeare's *The Tempest* and *Grimm's Fairytales* (various editions).

Magical Attack

If a magician has supernatural powers can they be used to attack his enemies? Certainly there is a widespread tradition throughout history of spells and curses being used to injure or even kill people, either enemies of the magician or conjuror, or enemies of the clients who pay him to make the attack. But the concept of a 'magical attack' has come to have a special meaning drawn from the traditions of Western magic. Occasionally ritual magicians have come into conflict and have engaged in 'psychic warfare', each performing rituals designed to cause harm to the other. Sometimes such rituals are intended to do actual physical injury to the victim, causing him to become ill, or suffer pain. On other occasions the rituals are intended to invoke supernatural beings who will attack the victim, or terrorize him.

When carrying out such an attack the magician is traditionally required to take precautions to protect himself, especially in cases where he invokes entities which may not only attack the victim, but also turn and attack the magician.

In general cases of magical attack, where there is no actual battle underway, the victim may be completely unaware of what is happening, merely feeling unwell, restless, exhibiting various physiological and psychological symptoms and suffering various psychic manifestations. The outward symptoms will be very much the same as in the case of an individual who is suffering from some form of influence or obsession. The attack may be launched for a variety of reasons, but usually either to cause suffering to an enemy, or to force a person to conform to the will of the magician.

The treatment of such an attack varies according to the symptoms and the source; usually the physical symptoms will have been treated medically, without success, before it is realized that they have a psychic origin. However, it must be emphasized that psychic or magical attacks are

75

comparatively rare (most would-be magicians have neither the knowledge nor the skill to initiate one).

While there are very few accounts of magical attack written from a serious occult point of view, two rather outstanding instances have been documented. The first, and probably the best known, is that related by Dion Fortune in her book *Psychic Self Defence*, where she tells of an attack upon her by the leader of a magical fraternity. The symptoms were extremely unusual – innumerable large cats began appearing in the neighbourhood, and eventually an enormous phantom cat manifested. Fortune was also attacked astrally when she left her body to undertake some occult work, and it was there that the real battle took place, with the attacker and the victim engaged in combat while out of the body. When she returned to her physical body, Fortune found she was badly scratched as if by a cat – a physical symptom of the astral battle. However, having triumphed over the attacker, the cats disappeared and all symptoms vanished.

The second account was given by the French novelist J-K Huysmans who was involved with an occult fraternity in Paris at the end of the nineteenth century, and who claimed to be the victim of magical attack by Stanislas de Guaita, the leader of a rival magical group. An account of this story is given by James Webb in his book *The Flight from Reason* (Macdonald, London, 1971). The outcome of Huysmans's claims led to a more physical attack, with the author being challenged to a duel by de Guaita!

SOURCEBOOKS

There are no books specifically on the subject of magical attack, and few which refer to it. The classic work in this field is *Psychic Self Defence* by Dion Fortune (Aquarian, London, 1972) which contains considerable details on the causes, symptoms and treatment for such attacks.

Various fictional works contain descriptions (often laughably and wildly, inaccurate) of the methodology of attacking; one of the most entertaining is *Moonchild* by Aleister Crowley (Sphere Books, London, and other modern editions) where the traditional pomposity of magicians launching such attacks is held up to ridicule; none the less the book is quite informative.

The occult novels of Dennis Wheatley contain several descriptions, often in vivid details of magical attacks, both on the physical and the occult plane – especially *They Used Dark Forces, The Gates of Hell, To the Devil a Daughter, The Devil Rides Out*.

The occult encyclopedia, *Man, Myth and Magic*, contains a good summary article on magical attack.

Sexual Magic

From the very beginning of his awareness of sexual experience man has realized that it brought him more than simply physical pleasure; in some mysterious, almost magical way it intensified his consciousness, expanded his awareness and heightened the experience not only of the physical body, but of something else as well. This was not the only factor that led to man's association of sex and magic. Sex, because of its link with pro-creation – the closest man comes to being in the godlike position of creating life – also held mysterious, powerful connotations. Ancient legends linked the creation of the earth with the sexual activities of divine beings; other myths attributed to the gods various characteristics of sexual prowess and desire, and rituals almost inevitably employed sexual imagery and stimulation, though often carefully disguised, to arouse and direct this basic human energy. Often the gods and their worshippers in ancient Greece were portrayed in states of sexual excite-ment, as the pleasure and intensified consciousness of sexual stimulation was shown to be a part of the ecstasy of religious worship. Often, it was held that the faithful became possessed (with all its sexual overtones) by the gods during the acts of sexual intercourse – states of ecstasy, visions, voices and experiences of the supernatural often accompanied the heights of sexual excitement. In this experience, in which the physical body seemed to fuse with a higher existence, man believed he came closest to the divine, to the creative life processes of which sexuality is a manifestation.

With the coming of Christianity, and the subsequent development of a strangely puritan approach to sexuality, this avenue of religious experience was forced to go underground, where it was rigorously persecuted by the church whenever and wherever it was found. Sexuality was linked with the devil, but its powers to heighten and intensify human consciousness and produce a variety of ecstatic effects was never denied; rather these were interpreted as powers given by the devil to his disciples. Hence, the witchcraft persecutions of the sixteenth and seventeenth centuries were based largely on evidence of sexual behaviour associated with devil worship, and psychologically can be seen to derive largely from the sexual frustrations and imbalances of men and women living under an abnormally repressive morality. Naked dancing, 'abnormal' sexual behaviour, intercourse with the devil, the use of stimulating drugs – these were characteristic of the evidence given against the accused.

Various other movements from the early history of the Church onwards through the Middle Ages perpetuated the ancient traditions of sexual religious experience. It was often suggested, for example, that the Knights Templar engaged in sodomy, and that this was part of a magical ritual technique.

The notorious Black Mass of traditional satanism was largely a sexual rite during which the celebrant had sexual relations with a prostitute who served as an altar, and in which a variety of forms of sexual stimulation were employed to arouse the congregation.

Although many peoples and religious traditions had connected sexual behaviour with religious experience, there were only a few groups which actually came to use sex as a technique of gaining religious or magical power. In the Orient, the tantric traditions of Hinduism gave various techniques of sexual behaviour which were believed to elevate the consciousness and lead to religious attainment. The teachings of tantrism were traditionally kept secret, and passed only from a guru to a disciple. Similar tantric traditions developed amongst various schools of Buddhism.

Tantrism became best known in the West through the activities of Aleister Crowley, the English magician, who practised a variety of sexual techniques expressly for the purpose of obtaining magical power and experience, ranging from ritual masturbation, to homosexual and hetero-sexual acts, bestiality, sadism and masochism. He derived his sexual magical teachings both from his own research and experimentation, and also from the traditions of the Ordo Templi Orientis, a magical fraternity of which he was a member. The OTO as it was known was an occult fraternity based upon sexual magic, and had been founded in Germany in 1906 by Theodor Reuss. It is still in existence today.

From the traditions of Crowley a variety of subsequent approaches to sexual magic developed, largely through his disciples. The main groups of contemporary magicians perpetuating what they believe to be the traditions of sexual magic include:

(1) Groups claiming to continue the traditions of the Ordo Templi Orientis, of which there are a variety throughout the world – in the USA, Scandinavia and Europe;

(2) Groups claiming to perpetuate the 'Thelemic' traditions of Aleister Crowley (often these are the same as 1) – these groups exist in the USA and Europe;

(3) Some witchcraft groups practising deliberate sexual techniques for magical purposes;

(4) Tantric yoga groups – principally in the USA, perpetuating teachings supposedly brought from India;

(5) The GBG group of Louis Culling within the USA.

(6) Some groups within the Church of Satan in the USA.

With the increasing popular contemporary interest in both the occult and sex, there is a growing interest in the traditions of sexual magic, and many books are featuring themes which purport to convey its teachings – *Seduction through Witchcraft*, *Astrology for Lovers*, *Magic Power through Sexual Attainment*.

Sexual magic is based upon a number of principles:

(1) Man possesses hidden powers (often identified with the sub-conscious mind) which give him greater perception, raise him to states of ecstasy, expand his consciousness, stimulate increased physical, emotional and mental powers;

(2) These powers lie 'buried' beneath some 'barrier' which conscious control cannot penetrate, but which can be overcome through a variety of techniques, including to some extent drugs and alcohol;

(3) This 'barrier' can be penetrated through heightening the physical, emotional and intellectual focus of the body by sexual stimulation, leading up to a 'break through' at the point of orgasm, at which energy is released;

(4) This release of energy can be used for many purposes – the attainment of an ecstatic state of consciousness (a sense of liberation and union, usually the aim of tantric yoga), or for some magical purpose (e.g. the casting of a spell);

(5) This energy can be focused and contained to some extent in various objects and substances – for example, in talismans upon which the sexual fluids have been poured, or in objects which are consecrated or 'charged' at the moment of orgasm, and these objects will remain as potent 'batteries' of power.

Deriving from these principles, various techniques of sexual magic are employed:

(1) *Autosexual* – techniques of masturbation have been widely used to heighten the consciousness of the magician and focus and stimulate his magical power, culminating in the release of energy in the orgasm, concentrated in the semen; this technique was advocated and practised by the

English magician, Austin Spare, who often employed a vessel of pottery as a mechanism with which to masturbate, and in which to concentrate and contain the magical energy thus obtained.

(2) *Heterosexual* – techniques of intercourse for magical use vary, although heterosexual stimulation leading to orgasm for magical purposes need not result in intercourse; magical use has traditionally been made of the sexual fluids of both men and women, and much alchemical symbolism derives from the imagery of sexual intercourse for magical purposes.

(3) *Homosexual* – various magical techniques have employed homosexual relations as their basis, both fellatio and anal intercourse; in some traditions of magic, these, being the 'inversions of the natural' expression of sexuality have been linked with devil worship and black magic. A number of magicians, notably Crowley, have employed homosexual activities, and the Knights Templar, are said to have used them for occult purposes according to some theorists.

The techniques of sexual magic have centred on a number of physical and intellectual procedures:

(1) The stimulation and excitation of the body, the emotions and the mind by every possible means, providing that conscious control is retained at all times – this may include moderate use of drugs, alcohol, food, the use of music, imagery, sensation;

(2) The maintenance of this stimulation and excitement for a period of concentration, during which the individual will be aroused to a 'fever pitch' of energy and arousal;

(3) The focusing of the conscious mind, and the whole of the individual's imagination onto the desired end of the act of magic – for example, if the act was directed towards the gaining of physical health, the image of the body must be seen as healthy, vibrant and energetic; the image must be carefully and accurately formed and held, throughout a period of stimulation, so that it is most completely structured and most 'tangible' at the point of orgasm. Where the consecration of a talisman is the object, the whole of the consciousness would be focused on the talisman, so that at the point of orgasm the whole of the aroused energy would be poured into it;

(4) The release of all the stimulated energy into a previously prepared and structured channel, in which it can be focused into the specific will of the magician – either into an actual object, or intellectually towards a specific end;

(5) A period of release and relaxation, during which the desired end should still be held in the mind, to 'firm' the image, and the body, the emotions and the mind allowed to relax and re-energize.

It is interesting to note that a number of modern psychologists and sexual counsellors have employed these very techniques in the treatment of a number of sexual problems (e.g. fetishism), where the patient is trained to use the aroused sexual energy gradually to redirect his sexual orientation.

SOURCEBOOKS

GORDON WELLESLEY: *Sex and the Occult*, Souvenir, London, 1973.
    Contains general background to the idea of sex as a magical force, with interesting comments on contemporary trends.
BENJAMIN WALKER: *Sex and the Supernatural*, MacDonald, London, 1970.
    Another interesting general introduction to the field, which includes material on a wide range of traditions.
FRANCIS KING: *Sexuality, Magic and Perversion*, Spearman, London, 1971.
    The best general study of magic and sexuality, both traditional, historical and contemporary. Covers a range from primitive fertility cults, to the Knights Templar and Aleister Crowley, and contemporary American groups.
JOHN SYMONDS: *The Magic of Aleister Crowley*, Muller, London, 1958.
JOHN SYMONDS (ed.): *The Magical Record of the Beast 666*, London, Duckworth, 1972.
    Both of these books cover Crowley and his sexual magic.
KENNETH GRANT: *The Magical Revival*, Muller, London, 1972.
    A survey of the subject from a distinctly Crowleyan viewpoint, this includes very interesting and significant material on Crowley, Austin Spare, Dion Fortune and witchcraft.
LOUIS CULLING: *A Manual of Sex Magick*, Llewellyn, St Paul, 1971.
    Deriving from the traditions of the OTO, the GBG in the USA has its principles summarized in this book.
The classic works on the Tantric tradition are those by 'Arthur Avalon' (Sir John Woodroffe), which include: *The Great Liberation* (1952); *Principles of Tantra* (1955); *The Serpent Power* (1958) – all published by Garesh, Madras.
AGEHANANDA BHARATI: *The Tantric Tradition*, Rider, London, 1965.
    A more recent study of Tantra.

Aleister Crowley:
Lord of the New Aeon

Aleister Crowley, known variously as the Laird of Boleskine, The Great Beast 666 and 'the wickedest man who ever lived', is probably one of the most unjustly maligned figures in the history of the occult. It is true that Crowley had sadistic tendencies in his childhood – he once executed a cat in a number of ways to prove that it was really dead – and suffered undoubtedly from megalomania as shown by his efforts to surpass all rivals in the occult order of the Golden Dawn. But he was also a magician of considerable style and originality, and some of his concepts may well prove eventually to be significant in the history of psychology. As early as 1929, Crowley published in Paris, his work *Magick in Theory and Practice*, one part of which was devoted to a systematic tabling of subconscious imagery in the mind.

From the beginning Crowley's life was full of contrasts. Born in 1875, he was raised in a strict Plymouth Brethren home, studied at Cambridge and meanwhile pursued interests as varied as mountain climbing, rowing and chess. He became a friend of Allan Bennett, and embroiled himself in a deep study of magic and mysticism. He was to become one of the most spectacular figures in the history of contemporary magic.

Evicted from Cefalu in Sicily by Mussolini where he had established an Abbey for practising ritual magic, constantly involved in legal disputes over the publication of Hermetic secrets, famous for his escapades with women, Crowley became notorious after acclaiming himself the Anti-Christ in 1904.

Prior to this pronouncement, Crowley had pursued an orthodox training in the magical arts in the Hermetic Order of the Golden Dawn. Introduced to the Society in 1898, Crowley soon grasped that those with the loftiest grades were able to wield profound spiritual authority over their minions, while claiming rapport with Secret Chiefs emanating from higher planes of being. In *Magick* he wrote 'Every man is more or less aware that his individuality comprises several orders of existence. . . .' Magick (Crowley spelt it with the additional 'k') was a means of transforming the consciousness under will, to allow union with the supreme spiritual forces in the cosmos.

Crowley was initiated as a Neophyte in the Golden Dawn on 18 November 1898. In December he took the grade of Zelator, and those of Theoricus and Practicus in the following two months. He was keen to ascend through the occult grades of the Tree of Life, as quickly as possible. Crowley was also the first magician to attempt the lengthy six-month Abramelin ritual which had been translated from the French by MacGregor Mathers, co-founder of the Golden Dawn. During the rituals, Crowley had visions of Christ, and then saw himself crucified. John Symonds writes:

He stood within the Divine Light with a crown of twelve stars upon his head; the earth opened for him to enter into its very centre, where he climbed the peak of a high mountain. Many dragons sprang upon him as he approached the Secret Sanctuary, but he overcame all with a word. This was an alchemical vision of his success in the Great Work. Crowley realised that he was born with all the talents required for a great magician . . . (*The Great Beast*, 1973, p. 43).

Certain events occurred in 1904, which suggested to Crowley that his genius and role in the world were even more far-reaching. Having failed to dislodge W. B. Yeats as head of the Golden Dawn in England, Crowley suddenly and impetuously embarked upon a series of travels through Mexico, the United States, Ceylon and India. He arrived finally in Cairo, which was to be a major milestone in the building of a new magical universe.

On the 14 March 1904 in his room near the Boulak Museum in Cairo, Crowley performed a magical ceremony invoking the Egyptian deity Thoth, god of Wisdom. His wife appeared to be in a dazed state of mind, and four days later, while in a similar state of drowsiness, announced that Horus was 'waiting' for her husband. Crowley was not expecting any such announcement. He was even more surprised when she led him to a Museum he had not previously visited. Meanwhile she pointed to a statue of Horus in the form of Ra-Hoor-Khuit and Crowley was amazed to find that the exhibit was number 666, the number of the Great Beast in the book of Revelations. Crowley regarded this as a portent and returned to his hotel where he performed a ritual for Horus. His wife again fell into a state of trance and began to dictate a series of statements emanating from a semi-invisible Egyptian spirit named Aiwass. In the communication, to be known later as *The Book of the Law*, Crowley was instructed to drop the ceremonial magic he had been taught in the Golden Dawn, and to pursue sexual magic instead. In so doing, he had to discover the whereabouts of the Scarlet Whore of Babylon, as mentioned in the Book of Revelation for it had been confirmed that he was indeed the Anti-Christ to succeed Jesus. In fact he was to be the Lord of the new Aeon: 'Now ye shall know that the chosen priest and apostle of infinite space is the prince-priest the Beast,' proclaimed Aiwass, '... and in his woman called the Scarlet Woman is all power given ...'. It seemed to be a curious parody on Christ and the Virgin Mary.

Crowley realized that an event of the magnitude of his cosmic initiation only occurred every 2000 years, and constituted a new phase in the evolution of mankind. He would incarnate in the world the mystery of the sexual union of the great Egyptian gods Nuit and Hadit; he would be the god-child. He was the successor to Osiris, Christ and Mohammed: 'With my Hawk's head [i.e. Horus) I peck at the eyes of Jesus ... I flap my wings in the face of Mohammed ...'.

His encounter and illumination at the hands of Aiwass conferred upon Crowley a new sense of authority. He had tapped the highest spiritual energies in the universe, and had done so in Egypt, the legendary home of magic. He wrote to Mathers to inform him that *his* ritual formulae were obsolete. Crowley notes, 'I did not expect or receive, a reply. ...'

Ever fond of structure and authority, Crowley decided to form his own occult Order, calling it the Argentinum Astrum or Silver Star. To begin with, its structure imitated that of the Golden Dawn, although after contact with the German Ordo Templi Orientis, he did include some sexual magic in his rites.

The A.A., as the Society was known esoterically, initiated close to a hundred people. Among the most impressive were Norman Mudd, Professor of Mathematics at Bloemfontain; Victor Neuburg, who was a 'father-poet' to Dylan Thomas and Pamela Hansford-Johnson, and the visionary artist, Austin Spare. Crowley also inspired a series of sexual magic societies in the USA, namely the Choronzon Club (named after the demon of Chaos); Louis T. Culling's *Great Brotherhood of God*; the Californian OTO (which included L. Ron Hubbard – founder of Scientology, in its membership); and the Fellowship of Ma Ion, a blend of Catholicism and Crowley.

Aleister Crowley died a confused man in December 1947. He had failed satisfactorily to locate the Whore of Babylon. He did however leave behind him a prodigious output of magical writing. His books included works on the Tarot, the Qabalah, the I Ching, Yoga, the Enochian calls of Dr Dee, and the symbolic meaning of ritual. He remains one of the most influential occultists of the century, and his works continue to be re-published at a prodigious rate under the auspices of editors like Israel Regardie, Francis King and John Symonds.

SOURCEBOOKS

Works by Crowley

Magick in Theory and Practice.
   Crowley's most important work, this volume contains all of the main points of reference in Crowley's magical philosophy, and in particular, his outline of magic as a means of changing consciousness by will. Included are summaries of the Banishing and Invoking Rituals of the Pentagram and Hexagram and an outline of astral projection rising on the planes techniques. One of the most important sections is an Appendix on the Principal Correspondences of the Qabalah, which outlines the relationship of the deities of different pantheons of gods to each other, and their 'position' on the Tree of Life. Also correlated are sacred animals, stones, plants, magical weapons, perfumes and Tarot symbols.
A larger edition of this book, including *Book Four*, was published under the title *Magick* by Routledge & Kegan Paul, London, 1973.
Book Four, Sangreal Foundation, Dallas, Texas 1972.
   Contains a detailed account of all the magical implements and their symbolic meaning in ritual. These implements include: the altar, the scourge dagger and chain, the holy oil, the wand, the book of rites, the bell, the lamen or breastplate, and the incense burner. There is also a short account of the relationship of yoga postures and exercises and magic.
The Qabalah of Aleister Crowley, Weiser, New York, 1973.
   This volume supplements the above, and includes three of Crowley's essays: *Gematria* – the study of the interrelated meanings of words whose numerical totals are the same, *Liber 777* an elaboration of Crowley's tables of correspondences in the magical universe, and *Sepher Sephiroth*, a short Qabalistic dictionary.
The Vision and the Voice, Sangreal Foundation, Dallas, Texas, 1972.
   In 1909 Aleister Crowley and Victor Neuburg journeyed to the deserts of Algeria to attempt to invoke the thirty Aethyrs or spirits annotated by Dr John Dee. These entities had made their appearance originally manifest in a 'shewstone' or looking crystal and had communicated passages in a language known as 'Enochian'. Crowley wished to re-establish contact with them, and he used as his meditative equipment a large golden topaz set in an ornamented Rosy Cross. In certain locations he would concentrate upon the topaz, and Neuburg would write down any of Crowley's ritual utterings. The documented Aethyrs include symbolic references to the Qabalah, Gnostic writings, the Mysteries of Eleusis, the Celts, the Scandinavians and other sources. The book is an invaluable compilation of magical influxes using a type of trance-method.

The Book of Lies, Hayden Press, Ilfracombe, Devon, 1962.

A book of condensed Qabalistic sayings with a paragraph by paragraph commentary. The book is fairly obscure but is of historical interest since it contains a sequence on The Star Sapphire which refers to the magic of sexual polarities disguised beneath the symbols of the rood (phallus) and the mystic rose (vagina). It is because this text purported to describe a sexual magic practice that Aleister Crowley was invited to join the OTO by Theodor Reuss.

The Book of Thoth, Weiser, New York, 1969.

First published in 1944, this book contains a detailed account of all of the Tarot trumps, that is to say, both the Major and Minor Arcana. Also included are the illustrations designed by Crowley and executed by Lady Frieda Harris, which constitute one of the most dramatic and visually impressive Tarot decks.

The Confessions of Aleister Crowley, Hill & Wang, New York; Cape, London, 1969.

The Magical Record of the Beast 666, Duckworth, London, 1972 – both edited by John Symonds and Kenneth Grant, these two books present valuable insights into the personality of Crowley. The latter is not as notable, as an account of magical experiences, as might be expected, and is useful mainly for its inclusion of the full text of *The Book of the Law*.

Moonchild, Sphere, London.

Diary of a Drug Fiend, Sphere, London.

Crowley's novels are both amateurish in style but relate strongly to his own magical experiences. *Moonchild* incorporates parodies on a number of figures from the Golden Dawn including Edwin Arthwait, who is a thinly disguised personification of A. E. Waite. Crowley describes him in his novel as 'pedantically pious' and compares his mind with a 'rag and bone shop of worthless and disjointed medievalism'. There are also references to Victor Neuburg, MacGregor Mathers and W. B. Yeats, whose poetry Crowley was keen to emulate.

Diary of a Drug Fiend is Crowley's novel of his drug practices and was first published in 1922. Crowley had especially difficult times with heroin and cocaine, but he discovered that ether, hashish, anhaolonium, opium and morphine had no habit-forming effect upon him whatever. A related work is Israel Regardie's *Roll Away The Stone* (Llewellyn, St Paul, Minnesota 1968, 1974) which includes Crowley's essay on 'The Herb Dangerous'.

Works on Crowley by other writers

John Symonds: *The Great Beast*, Mayflower, St Albans, 1973.

The most interesting and complete biography of Crowley and also the most humorous. Unlike Kenneth Grant, with whom Symonds edited and reissued some of Crowley's writings, Symonds looks at Crowley as an interested but not always impressed bystander. The new edition enlarges upon the old, and incorporates *The Magic of Aleister Crowley*, previously issued as a separate volume (Muller, London, 1958).

Israel Regardie: *The Eye in the Triangle*, Llewellyn, Minnesota, 1971.

Kenneth Grant: *Aleister Crowley and the Hidden God*, Muller, London; Weiser, New York, 1973.

In the face of criticism of Crowley as the latter gradually developed into a cult figure, writers have felt obliged to come to his defence. Consequently neither is as clear sighted or objective as John Symonds, although both present interesting background information. Kenneth Grant currently heads one branch of the OTO in England, although this has been challenged in terms of validity. Grant's main concern is the variety of sexual magic which Crowley developed after his illumination in Cairo in 1904.

Francis King: *Ritual Magic in England*, Spearman, London, 1970.

A readable and authentic account of the history of the Golden Dawn, Crowley's Argentinum Astrum, the Cromlech Temple, the Fraternity of the Inner Light and other recent occult groups.

Ḣypnotism, Auto-suggestion and Relaxation

Hypnotism, as a device for inducing a sleep-like trance, is an age-old technique. In general it depends on the abilities of the hypnotist to relax his patient and allow him to enter a mental state where he becomes more suggestible to commands. In most cases a skilled practitioner can induce a hypnotic state in around ten minutes, and the effects can be startling.

As an object of amusement post-hypnotic suggestion has often been used as a stage act. A person may, for example, be given an instruction while under hypnosis, that he should violently cough ten minutes after awakening. He returns to his seat as one of the audience, and then quite without knowing why begins to splutter and choke as commanded!

There is however a more serious side to hypnotism, and this is a medical therapy. Dr Harvey Doney of the Toronto Rehabilitation Centre has used hypnotism to suggest to heart victims that clean fresh air was coursing into their lungs and filling their bodies with oxygen and energy. Electrocardiograms have shown that after a six-month period, these patients were as healthy as another group who had to practise regular physical exercise.

Hypnotism has also been successfully used as an anaesthetic in surgical operations, and by dentists. It has also been found that very difficult childbirths can be rendered painless by hypnosis. Dr George Newbold, a British gynaecologist stated: 'After witnessing many labours during which the patient is restless and distressed from pain and discomfort, the sight of one conducted under hypnosis may well seem to the onlooker to be something in the nature of a revelation' (Van Pelt (ed.), *Medical Hypnosis*).

As an occult technique, hypnotism has not attracted as much attention as might be expected, mainly because it places the 'patient' in a state of passive helplessness. Currently, disciplines like yoga, and meditation, which stress that man has to achieve higher states of awareness by *himself*, have proved more relevant, and the same is true in the occult.

88

However, the technique of auto-suggestion, which is a form of self-hypnotism, does play a significant part, both as a relaxation exercise and also for visualization purposes.

One of the best methods is a relaxation method used in modern-day Mind Dynamics training and in similar groups. It is also found in a related form in practical Gurdjieff training. We include it here because the meditator has to *tell himself that certain things are becoming real to him*, and that his consciousness is moving, as it were, into 'new areas'.

The method is as follows: The person first informs himself that he is becoming drenched in beautiful red colours, and that as he relaxes each part of his body in turn, from his head down to his toes, he is becoming filled with 'redness'. Then he imagines that as he becomes more restful, his body is now filled with exquisite orange, and he gradually works his way downwards, passing through all the colours of the rainbow. He becomes increasingly relaxed in turn.

According to the Mind Dynamics Organization, this produces an *alpha* state of mind which allows a much greater mystical awareness. They have established a visualization exercise in which the meditator 'builds' a 'workshop' in the yellow colours, in an imagined, peaceful environment called 'the passive scene in nature'. In this workshop, are placed time-control devices, special medicines and equipment and an inexhaustible library, all of which are 'imagined into reality'. They become useful mental aids for reaching into the subconscious and finding solutions to problems which perhaps could not be solved at all in the conscious, awakened state.

Magic makes use of similar techniques of relaxation (see pp. 91–4). Once in the relaxed state, the magician has to imagine himself into a context which he wishes to enter. If he wants to 'balance' his personality with intellect, he may will himself to see the form of Michael, the Arch-angel of Fire (Intelligence), and to converse with him. He builds up a visual impression, calling him forth in a type of mental invocation. What is really occurring, is that the magician is asking a particular facet of his mind to appear in a visual form. He is bringing into consciousness certain faculties and energies that were hitherto unconscious.

Again, by means of autosuggestion when in a relaxed state the magician may wish to explore his mind by travelling along the symbolic Tarot paths (see pp. 63–8). He has to tell himself that the imagery of say, The Star, or The Charioteer, is becoming increasingly real to him in all its detail. He visualizes the environment in the symbolic form as portrayed on the Tarot card. He then finds that his consciousness has uncovered new, mystical areas of his mind that he might never have suspected were there!

Thus, magic makes use only of hypnotic suggestion as an adjunct to visualization. It places the meditator in control, not another person. It operates with certain visual aids in mind, like the Tarot cards or images from mythology, and it is used primarily to achieve transcendental states of awareness.

SOURCEBOOKS

J. J. VAN PELT: *Medical Hypnosis: New Hope for Mankind*, Gollancz, London, 1953.
    Contains interesting medical cases of hypnosis applied to relieving pain whether in child-birth, from migraines, or in surgical operations.

R. E. L. MASTERS and JEAN HOUSTON: *Mind Games*, Turnstone Books, London, 1973.
    An instruction book for group exercises designed to enlarge consciousness. The authors have researched relaxation and meditative techniques used in yoga, and also the altered states of awareness produced by hallucinogenic drugs. This book, however, deals with mental exercises alone. One person in the group takes the role of 'guide'. The authors started the New York Foundation for Mind Research in 1964.

Trance Consciousness

The main viewpoint underlying trance methods in magic is that we all have a number of bodies of perception, not merely the one which we use in our daily living. If by some means we are able to put our physical body to sleep as it were, we than have open to us other optional realms of perception. Trance is a means of rendering the physical body inert so that the consciousness is then freed to go on a mystical journey. It is an area which is thus strongly related to both out-of-the-body experiences and shamanism.

Trance consciousness has been traditionally more important in native societies, as in South America and also Indonesia, but it plays an important role in modern magic. It was the major method employed by two remarkable trance occultists, Austin Spare and Victor Angel, both of whom relied on trance inspiration for their painting (see pp. 192–3).

The occult technique for entering the trance state is actually an extension of a gradual relaxation exercise in which the body is 'put to sleep' in stages. However, it is equally important that one should retain the full spectrum of consciousness even though the physical organism is gradually made inoperative. Occultists who use the Tree of Life symbol in their meditations regard the Tree, in one sense, as growing within them. It becomes a representation of the divine energies which dwell in all of us. For this reason, it is also connected with energy centres known in yoga as chakras. The occultist tries to activate his chakras, to allow him greater visionary activity, while at the same time his body sinks deep into trance-relaxation.

The activation comes first. The 'magician' imagines white light descending from above his head and he vibrates to himself the mantra Eee-Hee-Yeh, a sacred name taken from the Qabalah.

The light now descends to his throat and is imagined to radiate forth in the form of mauve light. This time the mantra is Ye-Ho-Waa-El-Oh-Him. . . .

Descending further, it reaches the region of the heart and solar plexus. It has now transformed to golden yellow light, and the mantra is Ye-Ho-Waa, Al-Oaa, Vaaa Daath. . . .

Now from the heart down to the region of the genitals . . . and the light changes from yellow into a rich, deep purple: Sha-Dai-El-Haiii. . . .

Finally, the light reaches the feet and the colours of earth; russet, citrine, black and olive are visualized. The final mantra is Aaa-Doh-Naii, Haaa, Aaa-retz. . . .

All of these mantras are the names of God in the Qabalah and they are used because of their uplifting, vibrationary qualities. *Thus, the first stage of activation is completed.*

The magician now imagines white light streaming down his left side, beneath his feet, and up his right side to the top of his head. He then visualizes a similar band of light energy travelling from his head down along his nose to the chest and legs, once again beneath the feet and up past the back of the legs to the head. In his mind, he has thus enclosed his body, which may be lying horizontally or seated in meditation. His breathing is deep and regular. He imagines that the boundaries of light define a type of translucent container which is actually his 'consciousness'.

The second, crucial stage, is to transfer the consciousness out of the body. The person meditating now has to imagine that his 'container' is filling up, perhaps with liquid, and that the remaining space inside his container, the 'air' if you like, represents the extent of his consciousness. As the liquid fills the body slowly that part relaxes and goes to sleep.

At first, the legs fill and one is aware of the body only above the knees. Then the level rises and consciousness extends only to that part of the body above the chest. Soon, the only conscious part remaining is the head, for the rest has fallen into trance and is to all extents and purposes, 'inert'.

It is at this last stage, when the consciousness or 'mind' is leaving the body that the act of astral projection occurs. As mentioned in the opening paragraph, occultists believe that if the external physical body becomes inactive, the next 'inner body' is awakened. All of the perceptive processes are now transferred to an area of the mind which would normally be unconscious. But to all extents and purposes it is like transferring one's perception into a living dream. One is no longer bound by the body, and can travel according to will. Sometimes, fantasy elements from the unconscious also appear, and these will seem to be equally as real as 'normal' reality.

Meanwhile, the body remains in a state of trance. Some projectionists claim that a silver cord can be seen connecting the physical and 'astral'

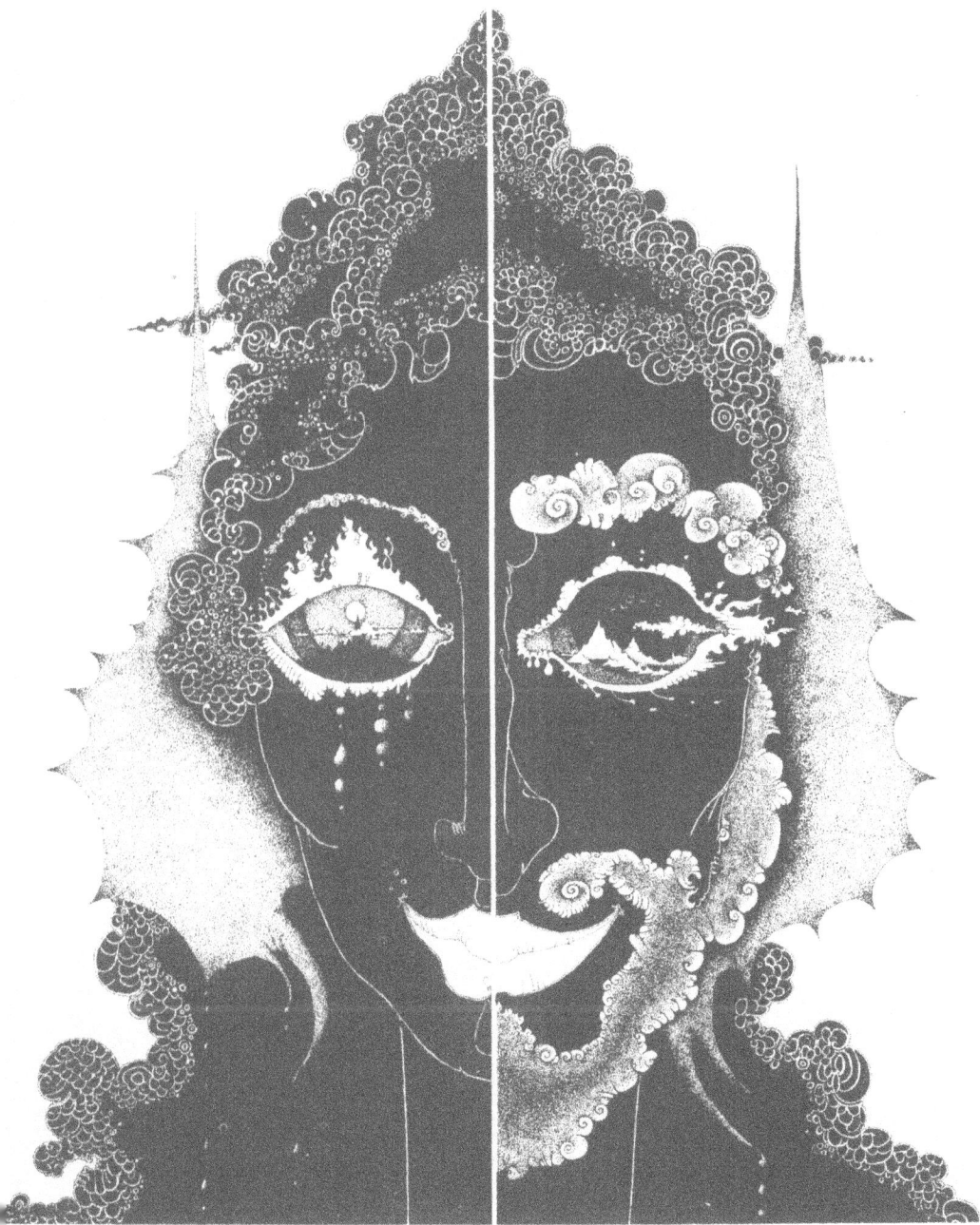

bodies, although according to Dr Celia Green, a prominent researcher into out-of-the-body experiences, this is not always the case.

Magicians using the Qabalistic mantras usually find that this act in itself becomes a type of directive to the unconscious mind to unleash certain visionary experiences. It becomes possible at this stage to imagine oneself into locations which are totally subject to the will of the practitioner, and it is this faculty of creative imagination that is really what magic is all about.

If the occultist is using the Tarot cards as his stepping stones he will try to imagine himself confronting the maiden of the 22nd Tarot card, *The Universe*. He can then travel by the paths represented by other cards in turn, until he gets deeper and deeper into the spiritual areas of his mind.

Meanwhile, the person's physical body remains in a state of trance. Should the magician wish to return, he gradually eases himself back into his body and awakens. The controlled act of projection has led a number of writers to theorize that perhaps this trance technique resembles the act of dying.

SOURCEBOOKS

W. E. BUTLER: *The Magician, His Training and Work*, Aquarian Press, London, 1959 (several impressions).
ISRAEL REGARDIE: *The Middle Pillar*, Llewellyn, Minnesota, 1974 edn.
    W. E. Butler is the present head of the Servants of the Light, an occult group descended from the Stella Matutina, itself an off-shoot of the Golden Dawn. A number of relevant occult techniques, including the projection exercise, and other visualization methods, are described. Israel Regardie belonged to the Stella Matutina, and similarly stresses the importance of the projection technique and the activation of the chakras. The title of his book is a reference to the 'middle pillar' of man, which extends from the crown of his head down to his feet, and is the column on which certain important chakras lie.

Out-of-the-Body Consciousness

In recent years the phenomenon originally known as 'astral projection' among occultists, has assumed a position of prominence in parapsychological circles. It is currently under special investigation by researchers like Professor Charles Tart of UCLA, Davis and Dr Celia Green, head of the Institute of Psychophysical Studies at Oxford.

An out-of-the-body experience is one where the person feels he is observing his surroundings from a position away from his body. One of Celia Green's subjects suddenly felt himself floating high in the sky while riding a motorbike at speed through the countryside, but normally the body is more passive.

Usually an out-of-the-body experience takes place during drowsiness, relaxation, sickness or bodily inertness. Electroencephelograph readings (EEGs) have revealed that these experiences share some characteristics with dreams but there is one important distinguishing feature: they seem to be subject to *will*, unlike a dream which incorporates random images, and they are characterized by a perceptive quality as clear as normal waking consciousness.

Ernest de Martino, an Italian ethnographer, believes that the out-of-the-body experience in primitive societies has been documented in myths and legends as the 'wandering of the soul', and that the world-wide belief in an afterlife may also be a folk memory of this phenomenon. In Western society it is only in the present century that astral travelling has been documented in detail, although several references are found in classical literature.

The three most noted modern pioneers of the out-of-the-body experience are Sylvan Muldoon, Oliver Fox (The pseudonym of Hugh Callaway) and recently, Robert A. Monroe, although other researchers like Ralph Shirley, former editor of the *Occult Review*, and 'Yram' (Marcel Fohan) have also made significant contributions.

Sylvan Muldoon came from a family interested in spiritualist matters and it was while attending a Spiritualist meeting in Clinton, Iowa, at the age of twelve that he had his first out-of-the-body venture. He felt that he had fallen into what he called a 'silent, dark and feelingless condition' and then suddenly found that he could project a part of himself outside his body: 'I managed to turn around . . . There were two of me . . .!'

Muldoon also describes a feature regarded by many as characteristic, and that is the silvery elastic chord which is said to join the astral body to the physical body. As Muldoon 'walked around in the air' this chord maintained a connection between his astral consciousness and his inert slumbering body. He had merely transferred his perception outside his normal frame of reference. Muldoon believed that the astral body was in a sense more real than the physical body, and in fact constituted the 'life' element. On death the astral body would sever the cord-link with the physical body and would not return. Russian parapsychologists have similarly formulated the idea of the 'bioplasmic body' – a type of energy prototype of the physical which like the DNA code, regulates and maintains the physical organism. (See S. Ostrander and L. Schroeder: *Psychic Discoveries Behind the Iron Curtain*, Bantam Books, New York, 1971.) This view has also found support from the American researcher, Dr Stanley Krippner.

Sylvan Muldoon, however, not only described his subsequent experiences in his important work *The Projection of the Astral Body* (1929), but he went on to describe means of achieving this state of consciousness. Anticipating Dr Tart, he evolved a technique of *dream* control whereby a person would try to will himself to dream a sequence of events which would involve the separation of the astral and physical bodies. One of these was to imagine oneself ascending in an elevator and alighting on the top floor. Another was to swim, fly, or ride in a balloon.

Muldoon highlighted another important aspect of the out-of-the-body experience. Usually the surroundings perceived in an o-o-b-e are exactly similar to reality. Sometimes one may feel one has travelled to a friend's or relative's house and is observing current situations which can be subsequently verified for accuracy. The second major category of experience, however, entails *phantasy* elements from the subconscious mind. These were present in the accounts of both Oliver Fox and Robert Monroe.

Oliver Fox's accounts of his experiences outside the body, first appeared in the *Occult Review* of 1920. Like Muldoon, there was a strong emphasis on dream control. Fox believed that the o-o-b-e occurred with the 'dream of knowledge', which occurred when one *realized* that one was dreaming and could then act within that framework. (This type of dream has recently been referred to by Celia Green as the 'lucid dream'.) The dreamer could now enter the realm which had hitherto been *unconscious*. He often found himself observing people shrouded in an aura of rich and dazzling colours. Similar descriptions of auras are given in Bishop Leadbeater's book on clairvoyance and the astral planes.

Initially Fox considered that the 'dream of knowledge' was the only means available for attaining the out-of-the-body state. Later he realized that the relaxation of the body could produce a similar effect. During the relaxation one would feel oneself overcome autohypnotically by a sense of numbness. Then it was almost like escaping through a trap-door in the brain. Fox called it the 'Pineal Door' method. On one occasion Fox felt that he was falling down a long shaft, and as Celia Green indicates, the tunnel is a common motif in o-o-b-es. Fox was overcome with a sense of darkness and silence, and then noticed that he seemed to be naked and bleeding, as if from wounds. It occurred to him that he was dying. Then, as if he had suddenly entered the realm of Greek mythology, he heard a voice demanding: 'Say thou art Theseus. I am Oliver Fox.'

Strange, mythological encounters and visions are commonly reported in the out-of-the-body state and lend some credence to the view of *The Tibetan Book of the Dead* that on death one's consciousness leaves the body and has visions of heavens and hells which are, in reality, states of harmony and disorder in the mind.

Robert Monroe's account in his work *Journeys out of the Body* has stimulated renewed interest in projection phenomena, and Monroe himself has been assisting in parapsychological experiments with Charles Tart at UCLA.

Monroe's o-o-b-es began suddenly in Spring 1958, during sessions while assimilating tape-recorded data during sleep. During his relaxed state he observed the same numbness that Fox had described, and says that it felt rather like being trapped in a vice. Meanwhile he had the strange sensation that he could extend his body in an elastic way, beyond its normal confines. He was able to feel things outside his normal reach. But another strange fact presented itself. His fingers were not feeling in the orthodox sense but were passing through physical objects! A number of recent subjects have similarly claimed that during o-o-b-es they have floated upwards through walls and ceilings and have observed with remarkable clarity, the night sky and surroundings, as if seen from a considerable height.

Monroe subsequently discovered that he could travel to see his friends in the out-of-the-body state. On one occasion he observed a friend loading an unfamiliar mechanical device into the back of his car, and when discussing the incident later with him, he found that it was a Van de Graaf generator. Like Fox, however, Monroe also entered strange inner plane locations which he designated Locale II and Locale III. Locale I representing the more ordinary everyday imagery. He found himself on the former occasions, involved in time-warp phenomena, Hell-like scenery and on one occasion in a symbolic location similar to the details of the tarot card *The Judgment*. Some of his descriptions parallel those found in the literature of the hallucinogens and psychedelics.

The basic characteristics of the out-of-the-body experience are as follows:

(1) The consciousness component (mind, or 'soul') appears to leave the body, and the latter remains apparently inert, as if in a state of deep sleep or trance.

(2) Sometimes, but not always, the person seems to have a second body, connected to the first by means of a silver chord.

(3) It becomes possible in the astral state to travel through physical barriers, and to travel considerable distances 'at the speed of thought'. The *will* is an important feature since it determines the form which the experience will take, or the location one will visit.

(4) Astral travelling can involve purely physical locations, or phantasy locations of the mind, including Heaven and Hell experiences, or episodes apparently taken from mythology. In such instances they become as real to the observer as reality in waking consciousness.

SOURCEBOOKS

SYLVAN MULDOON and HEREWARD CARRINGTON: *The Projection of the Astral Body*, Rider, London, 1929, 3rd impression 1971.

This work is more important than the author's companion volume *The Phenomenon of Astral Projection* and describes Muldoon's o-o-b-experiences and his techniques of dream control. A summary of the book and a comparison with other sources may be found in H. P. Prevost Batterby, *Man Outside Himself*, University Books, New York, 1969.

OLIVER FOX: *Astral Projection, A Record of Out of the Body Experiences*, University Books, New York, 1962.

Contains details of both Fox's dream control and Pineal Door methods, and represents one of the earliest classical accounts of modern astral travel.

ROBERT A. MONROE: *Journeys Out Of the Body*, Doubleday Anchor, New York, 1973.

Descriptions are given of Monroe's initial discovery of extended bodily sensations and his wanderings in Locales I, II and III. While similar laboratory work has been done with sensitives like Ingo Swann, Monroe is one of the most significant contemporary proponents undertaking parapsychological testing, and was mentioned by Dr Charles Tart in an interview with *Parapsychology Today*.

Related Sources

CELIA GREEN: *Out of the Body Experiences* and *Lucid Dreams*, both Hamish Hamilton, London, 1968.

The first of these books provides analytical breakdowns of the conditions accompanying the o-o-b-e such as bodily relaxation, preference for darkness over light, and descriptions of subjects' feelings e.g. 'Like dying'. Professor Price called it a 'notable contribution to psychical research'. The second book deals primarily with dreams which include the faculty of consciousness and decision. It is clear from the accounts of Muldoon and Fox that this relates lucid dreams to the o-o-b.

RAYNOR C. JOHNSON: *Watcher on the Hills*, Hodder & Stoughton, London, 1959.

Relates drug, mystical and religious experience to altered states of consciousness. One of the best general accounts.

ROBERT CROOKALL: *The Jung Jaffe View of Out of the Body Experiences*, C.F.P.S.S., London, 1970.

Carl Jung, found the o-o-b-e difficult to account for in terms of his own view of the unconscious mind. He attempted to describe the latter as possessing 'luminosities' which allowed the faculty of clarity or perceptiveness to arise in the unconscious state. He was particularly puzzled by subjects who observed their medical operations in an out-of-the-body state while under an anaesthetic. Crookall proposes a standard astral-body viewpoint while relating it to the religious experience of heaven and hell. Crookall has devoted several books to documenting medical cases of o-o-b-e's. His other works include *The Supreme Adventure, Intimations of Immortality, Techniques of Astral Projection* and *During Sleep*.

NEVILL DRURY: *The Path of the Chameleon*, Spearman, London, 1973.

Contains a short account of the relationship of the out-of-the-body experience to the trance state and 'mythological consciousness'. Expecially relevant is the reference to Aristeas of Proconnesus, a Greek ecstatic from an island in the sea of Marmara, whose account is given by Pliny and Herodotus among others. Aristeas' long astral journey involved normal physical perception in the state of trance, and also phantastic elements relating to solar mythology.

BENJAMIN WALKER: *Beyond the Body*, Routledge & Kegan Paul, London, 1973.

One of the best recent general works on out-of-the-body experiences and their connotations for the study of comparative religion and parapsychology.

Drugs and Mystical Consciousness

In Western countries psychedelic drugs, because of their dangerous random use have understandably been the cause of considerable controversy. However, they have been used in a number of native cultures (e.g. the Mazatecs and Jivaro of Central and South America) as a sacrament allowing the user special access to magical territory.

According to anthropological accounts the shaman feels that his universe has become sacred and throngs with awesome beings and presences. Perhaps his 'soul' soars away from his body and he converses with the ancestor of the first dawn. Perhaps his hallucinatory state allows him to see another person as a collection of 'luminous fibres' as Don Juan, the Yaqui shaman told Carlos Castaneda. Hallucinatory drugs cause altered states of awareness, which in the shamanistic societies are often used for positive purposes like healing (see pp. 106–8). In modern Western society their main medical function has been in the treating of terminal cancer patients, where drugs like LSD may be used as an illuminant and pain killer. However, the incursion of the psychedelics – LSD, DMT, mescalin and marijuana has had a chequered history in America, Britain and other Western countries.

One of the first contemporary drug-explorers was Aldous Huxley, the British novelist, who was later to be hailed by Timothy Leary as 'the father of the psychedelic revolution'. Huxley, of course, had been preceded by literary figures like Thomas de Quincey, Theophilus Gautier, Charles Baudelaire and other celebrated drug imbibers, but Huxley approached the subject from a different viewpoint. He had asked Dr Humphrey Osmond to overview a medically directed mescalin session in which quantities and effects were carefully gauged. For Huxley, the mescalin trip was like a mystical revelation: he began to discover a profound richness in the kaleidoscopic imagery unfolding before his eyes: 'Mosaics lighted from within, glowing, moving, changing . . .'. In the latter part of his life, Huxley was interested in the correlation between the drug experience and the dying process, and he was especially drawn to the exposition of the *Tibetan Book of the Dead*, which described the altered states of awareness in the after-death dream. Huxley was himself a Mahayana Buddhist, and he accepted the Buddhist view that there was an art to dying which would allow the spiritual rather than the demonic images of the mind to take precedence as a pathway to liberation. On his deathbed, his wife gave him a dose of LSD to allow him to ride out his life on a wave of transcendental experience.

The pioneers of what was to become the psychedelic revolution in the 1960s, regarded Huxley with awe. Timothy Leary, Ralph Metzner and Richard Alpert, the triumvirate of Harvard PhDs who began to research the relationship of drugs to enlightenment, found themselves similarly adopting Hindu or Buddhist frameworks. Leary himself had had a profound religious experience when he ate seven sacred mushrooms in Cuernavaca in August 1960. He found himself perceiving the motions of the universe at the atomic and subatomic levels. A new, pantheistic horizon had opened. Finite imagery had been left far behind. The experience was quintessentially religious. 'I came back a changed man,' he wrote '. . . you are never the same after you have had that one flash glimpse down the cellular time tunnel. You are never the same after you have had the veil drawn . . .!'

Leary began to gather colleagues in his academic circles, who were interested in researching inner space, and through the autumn of 1960 spent most of his spare time researching the hallucinogenic qualities of psychotropic mushrooms.

With Metzner, one of his most outstanding students, he studied the effects of psilocybin on prison inmates and found that it promoted a feeling of 'one-ness' among them, although the effects were not enduring. Meanwhile, Leary learned of LSD from an eccentric English writer and yoga practitioner named Michael Hollingshead. Leary was wary at first, regarding the drug as artificial by contrast with the mushrooms which were 'natural'. Hollingshead insisted, however, that LSD could produce mystical effects. Leary found himself experiencing the same primal energy processes that he had felt during the mushroom sessions, but there was also the sense of non-ego, and rebirth.

Meanwhile, Leary explored other hallucinogens as a means of entry to these states of realization. He took DMT with Richard Alpert and discussed it with theologian Alan Watts, and with William Burroughs who had chronicled at length the effect of yage in the South American jungle.

Meanwhile another of Leary's students, Walter Pahnke, proposed an experiment which was to become famous as a psychedelic test case. He wished to test the drug experience against a number of attributes drawn up by the scholar W. T. Stace as characteristics of mystical illumination. In brief, these attributes were: a sense of unity with the world and within oneself; feelings of joy and peace; transcendence of time and space; the feeling of sacredness and awe; the intrinsic sense of authority within the illumination; the conquest of paradox; the inadequacy of words in describing the sensations; transiency . . . illumination as a 'peak experience'; and finally, lasting changes in temperament and personality.

Pahnke gathered together twenty Christian theological students in a private chapel. Ten had been given the hallucinogenic agent psilocybin, the active principle in psychotropic mushrooms. The others were given nicotinic acid, a vitamin which causes 'transient feelings of warmth and tingling of the skin'. The participants listened to a $2\frac{1}{2}$ hour religious service consisting of organ music, four solos, readings, prayers and personal meditation. During the weeks before the experiment, special care had been taken to reduce fear and maximize expectancy, and during the session none knew the nature of the substance he had taken.

Pahnke collected data for up to six months afterwards, and each subject had prepared by this time an account of his own personal experiences. The following are Pahnke's statistics, which condensed as percentages are admittedly clinical. They do, however, prove a point: Of those who had taken psilocybin 70 per cent experienced *inner* unity and 30 per cent external, 84 per cent had a sense of transcendence of time and space, 57 per cent feelings of love and joy, 53 per cent sacredness, 63 per cent the sense of authority and objectivity, 61 per cent the element of paradox, 66 per cent the inability adequately to express their awe in words, 79 per cent transiency, and an average of 50 per cent were substantially changed in psychological attitude, along the lines of the Stace/Pahnke framework.

The control group, that is, those who had not taken the hallucinogenic drug, for the most part had much less intense religious experiences. The most pronounced sentiment was the feeling of love (33 per cent). Otherwise the figures were: unity (7 per cent); time and space (6 per cent); joy (23 per cent); sacredness (28 per cent); objectivity and reality (18 per cent); paradox (13 per cent); ineffability (18 per cent); transiency (8 per cent) and pronounced psychological change (8 per cent).

Pahnke's experiment thus went a long way in showing that hallucinogens can intensify what would normally have been only a mild and rare religious experience. He does not, of course, claim that all people who take such psychedelic drugs necessarily have mystical or religious experiences. This, of course, is far from the case. Pahnke in fact claimed that appropriate aspirations and environment are crucial.

Following on from the pioneering work of Leary, it is now generally conceded that hallucinogenic drugs *can* precipitate peak experiences of a mystical nature. A widely prevalent attitude among practitioners of Eastern religion and yoga since the psychedelic heyday is that while drugs *can* cause these effects, it is much better to get there without them. While there is considerable merit in an attitude which derides 'artificial' means of attaining enlightenment, there are certain biological objections to the new view.

For example, LSD-25, the most powerful hallucinogen known in terms of quality and effect, is structurally similar to the substance serotonin, which is stored in the pineal gland in the brain. The essence of transcendental mysticism is to activate the 'chakras' or energy centres of the nervous system and in so doing open the 'third eye' (or pineal gland). While the drug technique replaces serotonin with LSD in the brain, the method of disciplined deep breathing used in yoga alters the amount of oxygen in the blood. As with LSD, this also has a chemical effect on the brain and causes similar visionary effects. Fasting and sensory deprivation (which occurs when a meditator stares fixedly at an image of contemplation) are also ways of enhancing these hallucinatory effects.

In summary, while psychedelic drugs are ostensibly 'artificial' they may be seen as biochemical agents in the brain which cause similar effects to those produced by 'natural' methods. The major argument against drugs from the mystical point of view (aside from arguments against the addictive qualities of drugs like heroin and opium, which cannot be discussed here) is that they produce effects of relatively short duration. Natural techniques of altering and expanding consciousness are likely to be more enduring.

SOURCEBOOKS

(Readers are referred to the books listed for shamanism which are of considerable relevance to this topic.)

ALDOUS HUXLEY: *The Doors of Perception/Heaven and Hell*; Penguin Books; Harper & Row, several eds; first published 1954-6 as separate volumes.

Familiar, and widely quoted, but one of the classic contemporary drug accounts and the best on mescalin. (Others include Colin Wilson's described in *Beyond the Outsider* and R. C. Zaehner's in *Mysticism Sacred and Profane* – Pan Books and Oxford University Press respectively.) Huxley's book is vital from the historical viewpoint, since it virtually precipitated the psychedelic-mystical enquiry.

TIMOTHY LEARY: *High Priest*, College Notes and Texts Inc., New York, 1968.

TIMOTHY LEARY et al.: *The Psychedelic Experience*, University Books, New York, 1964.

Arguably, Leary's most important books. *High Priest* covers Leary's early formative years of experimentation from 1959 to 1962, including background to the Pahnke experiment and the meeting with Michael Hollingshead. It also lays the basis for Leary's view of the psychedelic drug as a sacrament. *The Psychedelic Experience*, written with the aid of Ralph Metzner and Richard Alpert, relates the drug 'rebirth' experience, to the states of after-death consciousness as described in the *Tibetan Book of the Dead*. It is also intended as a manual for monitoring the drug experience for mystical effects.

WALTER PAHNKE: 'The Psychedelic Mystical Experience in the Human Encounter with Death', *Psychedelic Review*, 4034, 20th Street, San Francisco, no. 11, Winter 1970–1.

An important elaboration of the celebrated theological drug test which came to be known as 'The Good Friday Experiment'. Pahnke died prematurely in 1971. This is one of his major articles.

BABA RAM DASS: *Doing Your Own Being*, Spearman, London, 1973.

Ram Dass was formerly Dr Richard Alpert of Harvard and a colleague of Timothy Leary. Following his experiments with LSD he took his sacrament to India and showed it to a revered Indian yogi in the Himalayas. The latter consumed Alpert's entire stock – 900 micrograms – and was unaffected! This convinced Alpert that he should take up Eastern methods of altering consciousness. This book is a transcript of two lectures given by Ram Dass under the auspices of the Menninger Foundation in Kansas.

JOHN WHITE (ed.): *The Highest State of Consciousness*, Doubleday Anchor, New York, 1972.

Possibly the best single anthology of source writings on mystical states of consciousness, achieved both with and without psychedelic drugs. It includes articles by Stanley Krippner, Aldous Huxley, Robert S. de Ropp, R. D. Laing, Alan Watts, Lama Govinda, Walter Pahnke, Charles Tart, Abraham Maslow and Richard Wilhelm, among others.

DAVID EBIN (ed.): *The Drug Experience*, Grove Press, New York, 1961.

Resembles the White book described above, except that its sources are major accounts of the drug experience. Writings by Gautier, Baudelaire, Bayard Taylor, de Quincey, Aleister Crowley, William Burroughs, R. C. Zaehner, Allen Ginsburg and Havelock Ellis are included.

SIDNEY COHEN: *Drugs of Hallucination*, Paladin, London, 1970.

One of the most lucid and also one of the fairest accounts of psychedelics. Interesting for its references to LSD and terminal cancer patients.

JOHN C. LILLY: *The Centre of the Cyclone*, Calder & Boyars and Paladin Books, London, 1973; Julian Press, New York, 1972.

The most relevant book by the famous neurophysiologist. Lilly underwent extensive sensory deprivation testing both with and without hallucinogens and he describes the resultant mystical consciousness. Trained in computer analysis, Lilly is also noted for his theory of religious doctrines as 'programmes' of the subconscious mind. By this he means that a belief system can be fed gradually into the mind and under sensory deprivation states, and in moods of contemplation, may be re-manifested in the form of illumination and symbolic visions. Lilly has correlated the LSD programme with Buddhist and Gurdjieff gradients of consciousness.

Shamanistic Magic

Shamanism is the magic of ecstasy, of leaving the body and soaring to great heights of mystical illumination. Mircea Eliade, the famous scholar of comparative religion calls the shaman 'the technician of the sacred'. He is a person who is able to move by an act of will from one plane of existence to another.

In the strict anthropological sense, shamanism is best represented in Siberia and in South and Central America among the native Indian tribes. Usually a shaman is a magician or healer who claims to contact the deities and spirits sacred to his people. His world is alive with awe-inspiring and often terrifying supernatural beings, and it is up to the shaman to encounter these entities and learn their mysterious secrets. These will, in turn, confer upon him a profound respect for the 'sacred things', and in the case of healing, a divinely revealed remedy for the sickness or disease. Shamans frequently use hallucinogenic sacraments like datura, psilocybin or peyote, and in this state of altered consciousness they claim to perceive the vital processes or energy body of the person whom they are treating. Sometimes in shamanistic accounts the magician claims that the body seems to become transparent and he can look inside. If a magical object – a power stone or dart – has been sent by a sorcerer to cause illness in the body of the victim, it is the shaman's function to discover and suck forth the offensive object from its harmful position. And if the patient has lost his 'soul', the shaman must follow it on a visionary journey and bring it back to safety where it cannot be endangered.

Perhaps the most impressive role of the shaman, however, is his ecstatic flight into the world of his native mythology. He is lifted up, perhaps on a winged horse or eagle, and journeys to the land of the ancestors who live in the heights of the universe. For him, his gods are entities whom he can visit and converse with, and they in turn can bestow supernatural powers.

In the remarkable books of Carlos Castaneda we find one of the best contemporary accounts of the world of the native shaman. Castaneda spent ten years attempting to grasp the magical concepts of the Mexican shaman Don Juan Matus, whom he had originally met on an anthropological field trip to Arizona. Don Juan used a number of hallucinogens to encounter his supernatural allies, and such a spirit helper was one with 'a power capable of carrying a man beyond the boundaries of himself'. Don Juan reserved special reverence for peyote, and in particular its associated deity Mescalito, Castaneda describes his mystical encounter with this nature-being: 'His eyes were of the water I had just seen. They had the same enormous volume, the sparkling of gold and black. . . . Except for the pointed shape his head was exactly like the surface of the peyote plant. . . .'

Another anthropologist, Michael Harner studied the Jivaro Indians of Eastern Ecuador. When he partook of their hallucinogenic drink *natema* he found himself encountering their tribal gods: 'I met bird-headed people as well as dragon-like creatures who explained that they were the true gods of the World. I enlisted the services of other spirit helpers in attempting to fly through the far reaches of the Galaxy. . . .'

Superficially the world of the native shaman may seem to be of little relevance to the occult and the modern magician, but this is not the case. It is an interesting coincidence that the shamans of Siberia refer to the Cosmic Tree where all the deities live. The Qabalah, which is the main reference of all modern contemporary magicians also has its Tree – the Tree of Life. And just as the shaman journeys upwards to meet his gods, so too does the occultist perform rituals and meditative trance exercises which will help him scale the heavens of inner space.

In the Hermetic Order of the Golden Dawn, most of the practical magical work was of a ritual nature in which the members dressed and performed like gods, mostly of ancient Egypt, and tried imaginatively to become inspired by acting in their place. But there was also a shamanistic type of magic, which like the native variety, involved leaving the body in trance, and encountering the spirits and deities of the Tree of Life.

One of the most impressive modern 'astral journeys' is that of Aleister Crowley's vision of Jupiter, which was first published in his occult magazine *The Equinox*:

I perceived other suns rising around me, one in the North, and one in the South, and one in the West. And the one in the North was as a great bull blowing blood and flame from its nostrils; and the one in the South was as an eagle plucking forth the entrails of a

Nubian slave; and the one in the West was as a man swallowing an ocean.

And whilst I watched these suns rising around me, behold, though I knew it not, a fifth sun had risen beneath where I was standing, and it was as a great wheel of revolving lightnings. And gazing at the Wonder that flamed at my feet, I partook of the glory and became brilliantly golden, and great wings of flame descended upon me, and as they enrolled me I grew thirty cubits in height – perhaps more.

Then the sun upon which I was standing rose above the four other suns, and as it did so, I found myself standing before an ancient man with a snow-white beard, whose countenance was afired with benevolence. And as I looked upon him, a great desire possessed me to stretch forth my hand and touch his beard; and as the desire grew strong, a voice said unto me: 'Touch, it is granted thee. . . .'

I would have lingered, but I was dismissed, for the four other suns had risen to a height equal to mine own. And seeing this I stretched out my wings and flew, sinking through innumerable sheets of binding silver. And presently I opened my eyes, and all around me was as a dense fog; thus I returned to my body . . . .

Occultists use different methods for attaining these visions. Usually they relax the body and enter a state of trance. At the same time, they *will* themselves to enter the mind through different pathways. One of the most appropriate means is to use the Tarot cards as doorways . . . since these lead to different levels of consciousness on the Tree of Life. It was also common in the Golden Dawn for the magicians to use the Tattvas, or symbols of the elements (see pp. 72–4).

The basic assertion of the shaman or trance magician is that by encountering the gods of our minds in this way, we in fact discover ourselves. All of us have a vast, cosmic potential, which is for the most part untapped. The shaman offers a technique for discovering this sacred inner knowledge, and the gods once again come forth to life.

SOURCEBOOKS

CARLOS CASTANEDA: *The Teachings of Don Juan* (1968); *A Separate Reality* (1971); *Journey to Ixtlan* (1972); *Tales of Power* (1974); *The Second Ring of Power* (1977); all published by Simon & Schuster, New York. First four available also in Penguin books.

The Castaneda/Don Juan material is a unique encounter between the rational and to some extent narrow reasoning of the Westerner, and the awesome magical world of the Mexican *brujo*, or sorcerer. Don Juan, a

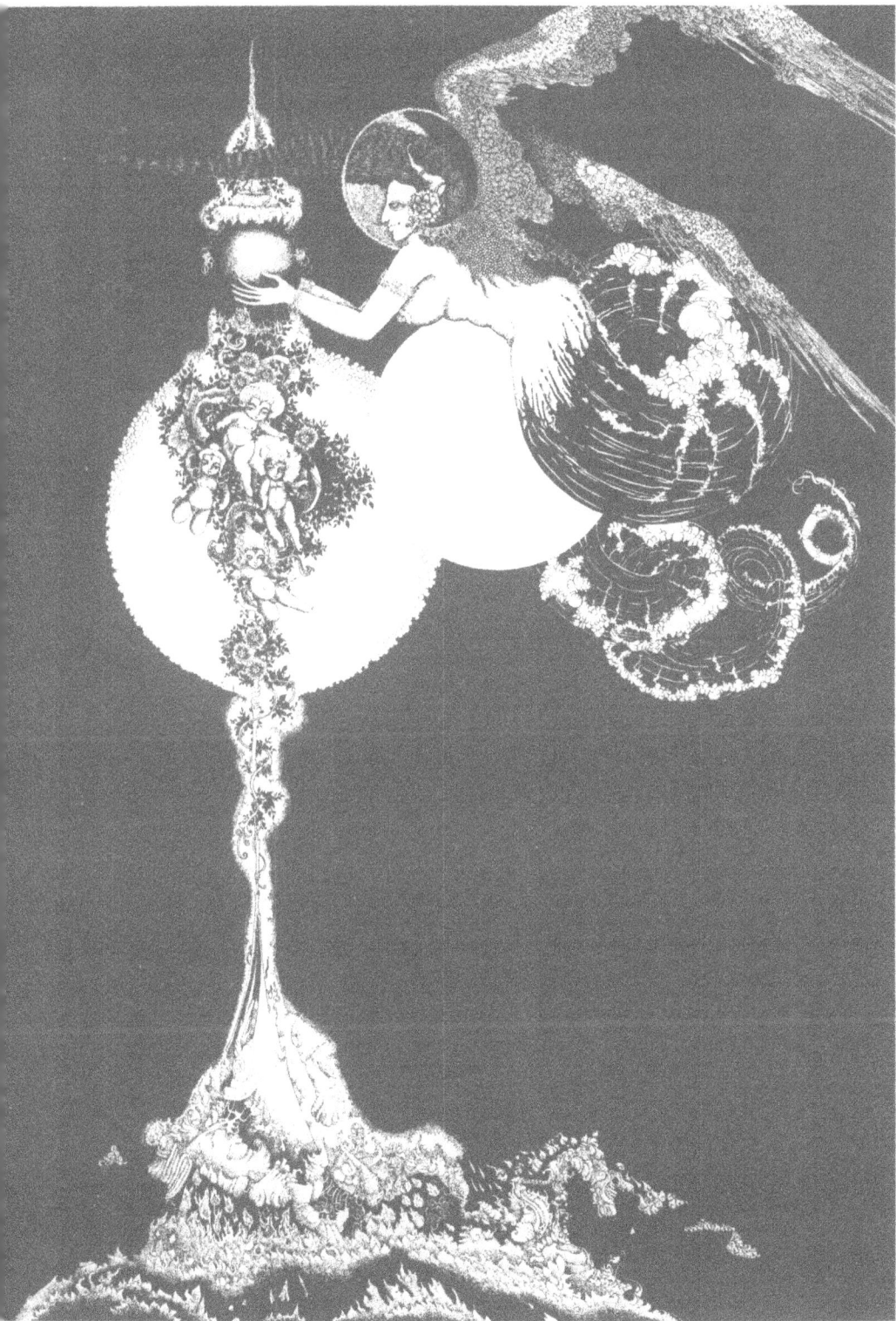

Yaqui Indian, is both a shaman and a warrior, who sees his magical techniques and 'allies' as aids towards becoming a 'Man of Knowledge'.

MICHAEL J. HARNER (ed.): *Hallucinogens and Shamanism*, Oxford University Press, London and New York, 1973.

PETER T. FURST (ed.): *Flesh of the Gods*, Praeger, New York; Allen & Unwin, London, 1972.

Both of these volumes are anthologies containing some of the best available anthropological accounts of shamanism. Harner's volume also contains a chapter on hallucinogens in witchcraft, and he shows how the flight on the broomstick was actually a sexual out-of-the-body phantasy aided by psychedelic drugs.

MIRCEA ELIADE: *Shamanism*, Bollingen Press, Princeton University, and Routledge & Kegan Paul, London, 1972.

The most complete treatment of shamanism on a world-wide basis, and an invaluable reference book.

NEVILL DRURY: *Don Juan, Mescalito and Modern Magic: The Mythology of Inner Space*, Routledge & Kegan Paul, London and Boston, 1978.

A detailed comparative analysis of Don Juan's magical trance techniques, and their relationship to the recent psychedelic movement (Timothy Leary, Baba Ram Dass et al.), contemporary magic and the Tarot.

Ghosts and Hauntings

Human history has been consistent in its fear of the unknown – especially when the unknown has to do with death. Every society has speculated on the fate of those who die, and most have believed it possible for some, if not all, the dead to return, usually in non-physical form, to haunt the living. Most societies have taken some precautions to prevent this, generally believing that the dead were dangerous – funeral rituals to drive the spirit away, or gifts to appease it, or tombs to trap it, all constituted part of the process of protection against the wandering dead. It was generally assumed that the dead, if restless and returned from the grave, would be attracted to either relatives or people with whom they had some close association during life, or to places which had special meaning for them. Therefore the relatives had to be especially careful, but so did anyone moving into a house in which a man had died. Some societies even forbade the mention of a dead man's name (echoed today in modern society's injunctions against 'speaking ill of the dead'), and shifted location to avoid their return.

In general terms, what are popularly known as ghosts, can be divided into several categories.

(1) *Influences* – the vague sort of 'feelings' that adhere to places (or occasionally objects), often unpleasantly, but which manifest in no more tangible form.

(2) *Poltergeists* – the noisy ghosts popularized in films, rather destructive outbursts of energy which cause physical manifestations of various types, usually involving the destruction of household objects, loud noises, etc. Research (for example, that of Harry Price and Carl Jung) tends to suggest these are not ghosts in the traditional sense, but psychic energy associated with adolescents.

(3) *Apparitions* – the traditional ghosts of popular fiction, the shadowy

figures which appear and disappear, usually in the semi-dark, and which are usually associated with historical locations.

(4) *Hauntings* – in which the characteristics of apparitions and poltergeists are combined to constitute psychic phenomena of alarming degree, with various manifestations.

Modern parapsychological research has investigated some ghosts in depth, and a number of scientifically based theories have been advanced as to the nature and functioning of these shadowy figures.

The term 'ghost' usually creates an image of the spirit of someone who has died, although some apparitions have been of the living. Apparitions can be classified into:

(1) 'Ghosts' – that is, appearances of persons who have died, and who are either: (a) associated with the person to whom they appear (for example the appearance of a relative to give a message from 'beyond the grave'); (b) associated with the place in which they appear (for example, the almost classic theme of a murder victim haunting the house in which he was murdered).

(2) 'Phantasms of the living', that is, apparitions of persons who are still alive, but who appear in one place whilst their physical body remains in another; such apparitions usually indicate: (a) a person who is on the point of death and who manifests to someone closely involved with him; (b) a person who is conveying some message or urgency (for example, the mother who appears to warn her son of impending danger); (c) a person who is asleep at the time and projects the astral body accidentally or intentionally.

(3) Apparitions of animals or objects, for example, ghost ships, phantom animals and mysteriously appearing and disappearing objects.

Although popular films and novels have characterized the ghost as a white, etheric figure drifting around terrifying spectators, ghosts are not necessarily visible, frightening, or indeed etheric.

Many have been mistaken for solid, physical individuals. And ghosts can be perceived in a variety of ways, often visible only to psychics, while non-psychics merely 'feel' the presence. Perception of ghosts can be by:

(1) vision – that is, the ghost appears physically in one form or another;

(2) sound – there are noises, voices, music or other sounds which suggest the presence of supernatural phenomena;

(3) intuition – the 'feeling' that someone/something is present;

(4) other sensory perception – for example, perception of temperature (often said to fall in the presence of ghosts), movement (often breezes are said to occur in otherwise still rooms), touch (invisible fingers running through the hair or across the face);

(5) psychic perception – where an individual possesses some psychic faculties he may perceive the ghost either in vision (clairvoyance), sound (clairaudience), feeling (clairsentience);

(6) indirectly by physical phenomena – as in the case of a poltergeist, the ghost may manifest in the movement of objects (psychokinesis or telekinesis), levitation of objects, mysterious appearance of writing, appearance of apports, or through any of the means employed in spiritualism.

Regardless of the question as to whether the individual actually perceives someone or something, there are questions as to what and how he perceives. Generally, theories of ghosts have employed one or more of the following premises:

(1) the discarnate personalities of individuals can remain in contact with the physical world after death (the spiritualist hypothesis);

(2) some type of energy mass can exist in association with places or objects or people which gives rise to various phenomena, but which is not human, although it may have been stimulated by human action (e.g. a murderer's anger and hatred remain once his crime is committed and may manifest in various phenomena) (this is one of the more frequent scientific explanations);

(3) events leave indelible prints on the total substance of the environment, and may manifest in various ways (a variation on (2));

(4) there is always a rational explanation for any such manifestations (the ultimate rationalist explanation);

(5) such manifestations have no existence in reality but are caused by psychic influences on the individuals who claim to perceive them.

SOURCEBOOKS

G. N. M. TYRRELL: *Apparitions*, reprint, Macmillan, London, 1970.
The classic work on the subject, and the one which more than any other stimulated continuing research.

DENNIS BARDENS: *Ghosts and Hauntings*, Fontana, London, 1967.

T. C. LETHBRIDGE: *Ghost and Ghoul*, Routledge & Kegan Paul, London, 1961.
An interesting study, based on historical material, and written by one of the best authorities in the general field of occultism.

ERIC MAPLE: *The Realm of Ghosts*, Pan, London, 1964.

DOUGLAS HILL: *Return from the Dead*, MacDonald, London, 1970.
Includes material on ghosts, vampires, werewolves and poltergeists.

H. CARRINGTON and N. FODOR: *The Poltergeist Down The Ages*, Rider, London,
1953.
  The most important work on poltergeists.
  Interesting collections of accounts of ghosts and hauntings are readily
available.

Spiritualism

Every known society has held that, under certain circumstances, it is possible to communicate with those who have died. Opinions have varied as to whether this is good or bad, harmful or beneficial, either to the dead or to the one communicating with them. In some societies formalized institutions have been established to enable regular communication to take place – mediums, shamans and other psychics have important places in many cultures.

Basically, spiritualism involves:

(1) A belief in the continuity of the personality after death – that is, the person is more or less the same after he has given up the physical body, can communicate in words, remembers events and people, is capable of conversation.

(2) The concept that contact with the dead is possible – the dead exist in some dimension not totally separate from our own and can be contacted there, or, alternatively, can come into our dimension to contact us.

(3) People (usually known as mediums) with specific psychic gifts which facilitate communication with the dead by a variety of means – automatic writing, going into a trance, direct voice, etc.

(4) The idea that there is a valid purpose in taking advantage of the possibility of contact with the dead – usually justified on the grounds that they know more, are more enlightened, or, conversely, that they need help to adjust to their new state.

Spiritualism can be considered as:

(1) Philosophy – it offers a particular view of life and death, and offers a system of beliefs about the universe, which includes the possibility and the validity of contact with dead.

(2) Methodology – various techniques are employed to make contact with the dead.

(3) Results – what is achieved by supposed contact with the dead? The

results are usually verbal, and frequently of a poor standard; occasionally physical manifestations occur.

(4) Evidence – what evidence is there to support the thesis that the results derive from communication with the dead? Modern spiritualism differs from spiritualism in primitive societies in its emphasis on evidence – that is, on its claims that scientific research can and will validate its premises.

The questions that need to be answered are:

(1) Can it be demonstrated that the results are achieved by means which are not explicable in non-supernatural terms? For example, by conscious or unconscious fraud on the part of those involved, by natural phenomena of various kinds, or by the workings of the mind especially in its little known aspects (e.g. telepathy). There is considerable scientific evidence to support the thesis that at least some 'spiritualist' phenomena occur outside the realm of natural phenomena as presently understood by science. This involves such faculties as telepathy, psychokinesis (see pp. 3–11).

(2) Assuming it can be demonstrated that the results are supernatural, can it be shown that they result from communication with the dead rather than simply being the psychic powers of the living? This is the most difficult area for spiritualists, since it is difficult to find evidence to support the hypothesis that it is communication with the dead, which cannot also be explained in simpler terms as deriving from the 'non-dead'.

Spiritualism, in its modern manifestation, began in the USA in the second half of the nineteenth century, and rapidly expanded throughout England and Europe. The impact of wars – with large-scale loss of life and hence a preoccupation with death and the fate of the dead – increased its influence, and eventually churches specifically proclaiming a spiritualist philosophy developed. Some of these are Christian in orientation, others non – or even anti-Christian. With the current emphasis on life rather than death, spiritualism seems destined to fade away, especially as the manifestations which once astonished and amazed are now no longer its exclusive domain but are accepted, to a large extent, as phenomena for scientific study.

Spiritualism usually centres on some form of communication with the spirits of the dead – either though a *seance* (a meeting specifically for that purpose, usually in semi-darkness, with a number of people sitting in a circle, invoking the spirits), through a *ouija board* (a board with the letters of the alphabet and various basic words written on it, over which a glass is moved, theoretically by the spirits), a *planchette* (pencil holder on wheels, which, if lightly held in the hand is said to be moved by the spirits who will use it to write), *automatic writing* (a pencil lightly held in the hand of the medium is supposed to move at the direction of the spirits), *spirit photography* (an unexposed photographic film when developed shows a picture or a message), *clairvoyance* (where the psychic power of seeing spirits is possessed by the medium), *clairaudience* (where the medium hears things not audible to ordinary people) or *clairsentience* ('feelings' or intuitions). At a seance a variety of phenomena occur – generally the medium goes into a trance during which he (or more frequently she) is *possessed* by the spirit of a departed person, or usually by a *spirit guide* (a teacher, or advanced spirit who assists and protects the medium) who may speak using the vocal cords of the medium, whose voice may change. Sometimes *materializations* (the physical appearance in the seance room of a deceased person), *apports* (the manifestation of material objects with no natural explanation – e.g. stones falling onto the table), *rappings* (the spirits knocking on the table to communicate in code) and lights may appear in the room. Rarely, *ectoplasm* (said to be a primal semi-spiritual matter) pours from the medium's mouth or extends from beneath his clothing. Occasionally, *trumpets* (a speaking trumpet through which the spirit is supposed to communicate) will be used. *Psychokinesis* (the movement of objects without a natural explanation) sometimes occurs, with objects floating around the seance room. *Levitation* (the lifting of the body of the medium, or a member of the seance, into the air) is rare. Traditionally seances are held in darkness, since the presence of light is said to weaken the power whereby the spirits manifest. Spiritualist groups also practise healing, usually claiming to work as the agents of spirit guides with a particular interest in medical work – both the laying on of hands and various forms of massage are used.

THE EVIDENCE FOR SPIRITUALISM

Although spiritualism has to some extent been scientifically investigated its religious overtones and tendency to require conditions that make scientific assessment difficult, if not impossible, have precluded this. However, extensive studies have been made of numbers of famous mediums, especially during the early years of spiritualism in England. Mediums are generally classified according to the type of phenomena with which they most often work – mental mediums give information about what they see or hear, or are channels through which the spirits communicate by impressions; physical mediums are those who are actually possessed by the spirits, and who precipitate various physical phenomena.

Among the most notable mediums in the history of spiritualism were: Mrs Leonora Piper (1857–1950); Mrs Gladys Leonard (1882–1968);

Miss Geraldine Cummins (d. 1968); Mrs Eileen Garrett (1893–1970); Mr D. D. Home (1833–86); Mrs Eusapia Palladino (1854–1918); Mr Rudi Schneider (1908–57).

THE PHILOSOPHY OF SPIRITUALISM

The philosophy and theology of spiritualism has been derived through the teachings of the spirits communicated through mediums, and accordingly different teachings given through different mediums tend to be different not only in emphasis but in information. Therefore various schools of spiritualism exist, centring on the teachings of different mediums. For example, most French spiritualists and those in South America (who usually call themselves 'spiritists') follow the teachings of Allan Kardec, which included reincarnation. The majority of English spiritualists follow the philosophy of W. Stainton Moses (1839–92) expressed in his book *Spirit Teachings*, or the more recent and very popular writings of J. Arthur Findlay (cf. his *On the Edge of the Etheric Rider*, London, 1931). In general terms all these philosophies diverge in detail but share certain common characteristics:

(1) The soul is a duplicate of the body and resides in its natural state in a world which is similar to, although better than, this physical world – with houses, trees, rivers, etc.

(2) The soul is occupied by the spirit, the life-principle.

(3) There are a variety of 'worlds' coexisting in a hierarchical series differing according to 'vibration' and the aim of life is to progress from the lower to the higher worlds; often it is taught that these worlds exist in concentric spheres around the earth.

(4) After death the soul is drawn to that world for which it is suited by its vibrations – i.e. an evil man will be drawn to an unpleasant world.

(5) Either souls reincarnate until they attain perfection (as the spiritists, following Kardec say), or else there is continued progression in other worlds (as the English spiritualists say).

(6) God is not as central as in Christian theology.

This philosophy and cosmology draws heavily upon the writings of Emmanuel Swedenborg and has some relation to certain teachings of the Neo-Platonists.

While some spiritualist groups are expressly Christian, others are not. The Spiritualists National Union (Great Britain) summarizes its philosophy into a creed that is the basis for many spiritualist groups throughout the world, with some variation:

(1) The Fatherhood of God

(2) The Brotherhood of Man

(3) The communion of spirits and the ministry of angels
(4) The continuous existence of the human soul
(5) Personal responsibility for individual action
(6) Compensation and retribution hereafter for all good
and evil deeds done on earth
(7) Eternal progress open to every human soul.

Most spiritualist groups, as distinct from formally organized churches, have vague and undefined philosophies deriving from the teachings received through the medium leading the group.

SPIRITUALISM TODAY

With the increasing revival of interest in the occult and the modern interest of science in psychic phenomena, there has been a decreasing interest in spiritualism. Essentially a phenomena of man's concern with death and the hereafter, it has little place in a world essentially concerned with the present and with life. Spiritualist groups have become characterized by a predominance of elderly, widowed ladies and the absence of the young. A widespread awareness of psychic phenomena means that the seance room no longer offers the excitement and the wonder it once did.

SOURCEBOOKS

The literature of and about spiritualism is enormous, ranging from large volumes of communications received from the spirits, to vigorous denunciations of the whole thing as fraud or the work of the devil, to heavy scientific tomes reporting investigations of mediums.

One of the best general surveys of spiritualism is:

GEORGESS MCHARGUE: *Facts, Frauds and Phantasms*, Doubleday, New York, 1972.

Covers the entire history of spiritualism from the time of shamans to the case of Bishop Pike, and includes a glossary of terms and a bibliography.

There are several 'classics' in this field which will never really be outdated and which, although often rather pedantic and heavy-going, are essential reading. These include:

NANDOR FODOR: *An Encyclopedia of Psychic Science*, reprinted by University Books, New York, 1966.

Containing information on almost everything in the field of spiritualism and psychic research.

FRANK PODMORE: *Mediums of the Nineteenth Century*, reprinted by University Books, New York, 1963.

The 'classic' study of mediums, centred on those who really established spiritualism, and were the first to be investigated with any degree of scientific method, in the great 'age' of mediums.

SIR ARTHUR CONAN DOYLE: *The History of Spiritualism*, Doran, New York, 1926.

An examination by a firm believer, who was one of the 'key figures' in the development of spiritualism.

Additionally, there are a number of more recent general surveys which provide useful background:

G. K. NELSON: *Spiritualism and Society*, Schocken, New York, 1969.

General survey in sociological terms.

DOUGLAS HILL: *Return from the Dead*, Macdonald, London, 1970.

General survey of beliefs regarding the possibility of contact with the dead.

There are numerous books by mediums or about them, some of which provide interesting material on what they do, and what they believe. These include:

TREVOR H. HALL: *The Spiritualists: The Story of Florence Cook and William Crookes*, Duckworth, London, 1962.

A detailed study of one of the great figures in the beginnings of scientific investigation on spiritualism, and the medium he examined.

EILEEN GARRETT: *Many Voices: The Autobiography of a Medium*, Putnams, New York, 1968.

The autobiography of a woman who was described as a great medium, and subjected to considerable investigation.

JAMES PIKE and DIANNE KENNEDY: *The Other Side*, Doubleday, New York, 1968.

The account of Bishop Pike's search for contact with his son, Jim, who committed suicide, and the sittings with Arthur Ford.

W. STAINTON MOSES: *Spirit Teachings*, reprinted by Spiritualist Press, London, 1962.

One of the first books written to convey the philosophy and beliefs of spiritualism.

On the subject of survival after death generally, the great 'classic' work is:

F. W. H. MYERS: *Human Personality and its Survival of Bodily Death*, reprinted by University Books, New York, 1961.

A massive study on the basis of the author's investigation of spiritualism.

H. HART: *The Enigma of Survival*, Rider, London, 1959.

Also deals with this subject.

Possession

Throughout history and across a wide range of cultures and societies, various states of consciousness, specifically those associated with ecstasy – poetic and artistic inspiration, religious fervour, madness, epilepsy, drunkenness, sexual frenzy, trance and other states outside the usual range of ordinary experience – have often been classified as resulting from the influence upon the individual of forces, powers or beings outside his own personality. The cause of such influence has been given a variety of explanations – devils, gods, spirits, the dead, elementals, nature spirits, angels, ghosts, but inevitably it has led to the idea that man can be taken over by an external force which operates through the individual, without his conscious co-operation and against his will. This remains in popular exclamations like 'He is not himself today', or 'Something has got into him', implying that the individual can be, and is, sometimes literally 'not himself'.

Possession is neither a new concept, nor a specifically Christian one. Throughout history, virtually all societies have recognized that it was possible for a man to be 'taken over' by an influence, or entity, outside himself.

Two types of possession have been universally recognized:

(1) *Voluntary possession* – when the individual allows himself to be possessed by an entity, as do spiritualist mediums, to enable the entity to manifest when it could not ordinarily do so: this includes possession by the spirits of the dead, by spirits of nature, and by the gods, especially for the purposes of prophecy, but also the type of possession found amongst Christian Pentecostalists.

(2) *Involuntary possession* – when the individual does not freely allow himself to be possessed but is taken over involuntarily by an external force which is generally evil and destructive to the individual.

In popular terminology the word 'possession' covers a wide range of phenomena, but in more precise usage it ought only to be used for one category of a number of types. Individuals can be influenced by external forces in a variety of ways:

(1) *Influence* – the individual is aware of an influence, of varying degrees of power, which affects his thought or behaviour, and which does not originate within him; in some methods of divination the individual allows himself to be influenced by external forces. At its simplest level, influence includes the sorts of 'feelings' that many individuals get in certain localities and about certain people.

(2) *Obsession* – the individual is aware of an influence affecting his thought and behaviour to a more marked degree than simply 'influence', and is unable to liberate himself from the influence – it has, so to speak, become attached to him, but remains 'outside' him;

(3) *Possession* – where the individual's personality is displaced by another entity which thus gains control, to varying degrees, of the individual's body; the individual need not necessarily be aware that anything is happening, or have any memories after the possession is over since he was not 'there' at the time. Individuals come under the influence of external entities in a variety of ways, sometimes quite accidentally (e.g. shifting into a house in which a restless entity exists), sometimes due to their own action (e.g. playing with occult rituals), and the actual degree of influence varies in every case.

Whether or not individuals can actually be possessed by external entities remains a matter of speculation; nevertheless, there have been innumerable cases where it appears that they were, and where exorcism proved successful as a therapy.

The psychologically unbalanced, particularly those suffering from specific types of disorder (e.g. paranoia, schizophrenia) may believe that they are being persecuted by someone or something external to themselves, or even attacked from within by various forces. Individuals suffering from compulsive thoughts or desires may interpret these as originating from outside, being 'planted' in their minds by enemies or evil spirits and it certainly appears to the individuals so affected that they are being 'made' to do things against their will by someone or something else. A wide range of influences can cause the experience of believing oneself to be obsessed or possessed. Certainly sexual frustration or imbalance is influential in causing an upwelling of psychic energy seeking, unsuccessfully, an outlet, and therefore introverting and causing a variety of conflicts within the individual. This is especially evident in cases where devoutly religious and highly puritanical individuals suffer from what they interpret as obsession or possession, characterized by 'impure' thoughts

POSSESSION

and desires. It must be recognized that the majority of cases in which possession, or obsession, or even influence are alleged, can be explained in much simpler, psychological terms, and the terms relating to possession should be reserved only for cases in which all alternative explanations fail.

These would be characterized by:

(1) Symptoms which do not respond to the usual methods of treatment, either medical or psychological.

(2) Cases in which the individual is otherwise healthy and well-balanced and exhibits no indications of being mentally disturbed apart from the actual symptoms of the possession or obsession.

(3) Cases in which there is an indication that unorthodox (from a psychological point of view) treatment – in the traditions of exorcism – will cause a response and an improvement.

Whether or not they are accepted as cases of possession or obsession in the traditional sense, there are cases in which these conditions are fulfilled, and which respond to exorcism, but not to traditional medical or psychiatric techniques.

There are many case studies in the field, although some of them can be explained in terms other than those involving possession or obsession. Examples may help to clarify the concepts:

(1) *Possession* – a young boy, after a period of showing signs of disturbance and restlessness, nightmares, loss of appetite, uncontrolled aggression and loss of concentration, suddenly begins lapsing into states of violent anger during which his body is thrown into uncontrolled frenzy and he screams and shouts. In the course of these 'fits' he converses with onlookers, almost as though he is 'someone else'; when he returns to his normal state he is unable to remember anything that happened, but suffers nevertheless as a consequence of the contortions of his body. His physical condition endangers his health. Extensive medical and psychiatric diagnosis reveals that the symptoms are not caused by any physical illness (e.g. epilepsy, brain damage), and that the boy, in his normal state, is quite healthy psychologically. However he continues to manifest a secondary personality of a violent, destructive nature. Eventually, a rite of exorcism is performed, and after several repetitions the symptoms completely disappear. A case in which conventional medical and psychiatric treatment had no effect, and in which possession can be advanced as a reasonable explanation.

(2) *Obsession* – a woman begins to have thoughts intrude into her consciousness, encouraging her to go and live with an aunt she dislikes. The thoughts eventually manifest as voices, audible to the woman but not to anyone else. She is consciously aware that they are not her own thoughts,

but is unable to prevent them, or put them out of her mind; it is as though someone is actually talking to her. She begins to 'see' the aunt in her mind, and the image becomes annoying because of its frequent occurrence. She undertakes all types of activities, physical and intellectual, to distract herself from the obsession, but cannot do so. A physician determines that her health is good, but being undermined by this problem. She consults a psychiatrist who can locate no immediate cause of the problem; she has no guilt feelings about the aunt, and presents herself as a well-balanced, healthy woman. Despite both medication and psychiatric treatment, the problem continues. The woman eventually consults an occultist, who tells her that the aunt is involved in witchcraft, and has been employing an obsessing entity, created by some form of ritual magic, to try to get her to live with her. The occultist performs a magical exorcism, and all symptoms cease.

(3) *Influence* – a man consults a spiritualist medium, and thereafter feels he is being followed by a vague undefined figure, neither hostile or friendly, but simply annoying. There is no feeling of obsessive influence, the figure simply follows him, and this in itself is disturbing. Believing it to be a problem within himself, rather than an external reality (possibly relating to the fact that he, because of his Roman Catholic background, feels guilty about attending the seance) he consults a psychologist. After treatment for some time the figure remains. The psychologist refers him to a minister, who performs an exorcism. The figure disappears and never returns.

These three instances, simplified from the original cases, give clear-cut examples of types of possession; in detail, actual cases are rarely as straightforward, or as easily resolved.

Actual cases of possession, obsession and influence are exceptional; most alleged instances having alternative explanations. Unfortunately, with the modern revival of an often uninformed interest in the occult, there is a tendency to accept at face value every claim to be possessed, and to offer exorcism as an immediate and practical solution. It should be remembered that exorcism itself, when performed in cases where there is no possession or obsession, can be a factor in causing the individual to be opened to all manner of undesirable influences.

SOURCEBOOKS

Since possession is virtually inseparable from exorcism, all the books in the exorcism category will also be appropriate.

T. K. OESTERREICH: *Possession, Demoniacal and Other*, University Books, New York, 1961.

The classic study of possession.

I. M. LEWIS: *Ecstatic Religion*, Penguin, Harmondsworth, 1971.
Considers the whole concept of possession in religion and includes material on Christian Pentecostalism.

WILLIAM SARGANT: *The Mind Possessed*, Heinemann, London, 1973.
The most significant psychiatric study which includes material on hynosis, sex, drugs and possession.

ALDOUS HUXLEY: *The Devils of Loudon*, Harper & Row, New York, 1953.
A major source of material on traditional Christian concepts of possession and exorcism.

Exorcism

Any belief systems that allow for possession, or obsession, or for the influencing of individuals or places by evil forces necessarily includes provision for the destruction of the evil forces. Exorcism – the casting out of evil forces, or devils – has been a part of human history ever since man first personified the forces of nature, and divided the powers around him into good and evil. Every society which recognizes possession, recognizes, and makes provision for, some form of exorcism in which a superior power or skill is brought in to combat the evil. Essentially, exorcism refers to people, but it can also refer to the casting out of evil influences from places (e.g. haunted houses).

Traditionally, exorcism has worked on several basic principles:

(1) make things unpleasant enough for the possessing entity and it will go away;

(2) use reason to trap the entity into doing something rash and thus force it to go away;

(3) summon a greater power and invoke it to force the entity to leave.

Several primitive societies burn leaves, whip the possessed individual, create large amounts of noise in expectation of frightening the entity away; or they try to trick it away from the body by placing tempting objects – food, or sometimes animals – around; or, finally, they summon the gods to banish the entity. Christian exorcism, although working on the basis of a different world view, employs traditionally the same procedures. Incense, holy water and bells may be used to discomfort the entity; interrogation, challenging and threats are applied to persuade the entity to leave; and, finally, God or the Holy Spirit is invoked to drive it away.

It is almost everywhere assumed that possession is accompanied by physical symptoms – including extreme loss of energy, nausea, pain, bleeding – and may give rise to supernatural powers on the part of the possessed (e.g. speaking in unknown tongues, levitation). Most societies also recognize that not all men can exorcize – some do so by virtue of their natural skills (a charismatic ministry), others by virtue of authority given to them (e.g. the priesthood). Either way, the exorcist is in very real danger. The methods actually employed vary from tradition to tradition, and are usually chosen to suit the beliefs of the possessed person.

With the resurgence of interest in things occult, psychiatry is taking a fresh look at possession and exorcism – not so much as an explanation, but as a technique which, even if founded upon non-scientific premises – tends to work.

Exorcisms, in general, tend to operate on the basis of a standard formula:

(1) the invocation of powers believed to be greater than those possessing the individual;

(2) the invocation of the possessing entity and an attempt to discover who or what it is, while being protected by the power previously invoked;

(3) the direction of the exorcist's power to drive out the entity.

The exorcist also casts around the possessed individual a 'protective field' to prevent the entity re-entering. Exorcism works on the basis of a belief in the existence of various powers in the universe, possessing varying degrees of strength, and engaged in a struggle for existence in this world, through the agency of man, who is thus caught in the midst of a cosmic battle. It is in the individual who is possessed and receiving exorcism that this battle is most clearly manifested – the struggle between darkness and light, good and evil, God and the Devil, life and death.

Exorcism is not necessarily a Christian phenomenon, and there are a wide variety of techniques and traditions by which it can be carried out. These can be basically classified as:

(1) *Christian* – deriving essentially from the power of Jesus Christ, and based upon the scriptural account of authority to cast out devils being given by him to his disciples; this in turn divides into:

(a) Catholic – the traditions of the Roman Catholic and Eastern Orthodox Churches, where the power and authority to exorcize is given to the individual by virtue of his ordination to the priesthood, and in which exorcism is performed sacramentally, in a ceremonial form, according to a carefully defined formula, with set rules and procedures;

(b) Protestant – where the power to exorcize is taken as having been given to all Christians by Christ, but which is believed to manifest especially through individuals who have received that particular gift of the Holy Spirit and thereby exercise a charismatic ministry; the exorcism tends not to have a prescribed formula, but will vary according to the wishes of the exorcist, and will generally not be ceremonial in form, or follow any specifically defined procedure.

(2) *Ritual magic* – the authority here derives from knowledge, as the magician works not by virtue of authority given to him, but by virtue of power he has acquired through self-preparation and learning; the exorcism will usually be ritual in character, making use of ceremonial forms and symbols, and often the invocation of powers, and leading ultimately to a confrontation between the entity possessing, and the will of the magician. In some magical traditions, the magician may invoke the aid of the particular Order or school to which he belongs. (Cf. *More Things in Heaven* by Walter Owen, Dakers, London, 1947.)

(3) *Witchcraft* – here the underlying principles are similar to those for ritual magic, although the emphasis is more explicitly a religious one, with the exorcist invoking the gods and powers of his religion, to drive out the possessing entity, and employing a range of traditional witchcraft rituals.

Other religious traditions – Judaism, Islam, Buddhism – have in various of their approaches provisions for exorcism, although they are not central to the concepts of the religions.

SOURCEBOOKS

FRANCOISE STRACHAN: *Casting out Devils*, Aquarian, London, 1972.
   One of the best introductions to the subject, covering a wide range of
   traditions from orthodox Catholic to contemporary witchcraft.
JOHN RICHARDS: *But Deliver Us From Evil*, Darton, Longman & Todd,
   London, 1974.
   Specifically Christian in approach and, indeed, designed for those
   working in the pastoral ministry. A useful source for material on exorcism
   in the modern church.
DOM ROBERT PETITPIERRE: *Exorcism*, SPCK, London, 1974.
   A briefer summary of this area is contained in this report of the
   controversial commission convened by the Bishop of Exeter in England.
MARTIN EBON (ed.): *Exorcism: Fact not Fiction*, Signet, New York, 1974.
   An interesting general collection of material on exorcism including a
   wide range of diverse cases.
   This includes the case upon which the book *The Exorcist* was based. The
   book by William Peter Blatty, as distinct from the film based upon it,
   presents an interesting, although not altogether accurate, portrayal of a
   contemporary exorcism.

Faith Healing

The term 'faith healing' is widely used to describe a range of healing methods many of which have nothing to do with either the faith of the healer, or the faith of the patient, but which employ methods which are either unorthodox, or presuppose some form of supernatural intervention in the healing process. They exclude such natural healing methods as naturopathy, osteopathy and homeopathy which employ something – chemical or natural – which may be described as 'medicine' and presuppose a physical origin and a physical cure for illness. There are exceptions and the Philippines healers, for example, could be classified into either category, since they employ physical, but supposedly supernatural, methods in their healing.

Disregarding the rather inaccurate phrase, 'faith healing', one can look at a tradition of healing from earliest times to which this term can be applied. In primitive societies shamans and magicians are called upon to drive out evil spirits which are believed to be causing illness; they were regarded traditionally as diviners, who could diagnose the nature of the sickness (usually a curse applied by another magician, the malevolence of any enemy or the invasion of an evil spirit) and then successfully cure it. These primitive faith healers used a variety of techniques, often characterized by exorcism, and sometimes gave natural remedies (such as herbs), or provided spells or rituals for healing. But faith healing is characterized by its emphasis on the mind – or, in some approaches, the soul or the spirit – as distinct from the body. The source of the power which healed through faith healing was believed to derive from a variety of sources, from God or gods, from spirits, from natural forces, or simply from the power of suggestion which the healer held over his patient. Usually, however, it was believed to originate *outside* the healer, who was thus merely a vehicle through which it functioned.

Persons with natural gifts of healing were originally a part of society, but with the increasing power of the Church they tended to disappear, principally because their gifts were inevitably interpreted as powers of the devil, and they as witches. The Church, holding to herself the power of healing through the sacraments, declined to recognize that such gifts existed outside her, except through the agency of Satan. There were individuals within the Church, including many of the great saints, to whom gifts of healing were attributed, or to whose remains or relics people flocked in search of healing. The miraculous – or allegedly miraculous – cures associated with places like Lourdes provide examples of faith healing within the context of the Church, but outside the established domain of the clergy.

It was Franz Mesmer who really began the fashion of faith healing in modern times. Mesmer, an Austrian living in the eighteenth century, claimed to cure his patients by placing them in contact with sources of 'magnetism' which he believed was the vital life force, the absence or depletion of which causes illness. His patients sat around tubs filled with iron filings into which metal rods were stuck, and these rods, held by the patients, were said to convey the magnetism into the patients' bodies. Convulsions, trances and comas were common among Mesmer's patients, and many of them afterwards reported their illness cured or significantly improved. Mesmer claimed that his cures were based on natural scientific principles, not on anything miraculous or on divine intervention. His disciples continued to employ his techniques, but eventually much of the paraphernalia of mesmerism, as it became known, disappeared and it became a purely mental process, without iron rods or tubs of filings.

In America it was continued by Phineas Quimby and later developed into Christian Science by his student, Mary Baker Eddy, who came eventually to deny the existence of matter, illness or death, believing them to be 'errors' of the 'mortal mind'.

With the development of spiritualism, a variety of healing techniques associated with it emerged, depending largely on mediums through whom various healers were said to manifest, some giving diagnoses and prescribing treatment, others actually giving treatment, such as massage and the laying on of hands.

An increasing interest in healing in the early years of the twentieth century stimulated a variety of approaches, and the Church also began to consider the restoration of the healing ministry which in primitive times had been so much a part of its work. The greatest interest amongst the churches came in the Church of England, but other churches, orthodox and unorthodox, began to undertake healing. And the revival of interest in witchcraft led to the emergence in that movement of healing techniques as well.

The techniques of faith healing can be classified into:

(1) *the laying on of hands* – this is traditionally the Christian method, and is used by a variety of churches in conjunction with prayer;

(2) *sacramental healing* – used in the churches of the Catholic tradition, involving anointing with holy oil and the laying on of hands, and known as Holy Unction;

(3) *prayer* – some groups use no physical actions at all, but simply pray, either silently or out loud, for those who are to be healed;

(4) *ritual massage* – this technique, which involves running the hands over the body, is not intended to affect the physical body in the same way as, for example, physiotherapy, but is believed to affect invisible forces and radiate healing power from the healers' hands;

(5) *ritual techniques* – as employed in witchcraft groups and by magicians, utilizing various symbols and ceremonies for the healing of the patient;

(6) *persuasion* – groups of the New Thought and Christian Science line employ nothing more than the intellectual method of persuading the patient that illness either does not exist, or is not a natural state, and therefore the mind is capable of overcoming it by right thinking;

(7) *psychic surgery* – used by some groups and healers, especially in the Philippines and South America, where the healer is alleged actually to open parts of the patient's body and remove diseased material physically.

There are a wide range of groups employing various methods of faith healing today. They include:

(1) Church groups – especially in the Church of England and other Protestant bodies, where prayer and the laying on of hands is practised. Various associations of healers, such as the Order of St Luke, have been formed as oecumenical groups in which healers from different churches can work.

(2) Christian Science and allied traditions, including New Thought, which have a decided emphasis in their teaching and work on the ministry of healing, which they endeavour to accomplish through an emphasis on thought and right thinking;

(3) Spiritualism – where the healing ministry is accomplished largely through mediums with spirit guides who have been physicians or healers.

(4) Witchcraft – where spells are cast and rituals performed for the healing of the sick.

Additionally, there are a number of individuals who claim gifts of healing around whom organizations have been established.

Does faith healing work? There are certainly sufficient instances of individuals who claim to have been cured of a variety of illnesses to suggest that it does. But there are a number of possible explanations:

(1) faith healing does not work at all – either those who claim to be healed were never sick, or else their healing was accomplished by quite natural processes unrelated to the healing;

(2) faith healing does not work in the sense of curing physical illness, but it is the applied effect of suggestion on the individual that leads to the cure, especially since many of the illnesses cured by faith healing are psychosomatic rather than 'organic' in origin;

(3) faith healing employs natural techniques of utilizing forces which are presently unknown to orthodox science but which are gradually being recognized as science advances (e.g. the Kirlian photographs);

(4) faith healing is dependent upon supernatural intervention by forces outside man, and is therefore outside the domain of natural law.

The scientific evidence, based on intensive studies of a wide range of faith healing techniques suggests that:

(1) there are some cases in which faith healing achieves the healing of disease;

(2) the majority of cures affected by faith healing are of diseases which are psychosomatic in origin, and not organic;

(3) there still remain a very few cases in which an organic disease, properly diagnosed medically, is cured by faith healing, contrary to the expectations of medical science.

(4) in the vast majority of cases of alleged healing there has been no adequate diagnosis before the healing, and claims of cures for all manner of terrible diseases are unsubstantiated because it cannot be established that the patient ever suffered from them.

Ultimately, it would be very difficult to prove a cure. First, the patient would have to be suffering from an organic disease of a serious nature, which would not cure itself by natural remission, and which had been accurately diagnosed by a number of physicians independently and, preferably recorded in some way (e.g. X-ray). This disease would not have responded to any medical treatment, and the patient would not have received medical treatment in any period sufficiently close to the alleged healing for the healing to be the result of the treatment. The healing would have to be total, complete and immediate – that is, the disease would simply disappear at the time of healing. And the patient would then be again examined extensively, and diagnosed free of the disease. Obviously, such cases are virtually unknown. And, as the purpose of healing is not the converting of the sceptical, but the relief of the patient, few healers would be interested in engaging in such scientific experiments.

SOURCEBOOKS

LESLIE WEATHERHEAD: *Psychology, Religion and Healing*, Hodder & Stoughton, London, 1963.

An excellent general summary of the field, from a psychological and religious viewpoint.

L. ROSE: *Faith Healing*, Penguin, Harmondsworth, 1971.

Another valuable introduction.

HARRY EDWARDS: *Spirit Healing*, Jenkins, London, 1963.

HARRY EDWARDS: *The Power of Spiritual Healing*, Jenkins, London, 1963.

The spiritualist view of healing is summarized by one of England's leading spiritualist healers in both of these books.

HAROLD SHERMAN: *Wonder Healers of the Philippines*, reprinted in a number of editions.

The Philippine faith healers and their South American counterparts are dealt with in a number of books, usually with credulity and little objectivity, but this is perhaps the best known.

Vampires

Although the vampire has been a figure of popular mythology in many countries throughout history, it was not until the publication of Bram Stoker's novel, *Dracula* in 1897 that the mythology of the vampire became firmly established. Stoker consolidated widely varying traditions about the vampire into the popular figure recognized today, portrayed in hundreds of novels and innumerable films, of whose characteristics most people are aware, and who still manages to inspire some strange fear.

Stoker based his novel on legends of blood-sucking ghosts, returning from the grave to cling to life by drawing vitality from the living, who, in turn would probably die and come back to haunt yet another generation. But Stoker's vampire was not simply a ghost, it was an un-dead, one who has died, been buried and risen from the grave in the physical body to walk abroad seeking the fresh blood which was necessary for his life. In Stoker's account, the vampire was a creature of the night, destroyed by the rays of the sun, unable to cross moving water, terrified of crucifixes and possessed of incredible occult powers. It is this figure – powerful, striking, sinister – that constitutes the vampire of modern myth. But there are a wide variety of other, lesser known traditions, from central Europe, through the Americas to Australia. And an obsession with drinking blood is not unknown to psychiatrists, suggesting that at least in some cases, historical vampires have been the demented and the insane, especially in societies where blood was given a sacred value and seen as the embodiment of the powers of life.

In simple terms, a vampire is a man (or woman) who has died, yet who rises from the grave, to become one of the un-dead, needing regular supplies of fresh human blood in order to remain undead. The causes of vampirism are uncertain: some traditions trace it to possession, to heredity, or to some action of the individual himself; most trace it to contamination by another who was already a vampire. Being bitten by a vampire is almost certain to infect the victim who then becomes a vampire. By day the vampire sleeps in his grave, rising only when the sun has set to stalk his victims, employing strange hypnotic powers to fascinate and ensnare.

The vampire can only be destroyed – in Stoker's tradition – by having a stake thrust through his heart; following this, the body should be burned if it doesn't, as in the best horror films, crumble to dust. In the coffin, the body of a vampire is characterized by the freshness and the suppleness of the skin, enhanced by the trickle of blood on the lips.

In addition to the physical vampire, many occultists have talked of 'psychic vampires', that is, of people who vampirize the vitality and energy of others, sometimes unintentionally, sometimes consciously. Garlic, crucifixes, holy water – such things are said to be effective against both the psychic and the physical vampire. But ultimately, he must be destroyed!

SOURCEBOOKS

BRAM STOKER: *Dracula*, (1897).
BRAM STOKER: *Dracula's Guest and Other Weird Stories* (1914).
>   The classic vampire story, and that which has, more than anything, shaped the popular mythology of the vampire.
RAYMOND T. MCNALLY and RADU FLORESCU: *In Search of Dracula*, Warner, New York, 1974.
>   The best modern study of vampires, beginning with the Dracula traditions, and moving from there into an exploration of the historical figure on whom Stoker based his novel (*Vlad the Impaler, 1431–76*). They conclude with an investigation of the vampire in fiction and films, including an excellent bibliography and 'filmography'.
RAYMOND T. MCNALLY and RADU FLORESCU: *Dracula : A Biography*, Robert Hale, London, 1974.
>   A detailed historical account of the historical figure of Vlad the Impaler.
BASIL COOPER: *The Vampire in Legend, Fact and Art*, Robert Hale, London, 1973.
>   A basic and comprehensive survey of the subject covering legend, literature, film and theatre and fact. In the latter sections of the book the characters of several notorious murderers (including John Haigh) are considered.
GABRIEL RONAY: *The Dracula Myth*, W. H. Allen, London, 1972.
>   The links between historical figures and the myth of the vampire are further pursued. Several cases of extreme cruelty and sadism are examined in relation to vampirism.
ORNELLA VOLTA: *The Vampire*, Tandem, London, 1965.
>   The sexual overtones of the vampire figure have long been recognized; an examination of the subject from an erotic viewpoint where the links between blood, sexuality and death are explored.

The Vampire: His Kith and Kin, Routledge, London, 1928 and *The Vampire in Europe*, Routledge, London, 1899 by Montague Summers suffer, as all his works tend to do, from his credulity, his failure to distinguish between significant and insignificant detail and his rather ponderous style. In their day they were pioneering works; today they have been superseded by more accurate and authoritative writings.

Traditional Witchcraft

It is often assumed that witchcraft traditionally constituted some sort of underground religion, usually identified with the worship of the devil and a cult of evil, which existed throughout England and Europe in the sixteenth and seventeenth centuries. This popular view identifies the witch with the old crone of legend and cinema, possessed of certain psychic powers, with a knowledge of herbalism and of an evil disposition, who met with other witches on dark nights to worship the devil. This view has been perpetuated in the literature and cinema, and been given support by several academics, notably Dr Margaret Murray. But the reality of history is far less exotic than the popular myth; there is no evidence to prove the existence of a religious movement in the Middle Ages which existed underground, or involved worship of the devil. And certainly the modern theorists like Gerald Gardner who claim that witchcraft existed as the continuation of a stone-age fertility religion are merely fantasizing.

There are several principal theories regarding European witchcraft in the Middle Ages:

(1) Witchcraft as a religion of devil-worship actually existed, and the Church undertook to oppose it, through the witchcraft persecutions of the sixteenth and seventeenth centuries; this theory assumes the existence of a devil and of the possibility of men and women worshipping him and entering into agreements (the traditional pacts) with him. The principal exponent of this view was Montague Summers who wrote extensively on the subject.

(2) Witchcraft was a continuation of an ancient fertility religion which had been the original religion of mankind, forced underground with the coming to power of established Christianity. This theory, basing its conclusions largely on the evidence of the witch trials and the documentation of the Church, accepts that this religion was widespread, organized and fairly consistent in its beliefs and practices. The principal exponent of

this line of argument was the English anthropologist, Margaret Murray, who wrote the basic textbooks for followers of this theory. Most modern witches advocate her view of witchcraft, and many have written in support of it, using the evidence she presented.

(3) Witchcraft was all hysteria and madness, and the trials and persecutions were simply a reflection of a widespread social delusion. This theory was first put forward in the sixteenth century by Reginald Scot in his *Discovery of Witchcraft*.

(4) The theory accepted by most modern authorities is that witchcraft, while not constituting an organized cult of the devil, was an amalgam of survivals of traditional folk religion and mythology, practised by individuals within societies throughout Europe, some in isolation, some collectively. It included such elements as herbalism, fortune-telling, simple folk superstitions, myths and legends, and remnants of older pagan religions which had been passed down through generations, becoming progressively less clear and more distorted with the passage of time. In an age of superstition and fear of the devil, anything outside the strict confines of orthodox Christianity was viewed as being supernatural and evil, and thus to be destroyed. Old women, herbalists, epileptics, those gifted with psychic powers, the strange, the deviant – all these were in real danger of being viewed as agents of the devil or witches. They were to be consigned to the inquisitors, and, ultimately, execution. Such social hysteria has not been confined to the Middle Ages, as purges, political, social and religious, in many nations throughout history, have demonstrated.

Witchcraft as such is very often identified totally with the popular view of the phenomenon of the Middle Ages in Europe; but witchcraft is widespread throughout societies and throughout history. In primitive societies it was generally a system of magical practices and beliefs held and practised by a few individuals within a group. Often it was seen as evil and dangerous (and generally known as sorcery), although many cultures have viewed it merely as an alternative to the orthodox religious system, or, indeed, an integral part of that system. Thus, for example, in many African societies, witch doctors perform important functions, in casting spells, in healing and in divination. Their activities are part of the overall religious system and, while it is recognized that they possess the power to do evil, their work generally is believed to be good. But some individuals, possessed of similar powers, are recognized as evil, and are known as sorcerers.

Witches in Europe were generally believed to be women (although men were involved), but in other countries the witch is almost inevitably male.

The word 'witch' derives from the Anglo-Saxon for 'wise' and implied a person possessed of supernatural abilities; in all societies such people have been recognized as constituting some sort of link between this world and another dimension, capable of influencing the present and of foretelling the future, capable of healing and of cursing. In many societies such gifts are believed to be hereditary, and the function of witch passes from generation to generation. In other societies it is believed that individuals singled out by various characteristics (many of which in modern society would be considered afflictions) possess these special powers – epileptics, homosexuals, the deformed, the insane.

In all societies, from England through Africa and Asia to South America, witchcraft can be divided into three areas:

(1) *Philosophy* – the beliefs behind the practice of witchcraft, the explanations given for how things came to be and the mythology of how the witch is able to fulfil his functions; this is usually some type of fertility religion, basing its beliefs on the cycles of nature and on a variety of myths handed down orally. It constitutes the world-view of the witch, and also the view of the witch held by members of the culture in which he lives. For example, in Europe of the Middle Ages, the world-view was largely Christian, and hence the witch was defined within that system as a devil-worshipper; the witch, on the other hand, interpreted his position by adapting the traditional myths of the pre-Christian era to fit into the Christian system.

(2) *Technology* – what the witch actually does, the casting of spells, the rituals of healing, the art of herbalism; such techniques are usually passed on, often in secret, from one generation to another. Various tools are used, chemicals are employed (both those with actual curative properties and also hallucinogenic drugs to stimulate visions of a supernatural dimension) and rituals are worked out.

(3) *Science* – the explanation of how the technology works, within the framework of the philosophy. While scientists may violently reject the use of the term 'science' when applied to witchcraft, none the less most systems of magical practice are internally consistent, and given the basic premises upon which they work, quite logical. It is the basic premises and not the logic that science should challenge. For example, the technology may prescribe the rubbing of red ochre over the body of a dying child; the science explains this by the laws of similarity – blood is red, blood gives life; ochre is red, therefore ochre will communicate the same life as does blood.

Witchcraft, in the traditional sense, continues to be practised in a few places today – principally in the remoter regions of the world, although in some newly emerging societies (for example, the new nations of Africa) witches have emerged to take their places in the new order of society, setting up as professional consultants, and thereby meeting the old needs in a new context.

SOURCEBOOKS

The 'classic' works on traditional witchcraft are by Margaret Murray: *The Witch-cult in Western Europe* (1921) and *The God of the Witches* (1933), both published by Oxford University Press. She argues for the 'continuation of a primitive religion' line. Her evidence is very convincing, but needs to be examined carefully.

It is thoroughly demolished by E. E. Rose: *Razor for a Goat: A Discussion of Certain Problems in the History of Witchcraft and Diabolism*, University of Toronto, 1962, which should be read after Dr Murray's books.

Montague Summer's vast number of books on the subject include: *The History of Witchcraft and Demonology*, Kegan Paul, London, 1926, *Witchcraft and Black Magic*, Rider, London, 1946, *The Discovery of Witches*, Cayme, London, 1928 – many of which are being reissued in modern editions. His scholarship is often suspect, and his prejudices intrude consistently into his work. But his influence on popular thinking about witchcraft has been immense.

Detailed histories of the 'witchcraft craze' of the sixteenth and seventeenth centuries in Europe, are found in:

H. R. TREVOR-ROPER: *The European Witch Craze of the 16th and 17th Centuries*, Penguin, Harmondsworth, 1969.
H. C. LEA: *Materials towards a History of Witchcraft* (2 vols), Pennsylvania, 1939.
CHRISTINA HOLE: *Witchcraft in England*, Collier-Macmillan, London, 1957.
PENNETHORNE HUGHES: *Witchcraft*, Penguin, Harmondsworth, 1952.

A reasonable general introduction to witchcraft in its traditional sense is found in –
ERIC MAPLE: *The Dark World of Witches*, Pan, London, 1962.
MAX MARWICK (ed.): *Witchcraft and Sorcery*, Penguin, Harmondsworth, 1970.
Witchcraft in a broader perspective is covered in this collection of readings which is an excellent introduction, and includes material from a wide range of cultural and historical settings.

Two other cross-cultural introductions are:
LUCY MAIR: *Witchcraft*, World University Library, 1969.
GEOFFREY PARRINDER: *Witchcraft*, Penguin, Harmondsworth, 1958.
R. H. ROBBINS: *Encyclopedia of Witchcraft and Demonology*, Crown, London, 1959.
A standard reference source, especially for material on European witchcraft.

Modern Witchcraft

The contemporary witchcraft movement constitutes one of the most widespread and active forces within the modern occult revival. Throughout England and the United States, Europe, South America and Australia increasing numbers of people are becoming involved in witchcraft in various forms, from the ritual magic of ceremonial robes and quite suburban ritual healings, to nude dancing, drug taking and animal sacrifice, as well as all possible variants between these extremes. Statistics are difficult to obtain, since most of the witchcraft groups are closed to outsiders; esimates of the size of the movement vary from scattered hundreds, to hundreds of thousands. Certainly there are many thousands of practising witches in England, Europe and the United States; there are few cities in the world today without witchcraft groups, and the movement continues to grow as it is increasingly widely publicized, and as it becomes more 'respectable'. Members of witchcraft groups, far from being the stereotypes of literature and mythology, range through all age groups, and include labourers, students, academics, doctors, lawyers, housewives and teachers.

BELIEFS

Although there is considerable variety in the beliefs of those calling themselves witches (and today that term is used for both male and female, with the traditional 'warlock' rarely in use), most subscribe to certain fundamental beliefs about the origins and nature of their religion:

(1) Witches believe that their religion is a continuation of the original religion of mankind, a fertility cult centring on worship of the forces of nature, usually personified into a female (the earth mother, the great goddess, the fertility deity) and a male (the horned god) deity, with numerous lesser entities, including elementals, or spirits of nature; this religion is claimed to derive from ancient times, generally the Stone Age

when man was closer to nature and more aware of his environment and the powers hidden within it;

(2) Witches believe that this primal religion continued unchanged throughout the centuries, some even trace its origins to the lost continent of Atlantis. With the coming of Christianity, and its enforcement as the official State religion, the 'old religion' as witchcraft is generally called, was forced underground, and obliged to continue as a secret tradition, generally within families. Modern witches cite the evidence of the witchcraft persecutions and trials of the sixteenth and seventeenth centuries as proof of the existence of this underground tradition;

(3) Witches believe that this underground tradition perpetuated teachings and practices of the 'old religion' including an elementary knowledge of medicine, herbalism, healing, a traditional ritual calendar, and secret, sacred names of the gods and goddesses; this traditional knowledge, together with the initiation into the religion was transmitted in a succession passing from male to female, and female to male;

(4) Witches believe that, with the general decline in the influence of Christianity and the power of the Church (symbolized for many in the repeal of England's laws against witchcraft, in 1951) the 'old religion' could again emerge from secrecy and practise more or less openly;

(5) Witches believe that their present-day religion is a continuation of this historic tradition, and represents a modern version of the faith of the medieval witches and the 'old religion' of mankind.

Such beliefs are unsubstantiated by historical or anthropological evidence; however, the witches generally argue that it is their secret teachings, rituals and words which 'prove' their authenticity, and as these things are secret they cannot be made available to satisfy the scepticism of scientists.

MODERN HISTORY

Contemporary witchcraft is largely the result of the work of three people:

(1) Margaret Murray, an English Egyptologist and scholar, who advanced the theory that a secret tradition of witchcraft had always existed, and continued up to present times in England; in her writings, the first of which was published in 1921, she 'reconstructed' the 'old religion', and her books have become sources for many followers of modern witchcraft, who see them as giving scientific validity to their faith. However, her theories have been virtually demolished by later, better informed scholars, and are now largely discredited.

(2) Gerald Gardner, an Englishman who travelled widely in the Far East and was interested in folklore. He claimed he had been initiated into

a traditional witchcraft coven in the New Forest in 1939 and was authorized to revive the old religion; he established a number of covens in England, wrote several books on witchcraft, and was widely publicized – he may be said to be the 'Father' of modern witchcraft.

(3) Alex Sanders, another Englishman, who claims to have been initiated by his grandmother when a young boy, thereby perpetuating an ancient family tradition; he went on to establish numerous covens throughout England, achieved considerable publicity, and proclaimed himself 'King of the Witches'. Despite some claims to independence, all modern witchcraft groups derive at least some of their teachings, ritual and tradition from these three sources.

Other modern English witches who have achieved some notoriety include Cecil Williamson, Eleanor Bone, Patricia Crowther, Monique Wilson (all former disciples of Gerald Gardner) and Doreen Valiente; in the United States the movement is widespread, and includes many individuals who have achieved widespread publicity, amongst them Leo Martello, Raymond Buckland, Sybil Leek, Louise Huebner and Joseph Wilson.

PRACTICES

Modern witches meet regularly in groups, known as covens, usually consisting of between six and twenty members (the traditional number being thirteen). The meetings are open only to initiated members, and are held both regularly for worship, usually on nights of the full moon, when healing work is undertaken, spells cast and new candidates initiated, and also on the special festivals of the year relating to the cycles of nature in the Northern Hemisphere (for example, the summer solstice, the autumn equinox, May Eve). On these special occasions rituals relating to the festivals are performed. Some covens undertake their work in ceremonial robes, others in the nude, some covens employ techniques of sexual magic in their work, others are highly puritanical in such matters. While the majority of witchcraft groups would describe themselves as 'white' (that is, as using their knowledge for 'good' purposes), there are some which are explicitly 'black' (using their knowledge for 'evil' purposes – for example, curses, destroying enemies). And there are, naturally, some pseudo-witchcraft groups which use the religion as a front to entice subjects for sexual activities, drug taking, and often blackmail.

In the United States witchcraft groups are less secret and tend to advertise for potential members (for example, the periodical *Gnostica News* contains a large number of such advertisements and details of contacts with covens); the movement in England tends towards greater secrecy, although magazines and newsletters specifically devoted to witchcraft are beginning to appear (for example, *The New Broom*).

SOURCEBOOKS
General

PETER HAINING: *Anatomy of Witchcraft*, Souvenir, London, 1972.
A good introduction to modern witchcraft, both 'white' and 'black', and including material on voodoo, American satanism, and the texts of a witchcraft initiation.

FRANK SMYTH: *Modern Witchcraft*, Macdonald, London, 1970.
A good introduction, with an emphasis on England, and with good background material on links between traditional and modern witchcraft.

ERIC MAPLE: *Witchcraft*, Octopus, London, 1973.
A large book, with numerous illustrations and colour plates, including material on traditional and modern witchcraft in modern and primitive societies, written by an outstanding scholar of witchcraft and the occult.

JOHN FRITSCHER: *Popular Witchcraft*, Citadel Press, New Jersey, 1973.
Specifically examining witchcraft in modern America, this book presents a view of witchcraft in the context of modern culture, 'the Age of Aquarius', and some interesting material on witchcraft and sex.

Margaret Murray

The Witch Cult in Western Europe, Oxford University Press, London, 1921.
Her first book in which she expounds her theories of traditional witchcraft and presents her 'reconstruction' of the religion.

The God of the Witches, Daimon Press, Essex, 1962.
A further examination of the 'horned god' and his religion.

The Divine King of England, Faber, London, 1954.
In which she advances a theory that the Kings of England were involved in witchcraft.

E. E. ROSE: *A Razor for a Goat: A Discussion of Certain Problems in the History of Witchcraft and Diabolism*, University of Toronto, 1962.
This book effectively demolishes the theories of Dr Murray and (in the process) of Gerald Gardner, carefully analysing the claims of modern witches in the light of historical and anthropological evidence.

Gerald Gardner

Witchcraft Today, Rider, London, 1954.
His first book claiming to be a factual study of witchcraft, in which he advances his own theories and tells of his own experience; it rapidly became, together with Murray's *The Witch Cult in Western Europe*, the textbook of early contemporary witches.

The Meaning of Witchcraft, Aquarian, London, 1959.
His final commentary on the craft, examining his theories of its history and ritual.
High Magick's Aid, Michael Houghton, London, 1949.
Gardner's first book, a novel, in which he advanced his theories – it was a failure at the time.
JACK BRACELIN: *Gerald Gardner, Witch*, Octagon, London, 1960.
The biography of Gardner, written by one of his disciples.

Alex Sanders

JUNE JOHNS: *King of the Witches*, Peter Davies, London, 1969.
A rather eulogistic biography of Sanders, including material on his teachings and rituals, and partial texts of his *Book of Shadows* and initiation rituals.
STEWART FARRAR: *What Witches Do*, Peter Davies, London, 1971.
Another eulogistic presentation of Sanders's teachings and rituals, with details of initiations.

Witchcraft in England

DOREEN VALIENTE: *Where Witchcraft Lives*, Aquarian, London.
An account by a modern English witch, presenting the theory of Gardner.
PATRICIA CROWTHER: *Witch Blood*, House of Collectibles, New York, 1974.
The biography of one of England's leading witches, with an account of Gerald Gardner.

Witchcraft in the United States

EMILE SCHURMACHER: *Witchcraft in America Today*, New York, 1970.
Includes a wide range of material on the movement in America, e.g. voodoo, satanism. American Indian witchcraft and possession – a very popular presentation, but interesting none the less.
MARTIN EBON: *Witchcraft Today*, Tomorrow Publications, New York, 1963.
A collection of articles on witchcraft and satanism from Salem to the present day.
RAYMOND BUCKLAND: *Ancient and Modern Witchcraft*, H.C. Publishers, New York, 1970.
RAYMOND BUCKLAND: *Witchcraft From the Inside*, Llewellyn, St Paul, 1971.
Two books presenting a Gardnerian approach from an American witch, who is also an 'anthropologist'.
LOUISE HUEBNER: *Power Through Witchcraft*, Bantam, New York, 1973.
A collection of rather simplistic techniques representing the sort of magic practised by modern witches, fortune-telling, healing, herbalism and similar skills, by a well-known American witch.
LEO MARTELLO: *Weird Ways of Witchcraft*, H. C. Publishers, New York, 1969.
A rather eccentric and vehemently anti-Christian presentation of modern witchcraft by an American who claims to be a traditional Sicilian witch; it includes a lot of odd and irrelevant material, but represents one of the extremes in modern witchcraft.

HANS HOLZER: *The Witchcraft Report*, Ace, New York, 1973.

HANS HOLZER: *The New Pagan*, Doubleday, New York, 1972.

Together these two books contribute a comprehensive if somewhat shallow coverage of modern witchcraft in the USA, the groups and individuals involved.

Numerous books have been, and are being published on witchcraft; virtually none of them say anything new, and almost all constitute variations on the themes of Murray and Gardner, with odds and ends of ceremonial magic and folklore thrown in; but they sell, and hence can be expected to continue to appear.

Traditional Satanism

Traditionally, satanism has been interpreted as the worship of evil, a religion founded upon the very principles which Christianity rejects. As such, satanism exists only where Christianity exists, and can be understood only in the context of the Christian world-view. Things are, so to speak, reversed – the Christian devil becomes the satanist's God, Christian virtues become vices, and vices are turned into virtues. Life is interpreted as a constant battle between the powers of light and darkness, and the satanist fights on the side of darkness, believing that ultimately this will achieve victory.

By this definition, there have been very few satanists throughout history. The Christian Church has often interpreted a wide range of non-Christian religions as satanism, and the activities of its own heretics as indicating adherence to satanism. This was especially true of the early Gnostics, whom many churchmen believed to be satanists, although they were not. Nevertheless, the idea and principles of the Gnostics have profoundly influenced later satanists especially through the dualistic philosophy (that is, the belief in two opposing forces – of light and darkness – interlocked in constant battle).

The Church, in its persecution of heretics and others who refused to conform to its rigid doctrinal confines, created a synthetic image of what it supposed to be the typical satanist: he was a Christian who formally renounced the vows of his baptism, rejected the Church and dedicated himself to those things which Christ forbade; he did not, obviously, reject the Christian world-view, since his own philosophy had meaning only within that context. The Church pictured exotic and sacrilegious rituals in which men and women rejected their faith, entered into a pact with the devil and engaged in all manner of abominable and immoral acts. Central to such behaviour was the Black Mass, an inverted celebration of the central ritual of Catholicism, in which the Host (believed to be the

Body of Christ), stolen from a church, or consecrated by an unfrocked priest, was desecrated. In this ceremony, every action that the Church forbade was believed to occur – from a whole range of sexual perversions, to the sacrifice of unbaptized infants, and the recitation of the Lord's Prayer backwards. The whole ceremony was directed towards inverting the Christian symbolism (centred in the inverted cross which stood upon the satanist's altar) and raising up the devil.

Although such images of satanism were largely the creation of the vividly imaginative Inquisitors, their practice actually developed, especially in France during the seventeenth and eighteenth centuries, when aristocrats engaged in an underground movement of satanism as a form of rejection of the values of society and, doubtless, as an excuse for unusually exciting self-indulgence. Generally, however, satanist groups have remained hidden – they have little to gain from publicity and much to lose, especially since many of the ingredients of their worship are intrinsically illegal (drugs, murder, violence, etc.), and are most positively unacceptable even in a fairly liberal society. Thus very little is known of the groups which have, throughout history, followed this path. Various accounts have been given of a widespread 'cult' of evil by such authors as Montague Summers, but these tend not to be grounded in fact. Groups have indeed existed, but most of them, far from being genuine satanists, have used the trappings of an anti-Christian religion for an exaggerated indulgence in hedonism (for example, the infamous English 'Hell Fire Clubs' – see reference to Francis Dashwood, p. 206).

Throughout history individuals and groups have employed the rituals of satanism either as a means of searching for worldly power, or as a symbolic rejection of the established values of their society, and it was this latter group, rather than true satanists (in the sense of those who literally worshipped the devil as Christians worshipped their God) that left their mark on history. And many groups (including, for example, Freemasonry) were labelled as satanists by the Church in its attempts to suppress them. Since satanism is essentially a reaction to Christianity, it is not known, in any real sense, outside the Christian world, although it has been popularly assumed that some oriental religions (for example, the worship of Shiva in India) represented satanism. However in a naturally dualistic religion, the worship of either the creative or the destructive aspects of the deity can be equally acceptable.

Many Western magicians (another category of people indiscriminately assumed by the Church to be satanists) approached the devil in this way, or saw him as a source of power which could be controlled and utilized for their own purposes without any connotations of actually worshipping him.

Such people were seen to be practising 'black magic' or the 'black arts – although since the church condemned all magical and occult practices this had little meaning, and tended to mean also satanism and devil worship.

However, the term satanism should be reserved for those who deliberately choose to worship and work with the power of evil, generally personified into an individual devil, known either as Satan or Lucifer, under whom many subordinate entities (paralleling the hosts of heaven) work. Those few who actually fitted within this definition evolved elaborate theologies of the devil to match the theologies of the church, especially concentrating on the names and natures of lesser devils over whom they could gain control, and through whom they could achieve their ends. It is, however, inappropriate to refer to the medieval magicians, whose grimoires popularly represent black magic, as satanists; they were not concerned with the devil so much as with forces of various kinds, personified into individual entities, with whom they undertook what virtually amounted to business relationships.

SOURCEBOOKS

RICHARD CAVENDISH: *The Black Arts*, Routledge & Kegan Paul, London, 1967.
A general reference book providing a good amount of background material, but one which appears to lump a wide range of subjects under the general heading of black magic.

MONTAGUE SUMMERS: *Witchcraft and Black Magic*, Rider, London, 1946.
A basic source for the popular (and mistaken) view of black magic and satanism.

H. F. T. RHODES: *The Satanic Mass*, Arrow, London, 1965.
The standard work on the Black Mass – an excellent survey of the subject, with a penetrating analysis.

JULES MICHELET: *Satanism and Witchcraft*, Tandem, London, 1965.
The standard work on French Satanism. Written in the vein of a particular prejudice which accepted the idea of a conspiracy of evil.

DANIEL MANNIX: *The Hellfire Club*, New English Library, London, 1961.
An account of the English aristocratic 'satanists' of the eighteenth century.

J. TONDRIAU and R. VILLENEUVE: *A Dictionary of Devils and Demons*, Bay Books, Sydney, 1972.
An excellent and concise sourcebook on Satanism containing a variety of entries on many related subjects.

Modern Satanism

With the general decline in the influence and authority of Christianity, traditional satanism – which had developed in opposition to that religion – also declined. But with the occult revival of this century there has been an upsurge of interest and involvement in satanism, and an increasing number of books and articles on the subject. Generally, however, contemporary satanists do not follow the traditional pattern of worshipping a devil in contrast to worshipping the God of the Christian religion; traditional satanism only held power where the Christian, and generally the Catholic, religion was accepted – it is difficult to commit blasphemy against the God, or violate the sacraments of a religion one does not believe in. Modern satanists fit into several categories, with some overlapping and a few groups which would claim to be outside any of these categories:

(1) The traditional anti-Christian satanists who worship a devil in orthodox Christian terms, who celebrate the black mass, profane the sacrament, desecrate churches and graveyards, and who believe that the devil will ultimately triumph over the God of Christianity (for example, the Order of Satanic Templars in England);

(2) A secular humanistic satanism, with neither a personal devil nor a personal god, which devotes itself to man and opposes the restrictions and inhibitions which Christian culture has imposed upon him, advocating, for example, the traditional Seven Deadly Sins as virtues, and using traditional satanic rituals as processes for liberating the individual from inhibitions (for example, the Church of Satan in California);

(3) A paganistic satanism which worships the 'forces of darkness' in contrast to the 'forces of light', interpreting its worship in terms of old mythologies and religion (for example, Greek, Egyptian, Roman), but having especial interest in Christianity; these groups generally call themselves 'pagan' and view their activities as a new religion, rather than the continuation of a traditional one (for example, Ophitic Gnostic Cultus).

(4) Satanic witchcraft which uses the traditions and rituals of modern witchcraft as a basis for a modified witchcraft tradition, in which the 'horned god' is seen as the devil of Christianity, a more powerful and more worth-while god to worship; they use the techniques of witchcraft (for example, cursing, casting spells) to practise what they interpret as a traditional, historic religion (for example, the Satanic Brotherhood).

(5) A hedonistic satanism in which rituals, drugs and sexual techniques are used to gratify the senses, proclaiming a morality founded on pleasure; there are vague religious overtones, but such groups are not philosophical, and view their activities as gratifying (more so because they are 'evil' in the eyes of society) rather than worshipping. Such groups tend to be small, privately organized and rarely publicized; they are increasingly being catered for by popular pornography.

BELIEFS

Satanists generally recognize the existence of two forces in the world, traditionally referred to as 'black' and 'white', and in Christian terms as 'good' and 'evil'; seeing 'white' as the religion of the establishment, the satanists reject it, and choose its opposite – for example, preaching gratification of the senses rather than abstinence, self-centredness rather than self-sacrifice. They believe that the 'powers of darkness' (whether they are personified or not) are life-giving forces, of which the 'white' religion is afraid. Sex is important because of its repression by Christianity and because of the power, gratification and pleasure it provides. Satanists naturally believe that the powers of darkness will ultimately triumph, and view themselves as powerful, virile, strong individuals, contrasting with the weak, inhibited, frightened masses. They believe that if there are powers within man to heal and bless, he also possesses the power to kill and to curse, and should use these for his own advantage. They reject morality in any conventional sense, believing that survival and self-fulfilment is the individual's most important aim, regardless of the cost to other people. Some satanist groups have evolved mythologies explaining their teachings, usually relating to the legendary fall of Satan from heaven, and his subsequent domination of the world, and future triumph and return to reign in heaven. They believe his power is gradually increasing, and work with him in the hope of rewards, both in the material sense here and now, and in some future life.

MODERN HISTORY

Satanists, rejecting the essential values and norms of behaviour in society, have always been obliged to maintain some degree of secrecy – the law and social sanction is against them. Groups have tended to be small, under-ground and secret, and so their history is poorly documented, except where conflict with the law has occurred. In modern times groups have emerged in England and Europe, and particularly in the United States, which, taking advantage of the permissiveness of modern society, have encouraged some publicity. The most famous of these has been the Church of Satan, founded in Los Angeles in 1966 by Anton La Vey, which currently has a membership of many thousands, and has established itself as a church throughout the United States. Several other groups in America have imitated it, and some groups have also been established as 'black witchcraft' covens. The Manson gang, in which a bizarre mixture of satanism and occultism was practised, gained a great deal of unfavour-able publicity for satanism in America, but in fact this resulted in a greater public interest in the subject. With more people rejecting the traditional values of society, its religion and its morality, the satanist movement will inevitably have greater appeal.

PRACTICES

Traditional satanists use inverted forms of orthodox Christian worship (for example, reciting the Lord's Prayer backwards, the Black Mass) to symbolize and focus their rejection of Christianity, and to invoke the powers of darkness. Other satanists use rituals based upon ancient mythology (usually Egyptian, Greek or Roman) to express their teachings, while the secular humanistic satanists like the Church of Satan view their rituals as psychological techniques for liberating the individual from his repressions, and enabling him to find freedom and pleasure. Tradition-ally, satanists have used ritual to gain material rewards, curse enemies and acquire power; such rituals are inevitably compounded of words and actions which invert the general values of their society (for example, 'perverted' sexual behaviour, use of excrement, inverted crosses) and symbolize the darkness they worship (using black vestments, black candles). To stimulate the senses drugs and sexual activities are employed, very often with some degree of sado-masochistic behaviour as well. Groups, usually called 'covens' or 'lodges' are strictly secret (with the notable exception of the Church of Satan where they are semi-secret), and admit only initiates who have been prepared over a long period of time. Some satanist groups follow traditional occult patterns in their ritual, holding ceremonies on nights of the full moon, and on the major festivals of the witchcraft calendar.

SOURCEBOOKS

General

ARTHUR LYONS: *Satan Wants You*, Granada, London, 1970.
   The best introduction to contemporary satanism, with historical background to its traditions, and details of its development in the United States, including the Church of Satan.
C. H. WALLACE: *Witchcraft in the World Today*, Tandem, London, 1967.
   Although the author confuses witchcraft and satanism, he none the less presents a comprehensive coverage.

Church of Satan

ANTON LA VEY: *The Satanic Bible*, Avon, New York, 1969.
   'The Bible' of the Church, a compilation of material from a wide range of sources, expressing the philosophy of La Vey.
ANTON LA VEY: *The Satanic Rituals*, Avon, New York, 1969.
   A sequel to 'The Bible', containing the rituals of the Church.
ANTON LA VEY: *The Compleat Witch*, Lancer, New York, 1971.
   A rather bizarre study of the powers of magical seduction and spell casting from a satanist point of view.

Satanism in America

JASON MICHAELS: *The Devil is alive and well and Living in America Today*, Award, New York, 1973.
   An account of satanism in the United States, informative and comprehensive.

Satanism in Great Britain

A. V. SELLWOOD and P. HAINING, *Devil Worship in Britain*, Corgi, London, 1964.
   A popular journalistic account of satanism in contemporary Britain.

Voodoo

Voodoo refers to the native religion of Haiti in the West Indies, stemming from traditional West African religions, brought to the West Indies by the slaves, and centring on an extensive pantheon of gods and goddesses, who take possession of devotees in religious ceremonies. This religion also spread with the slaves to some of the Southern States of the USA, to other parts of the Caribbean and to Brazil. Wherever the slaves went, they merged their traditional African religious beliefs with the local religion. Voodoo consists both of the traditional beliefs with their local variations, and also of various magical techniques employed to achieve certain ends, including the descent of the gods into individual worshippers to give oracles and to provide protection. These magical techniques are known as 'obeah'.

Voodoo is popularly seen as a mass of frightening superstitions and black magical practices. Certainly to the outsider it may appear as such, depending for much of its power upon the inculcation of fear into its adherents. Voodoo does, however, have an elaborate and complicated theology and constitutes a complex metaphysical system of explanations of man and the universe. Only the priests know this belief system in full, receiving it as they do in their training, and through a series of initiations. They are the agents of the 'invisibles' or gods (loa), who can to some extent control and direct them, and when possessed by the loa act as oracles. The priests are expected to be able to use black and white magic equally, according to the needs of the occasion, and must be ever aware that the loa are both powerful and jealous, and quite capable of destroying those who serve them. In order to possess the supernatural powers he needs the priest must take the ultimate risk of becoming involved with forces that are not necessarily benevolent, and which can change their attitudes to their people with surprising frequency. The pantheon of gods of voodoo includes many of the traditional West African tribal deities, together with some unexpected additions – many of the Catholic saints have been incorporated into the voodoo pantheon in areas where Catholicism is the dominant religion (or at least the religion of the respectable). Voodoo is never an exclusivist religion, and its method of dealing with other belief systems has been to fuse them into its own, so that a voodoo devotee can attend a Roman Catholic mass without any sense of alienation, simply interpreting the mass in a different way to other worshippers.

The typical rituals of voodoo include an emphasis on music, especially the beating of drums which has an hypnotic effect on the worshippers, and energetic and rhythmic dancing leading to ecstasy and often to collapse, or to possession by one of the gods. Some of the ceremonies are open only to initiated members, who have been through complicated ritual processes during which they have been taught the philosophy of voodoo, the names of the gods and the ritual techniques. As with all initiations this involves a ritual death and rebirth.

Although voodoo was originally the religion of the slaves, it has not died out with the disappearance of slavery, and continues to constitute a major religious movement in the Caribbean, especially in Haiti. The development of the Umbanda cult in Brazil emerged directly from the voodoo religion, and South American spiritism has been influenced by it. With the popular revival of interest in the occult there has been a revival of interest in voodoo, especially in the southern USA, where a number of contemporary voodoo groups (of varying degrees of authenticity) have been established, and shops set up to sell ingredients for the practice of voodoo.

SOURCEBOOKS

The three principal works on the subject, all of them detailed and scholarly, are:
MAYA DEREN: *Divine Horsemen*, Thames & Hudson, London, 1953.
FRANCIS HUXLEY: *The Invisibles*, Hart-Davis, London, 1966.
A. METRAUX: *Voodoo in Haiti*, Deutsch, London, 1959.

A more popular first-hand account is given in
MARCUS BACH: *Inside Voodoo*, New American Library, New York, 1952.

Eastern Mysticism

In recent years there has been an increasing interest by Westerners, especially young people, in the teachings and practices of Eastern mysticism, and a number of schools have emerged claiming to present these traditions, ranging from the brightly robed members of the Hare Krishna Movement, through Sikhs and Buddhists to self-proclaimed messiahs from India. This emergence of Eastern philosophy is not an entirely new phenomenon however; it began about the same time as the development of spiritualism, when Western scholars first began to consider that the East offered something more than barbarism and crude superstition. It was also at that time that the first material was made available for the general public on just what Eastern religions did teach and practise. This emergence of the East can be linked to two events – the founding of the Theosophical Society in 1875, and the Columban Exposition in Chicago in 1893. The former, because of its interest in oriental philosophy and the emphasis placed by its founders on India and Tibet as sources of occult knowledge, promulgated many oriental ideas (for example, reincarnation) and encouraged investigation into Eastern scriptures which had previously been the almost exclusive domain of the scholar and the academic.

The Columban Exposition included a world parliament of religions where a wide range of beliefs and approaches were given an opportunity for expression and dialogue. It was in the personality of Vivekananda, a Swami and disciple of Ramakrishna, an Indian mystic who died in 1836, that the first adaptation of the 'East for the West' was really made, and eventually the Vedanta Society of America was founded and quickly established throughout the country. It was the beginning of a missionary movement from the East to the West which in later years would have marked effects.

As an alternative to the traditional philosophies of the West, Eastern mysticism has proved very popular, and the success of the initial movements inspired others, of varying degrees of authenticity and importance, to undertake missionary work in the West. Today this activity is reaching almost a fever pitch as a whole range of groups engage in proselytizing activity. On the superficial level this has encouraged an interest in meditation and vegetarianism, incense and beads, in chanting 'OM' and in reading oriental scriptures. Doubtless, it has also had a much more lasting effect on the few disciples who have penetrated these shallows, to the depths beneath.

Amongst the groups and individuals claiming to follow the Eastern traditions, the following are important:

The Vedanta Society – the original group founded by Vivekananda, which today continues giving lectures and classes, and which has monasteries and convents throughout the United States. The philosophy it espouses is based on the 'Vedas'.

A'nanda Ma'rga – founded in 1955 by Shrii Shrii Anandamurtijii to spread the teachings of the ancient techniques of tantra and astanga yoga, and meditation. The movement has groups, communes and centres in many cities throughout the world. It also operates schools and engages in various forms of social work.

Baha'i faith – followers of the teachings of Baha'U'llah who declared in 1863 that he was the chosen manifestation of God for this age. The religion affirms the universality and validity of all religions and strives to establish a unified mankind, with one religion, one political and social order. The movement has a large membership and is spreading rapidly. (See *All Things Made New* by John Ferraby, Allen & Unwin, London, 1960.)

International Society for Krishna Consciousness – the Hare Krishna movement, dedicated to awakening the ecstatic state of 'Krishna Consciousness', whose disciples devote much of their time to chanting the mantra, 'Hare Krishna' and doing missionary work in the streets. The Society was founded in 1966 by His Divine Grace A. C. Bhaktivedanta Swami Prabhupada, who claims to be part of a long line of succession going back 500 years to Lord Caitanya, an incarnation of Krishna. (See *Bhagavad Gita As It Is* by the founder of the movement, and *Freedom in Knowledge* by Sri Isopanisad.)

Krishnamurti – an Indian philosopher and mystic who, after leaving the Theosophical Society which had prepared him to become the vehicle for a manifestation of Christ (see p. 216), established himself as a teacher in his own right, and who travelled widely lecturing on his own highly individualist philosophy. He rejects all attempts to proclaim him as a teacher, in the sense that he believes truth is something for an individual to discover for himself; he is opposed to all institutions and defined systems of belief.

Meher Baba – an Indian who claimed to be the incarnation of God, both Krishna and Christ, come again to redeem man. He has disciples and groups throughout the world. Despite his claims to being immortal, he died; however, most of his disciples have coped with this apparent disaster. The groups teaching his philosophy continue to operate.

Students' International Meditation Society – the group operated by Maharishi Mahesh Yogi which teaches 'transcendental Meditation', and which has spread rapidly throughout the world. The techniques taught by the Society have been favourably commented upon by those who have undertaken scientific assessments of their effects on individual efficiency and health. The system is based on an initiation at which a trained teacher, deriving ultimately from the Maharishi, gives the student a word upon which to meditate. A variety of scientists have written on the effects of the technique, and it has been approved for teaching in some schools and colleges in the United States.

Divine Light Mission – centring on the person of Guru Maharaj Ji, a 16-year-old Indian who claims to be God's representative, and who heads a world-wide movement, which he says is based upon the Vedantic tradition. A split has recently occurred between the Guru and his Mother, who now claims that her son has become too fond of material comforts and is no longer the 'perfect master'.

There is an increasing range of other Eastern teachers and traditions appearing in the West. These may be classified in general terms as fitting into one of the following categories:

(1) *Indian* – deriving from the philosophical traditions of India; emphasizing meditation, and using the Bhagavad Gita, the Vedas, and other similar scriptures; often these are centred on individual teachers who claim either to be divine or to be divinely inspired, and who claim the close master/disciple relationship with their students which characterizes Indian schools.

(2) *Yoga* – this includes groups which practise a wide variety of yogic traditions from hatha (the physical) to raja (the intellectual) and everything in between; the major teachers recognize that such divisions are largely artificial, and that any system of development must be based on an integrated view of man. Hatha yoga has become increasingly popular in the West as an alternative to the frenzied activity which has characterized Western systems of physical culture.

(3) *Zen* – Zen Buddhism has emerged from Japan as a system of some considerable interest to many people in the West, especially those who,

tiring of the heavy emphasis most philosophical schools place on the intellect, find in the 'no-mind' approach of Zen a refreshing change. Various Zen communities, centres and teachers have been established in the West to perpetuate this tradition.

(4) *Tibetan Buddhism* – Tibet has always been a place of mystery and fascination, from the beginning of contact with the West, and the claims of the Theosophical Society that it was the home of the Masters. Principally because it has been so inaccessible, and so little has been known about it, it has had an incredible appeal. Teachers offering the Tibetan traditions have ranged from such blatantly commercial 'Lamas' as Lobsang Rampa (see p. 223), to a number of legitimate Buddhist monks who have established centres in the West.

(5) *Buddhism* – Buddhism in the West has formerly been largely the domain of the educated intellectuals who found in it a religious system without the traditional Western concept of the supernatural or God. The Buddhist Society in England is an old and highly respectable organization, and its members have included a number of eminent scholars like Christmas Humphries. Because of its basic beliefs, the Buddhist religion has tended not to proselytize or engage in any of the more exotic activities which have characterized other Eastern groups.

SOURCEBOOKS

For general background on the Eastern tradition, the following books provide essential material:

P. SEN: *Hinduism*, Penguin, Harmondsworth.
C. HUMPHREYS: *Buddhism*, Penguin, Harmondsworth.
PETER GRANT: *Godmen of India*, Penguin, Harmondsworth.
CHRISTOPHER ISHERWOOD: *Vedanta for the Western World*, Allen & Unwin.
E. WOOD, *Yoga*, Penguin, Harmondsworth.
And for Eastern scriptures:
   The Bhagavad Gita; Buddhist Scriptures; Upanishads – all in the Penguin
   Classics series.
See also:
PAGAL BABA: *Temple of the Phallic King*, Simon & Schuster, New York, 1973.
J. NEEDLEMAN: *The New Religions*, Allen Lane, London, 1972.
   For a general coverage of the 'new' Eastern religions.

Eastern Influence
on the Occult

The present revival of interest in the occult is mirrored by its earlier upsurge in England a century ago. In many ways, the social and religious symptoms of the times are very similar. In the 1880s the debate between fundamentalist Christianity and science was taking place and those people who were unable to accept the total authority of science felt that they had to choose an alternative faith. Some turned to Mormonism and Christian Science while others felt that Theosophy offered a synthesis of scientific knowledge and comparative religion. In England, the Esoteric Section of the Theosophical Society studied the Hermetic sciences and writers like G. R. S. Mead, its leader, made a deep study of Gnostic literature. Meanwhile, the Hermetic Order of the Golden Dawn (see pp. 48–50) developed as a rival group and a person wishing to be instructed in the Western mysteries had to make his choice between one or the other!

The Golden Dawn incorporated some Eastern elements into its magical practices, like *I Ching* divination and the Tattvas, or Hindu symbols for the elements (see pp. 72–4). However, the occult sciences also assumed basically Eastern concepts of man, the sources of his cosmic energy, and his method for spiritual advancement.

Concept of Man

In the same way that Hindus and Buddhists accept that man's consciousness is a drop in the ocean of Brahman or Nirvana, contemporary occultists and magicians accept the view that man has upon his own shoulders the task of universalizing his consciousness. In his book *Magick in Theory and Practice*, Aleister Crowley wrote: 'every man and woman is a star. . . .' And like the Tantrics of India, Crowley believed that the harmonized man was one in whom both sexual polarities were apparent. For this reason, Crowley incorporated a homosexual degree in the occult rituals of the Ordo Templi Orientis. Victor Neuburg, poet and disciple of Crowley, noted that he laid special emphasis on the Divine Androgyne – the being who transcends duality and limitation.

Unlike Christianity which has tended to stress compassion and faith, and unlike Islam which has stressed man's inadequacy before Allah, modern magic followed Buddhism's precept that the root of all suffering is ignorance. Consequently, magic stresses that man has to know himself, and also make himself familiar with the more profound levels of consciousness open to him through meditation and similar methods.

SOURCE OF COSMIC ENERGY

Magic adopts the microcosm/macrocosm distinction found also in yoga and which postulates the raising of the Kundalini energy through the central nervous column until it reaches the crown (universal consciousness). The Qabalah, upon which modern magic is built, may have inherited some of its Eastern concepts as a result of trade-route inroads into the Holy Land centuries before Christ. Whether or not this is so, as a teaching it proposes a similar type of mystical framework. Adam Kadmon is the archetypal man and in his body are all levels of consciousness. The task is similarly for the mystic or magician to raise his consciousness to the point of *Kether*, the chakra transcending all duality (and equating with Nirvana).

What the yogis call the *Sushumna*, the central nervous column with its polar energies *Ida* (male) and *Pingala* (female) has a magical equivalent in what is known as the Middle Pillar. In an occult sense, this represents all the harmonized or 'neutral' levels of consciousness found in alignment in the middle of the Tree of Life. These levels are: *Malkuth* (ground or 'earth' level); *Yesod* (sexuality); *Tiphareth* (harmony, love, compassion) *Daath* (knowledge) and *Kether* (cosmic consciousness). Magic uses either ritual or meditation as its main methods for attaining these levels (see pp. 33-7).

Magic similarly uses the essentially Eastern concepts of posture and mantra. In yoga, the postures adopted by the chela to purify his body and develop muscular control are called the *asanas*. Whereas hatha yoga has a wider range of asanas than the West, magic still makes use of them. The main difference is that magic is based upon a ritual imitation of Western gods and mythology, particularly that of ancient Egypt. Consequently, in its rituals, magic uses the posture shown by the gods depicted in Egyptian sculpture and usually they are seated *on a throne*. By contrast, the ideal yogic asana is the 'full lotus' position in which the yogi sits *on the ground*, rather than in a seat. The buttocks rather than the feet are the point of contact with the ground.

Nevertheless, just as the yogi recites mantras like *Om Mani Padme Hum*, magic similarly uses the sacred power of sound. The mantras of magic are the so-called god names of the Qabalah. Mantras like 'Elohim', 'Shaddai', 'Adonai' are all terms relating to God, but in magic they are used to focus the consciousness on a spiritual ideal.

Finally, magic and occultism tend to adopt the Eastern concept of reincarnation rather than the specifically Western doctrine of the resurrection. Reincarnation suggests that man lives in order to learn certain spiritual lessons. He gradually evolves to the extent where subsequent physical incarnation is unnecessary. Magic teaches that man, in a sense, is in charge of his own mental and spiritual development. It is up to him to purify his life, and he is eventually responsible for all his acts, be they good or bad (karma). Rather than rely on an act of grace from God, the magician feels obliged actively to pursue greater levels of spiritual understanding. Like the yogi, he believes that the path is *inward*; he does not look to external gods or saviours for support.

Some claimed reincarnations carry with them an overtone of wishful thinking, and it is interesting that Aleister Crowley claimed to be a reincarnation of the occultist Eliphas Lévi, and the Elizabethan trance medium Edward Kelley, both of whom influenced him extensively. Modern magic is, for the most part however, pragmatic and reincarnation is regarded more as a working hypothesis than a fact. As with the Buddha, the emphasis is on testing all precepts by personal experience (as in meditation) rather than accepting them as literal dogma.

SOURCEBOOKS

RALPH METZNER: *Maps of Consciousness*, Collier, New York, 1971.
BABA RAM DASS: *Seed*, Lama Foundation-Crown Books, New York, 1973.
    Metzner and Ram Dass (Richard Alpert) are both former colleagues of Timothy Leary. Metzner's important volume contains long, but lucid, essays on I Ching, Tantra, Tarot, Alchemy, Astrology and a branch of Yoga called Actualism. The book is an invaluable source for comparing the meditative paths of East and West. Ram Dass's volume continues the direction set by *Be Here Now* (1970) and includes a section on the Qabalah and the Tree of Life.

Theosophy

In popular usage the term 'Theosophy' usually refers to the philosophy popularized by the Theosophical Society. In fact it is of much more ancient origin – the word derives from the Greek, *theos* (god) and *sophia* (wisdom) and was used by some of the ancient Greek philosophers, and later in the West. It was used to mean a special knowledge of the divine, similar to that which the Gnostics claimed. Gradually there emerged the idea that a tradition of secret knowledge had been transmitted throughout the ages, constituting an esoteric, or inner, philosophy – known as 'the ancient wisdom' or 'theosophy'.

This concept was popularized in the late nineteenth century by a Russian noblewoman, Madame Helena Petrovna Blavatsky, whose writings aroused considerable interest and controversy. Her monumental and voluminous *Secret Doctrine* constitutes the source of most of the teachings of the Theosophical Society. Together with Henry Steele Olcott, Madame Blavatsky founded the Theosophical Society in New York in 1875. The society was to prove one of the major catalysts of the occult revival which occurred in the last quarter of the nineteenth century, and was largely responsible for popularizing Eastern religion and philosophy in the West; its influence was considerable. The Society, although in theory free from doctrinal foundations, soon established a specific teaching which it promulgated. These doctrines, principally deriving from eastern, and specifically Indian philosophy, were said to constitute an 'ancient wisdom', deriving both from the historic tradition, but also from living authorities – of Masters – men who had attained perfection and now guided and taught others. In the early years of the society frequent contact with the Masters was claimed, including the alleged manifestation of mysterious letters said to have been written by the Masters.

Caught up in the occult revival, the Society expanded rapidly and spread throughout the world. Its headquarters were eventually established

at Adyar, India, where they remain today. The Society began its extensive publishing activities, and groups (known as 'Lodges') were established in most countries. Within the Society there developed an inner group, known as the 'Eastern School' or the 'Esoteric Section' to which only select members were admitted and in which secret teachings were promulgated.

After the death of Madame Blavatsky, the leadership of the Society was taken over by Dr Annie Besant, and the emphasis on Eastern philosophy became more marked. In the United States there were several breakaway groups. Today the Society appears to be in a period of decline, probably due to the lack of charismatic leadership of the nature of Blavatsky, Besant and Leadbeater. The Society was further disrupted by its involvement in a messianic movement centring on Jiddu Krishnamurti; after he renounced claims to messiahship many members left the Society in disillusionment. One major defection at this time was the German occultist, Dr Rudolph Steiner, who subsequently formed his own organization, the Anthroposophical Society.

SOURCEBOOKS

While the works of Madame Blavatsky may seem like essential source material, they tend to be both lengthy and complex and are difficult reading. Her principal works are:
Isis Unveiled (1877).
The Secret Doctrine (1888).
The Key to Theosophy (1889).
These are all available in various editions published by the Theosophical Publishing House, Adyar. *The Secret Doctrine* is probably best approached through an edited and annotated edition in one volume: *An Abridgement of the Secret Doctrine* edited by Elizabeth Preston and Christmas Humphreys, TPH, Wheaton, Ill. USA, 1968.
This includes useful introductory material and a bibliography.

Simpler introductory material on theosophy is found in:
C. W. LEADBEATER: *An Outline of Theosophy*, TPH, Adyar, 1963.
C. W. LEADBEATER: *A Textbook of Theosophy*, TPH, Adyar, 1971.
An excellent synopsis of the history of the Theosophical Society, together with an introduction to its philosophy.
HUGH SHEARMAN: *Modern Theosophy*, TPH, Adyar, 1954.
JOSEPHINE RANSOM: *A Short History of the Theosophical Society 1875–1937*, TPH, Adyar, 1938.
A detailed account of the early history of the Society. Compiled from official records.
The TPH publishes a considerable range of extremely cheap books on Theosophy, including the works of its most eminent teachers – Madam Blavatsky, Annie Besant, Charles Leadbeater, Geoffrey Hodson and others.

I Ching

The *I Ching* or *Book of Change*, is one of the oldest books in the world, and originated in China at least 1,000 years BC. Confucius and the Taoist sages thought very highly of it, treating it reverently as a sacred book and prizing its powers of divination.

With the upsurge of interest in prediction and prophecy as part of the occult revival, it is not surprising that the *I Ching* has come to be included among popular counter-cultural pastimes. At the superficial level this is an undoubted injustice to the *I Ching* since it was intended to provide a serious and penetrating guide to life, and not merely a source of venting idle curiosity or providing fortunes.

Several commentators, among them the famous psychoanalyst Carl Jung, and the well-known translator of Buddhist and Taoist texts, John Blofeld, have remarked that the *I Ching* seems to work infallibly. They add, however, that the Oracle seems to 'answer' in terms of the seriousness of the question, and the response – expressed symbolically as one of the meanings given in the *Book of Change* itself – needs to be interpreted with sensitivity and intuition.

Basically the *I Ching* is structured on the philosophy of alternating polarities of *Yin* and *Yang* in the universe. *Yin* represents the earth, and is regarded as passive, feminine, yielding, weak and dark. Overall, it is said to be *negative*. *Yang* represents Heaven, and is also active, masculine, firm, strong and light. Thus it can be said to be clearly *positive*. Other relevant concepts in the *I Ching* philosophy are *T'ai Chi*, meaning the centre of things – a type of Absolute and Divine Stillness – and *Tao*, meaning *the way*. The *I Ching* offers us the way for right action. Commentators skilled in its use say that what really occurs is that the question asked, and the spirit in which it is made, bring to light an intuitive response which in turn responds to the *tides* of change, of ebb and flow, in the world. Thus the future is not something static, but something which results from the here and now. John Blofeld says that the Oracle allows man to perceive the functioning of the Tao in him so that the serious and well-intended question about how one should act provides in return a symbolically expressed answer in tune with the most spiritual side of man's potential. Thus, the *I Ching* does not 'predict' in the crude sense of the word, but offers the seeker an appropriate course of action for the future based on the cosmic tides of positive and negative that shape our destinies.

To consult the *I Ching* a method of dividing small heaps of sticks or of throwing coins is used. In the first instance fifty short and long yarrow stalks are systematically divided in heaps until a resulting combination of stalks provides a combination which can be identified as one of the lines in a 'Hexagram'. The Hexagram is a combination of six lines, some representing Yin and some Yang, and the completed Hexagram spells the answer to the question asked at the time of the division of stalks, or fall of coins. In the latter case, three coins are thrown, and the side of the coin representing its value is taken to be its positive face. The coins are dropped from cupped hands spontaneously and their fall produces varying combinations of positive and negative.

In each method, the procedure must be applied six times, and the lines built up from the bottom to the top (from earth to heaven as it were). After the throws have been made, the specific meanings are found in the *I Ching* itself. There are sixty-four Hexagrams in all, but the variety of intuitive meanings far exceeds this number.

As a means of divination in the occult, perhaps Aleister Crowley more than any other Western magician, made most use of the *I Ching*. Crowley was noted for his keenness to adapt Eastern methods of posture (yogic asanas) and breathing to modern occult techniques and according to his Magical Record, he also consulted the Oracle regularly. However, when one looks through his account of his day-to-day activities, it is clear that much of his intuition was self-oriented rather than emanating from the *Book of Change* itself. Crowley became notorious for his 'sex-abbey' at Cefalu in Sicily and the following extract from his diaries shows how he consulted the *I Ching* before deciding whether or not to buy:

'Shall we buy real estate in Cefalu?'

———— = *Fang*, Fire of Sun

Large, abundant! What should be its physical characteristics? Water of Lingam. Leah says: in a high place. I say: water around it, and Phallus, a Pinnacle. This fits the Caldura like a glove; its promontory is washed by the sea for at least two thirds of it, and it has a magnificently phallic rock. (p. 227)

On another occasion, in 1921, Crowley asked the *I Ching* for a symbolic prediction of his magical work in the world (he had become Lord of the New Aeon in 1904). The answer was: 'Sudden rise to fame, though starting slowly . . .', which was probably true since Crowley's sexual magic and experimental drug-taking soon earned him notoriety in the British press.

More recently, the *I Ching*, along with Transcendental Meditation, Yoga and other forms of Eastern mystical philosophy, has been popular as a symbol of the rock culture. While she was Mick Jagger's special consort, singer and actress Marianne Faithfull frequently employed the *I Ching* for divination. At one stage she was particularly worried about the fortune of Brian Jones, the leading musician in the Rolling Stones. He had become alienated from his friends and was heavily dependent on drugs. Whenever she threw the coins with him in mind, the *I Ching* would suggest water and evil. 'Where the water is. A pit, a perilous cavity. There will be evil, it says', she told Jagger. In July 1969, the prediction came true. Jones, a Piscean by birth, drowned in a swimming pool.

SOURCEBOOKS

R. WILHELM: *I Ching*, Routledge & Kegan Paul (several editions).
J. BLOFELD: *The Book of Change*, George Allen & Unwin, London, 1971.
    The above are the classic texts in the field.

Astrology

From his very first perception of the universe around him, man has been overawed by the vastness of space, and the wonders of the sun and moon, the planets and the stars. Even today, when his scientific skill penetrates the depths of space, the wonders of the universe remain mysterious and powerful. In his personalizing of the universe, man attributed to the stars and planets relationships with and influences over his own life. Astrology is the study of the relationships between the heavens and the earth, between man and the planets, and as such is one of the oldest studies known, having played an important role in every highly developed civilization of the past from Egypt and Babylonia to India, China and South America. Astrological study of the heavens eventually led to the emergence of the scientific discipline of astronomy, and the rules, methods and principles of astrology have emerged over thousands of years of usage. Astrology works upon the basis that the planets exert influences on the earth which affect individuals, as well as groups. Individuals are especially affected by the cosmic situation existing at the time of their births, and the qualities inherent in the individual can to a large degree be determined by such a situation. In the light of knowledge about the influences of cosmic radiation upon earth, the theories of astrology are not so fantastic, although it can be argued that the important time as far as the individual is concerned is the moment of conception (at which the influence of the cosmic radiation begins) and not the moment of birth. Astrology attributes different influences to different planets and conjunctions of planets. A 'Map' of the heavens at the moment of birth is drawn up to determine the planetary influences upon an individual; this is known as a *horoscope* and its accuracy depends very much on an accurate knowledge of the location and exact time of birth. In general terms, individuals can be placed under the influence of the twelve signs of the zodiac according to the date of their birth, but the more subtle influences of planets and conjunctions mean that these basic types are subject to wide variation. The popular newspaper-column astrology presents only a rather crude parody of the science; scientific astrology is a mathematically precise technology, involving detailed analysis of astronomical data which is in every individual case unique (unless two individuals were born at exactly the same time at exactly the same place). There are two main types of astrology:

(1) *Mundane* – which concerns itself with large-scale phenomena, such as wars, natural disasters, political and social trends; this is based upon the premise that cosmic influences affect large groups of people, and in fact the physical structure of the earth. Horoscopes can be drawn up for nations, societies or even races, but these are necessarily far less accurate than those for individuals.

(2) *Horary Astrology* – is based upon the premise that a chart can be drawn up, not only for an individual born at a specific moment in a specific place, but indeed for anything to be 'born', or inaugurated at that place at that time. Hence horoscopes can be used to determine the advisability or otherwise of undertaking particularly activities at particular times.

Astrology being by its own claims an exact science, it is difficult either to support or condemn its premises in simple terms, and it should not be judged on the basis either of newspaper columns or the popular astrologers.

The basic premise upon which astrology is founded is that the universe is not a fragmented collection of individual pieces, but a unified, organic whole, in which every part is dependent upon and in some way connected with every other part. The universe is seen to be coherent, meaningful and ordered; it has pattern and rhythm and is to a large extent predictable. Man first gained this feeling of order and rhythm by his close relationship with the cycles of nature and his observance of the movement of the planets and the stars. Gradually he also came to the conclusion that these patterns could be interpreted and understood, and could be anticipated.

It has often been said that the reasoning behind astrology is therefore *analogical*, rather than *logical* – it works on the ancient occult theorem, 'as above, so below'. This idea has gained increasing support as a result of modern research into the nature and working of cosmic influences on the earth, and on human behaviour. As science investigates the effects of cosmic radiation – not only the obvious things like sunspots, but more subtle emanations from outer space – the premises of astrology are receiving more and more support. Even the old story that the moon affects sanity has received some measure of support from modern research into the influence of that body on human behaviour.

Astrology works on the assumption that the earth is the centre of the solar system and the universe – and for all practical purposes this is a valid assumption. As far as man is concerned, the universe does revolve around him. Astrology pictures the earth as the centre of a series of concentric circles, the paths of the planets and the signs of the zodiac. The zodiac is a hypothetical sphere around the earth, divided into twelve signs – the popularly known signs of the zodiac. Each of the signs is classified as being either positive or negative, and is attributed to one of the base elements of traditional occultism (earth, air, fire and water). The sun appears to move around this zodiac, passing through the various signs, and the sign against which it appears to rise on the day of an individual's birth dictates the sign under which he is said to be born. Thus a man born on 4 November will be a Scorpio because the sun is in the sign of Scorpio at that time. And the sun, representing the powerful energetic, creative principle, is seen as the most important factor in the horoscope.

But the earth also revolves on its own axis, and so there is also a rising sign (that is, the sign against the eastern horizon at the moment of birth), and this is said to be the second most important factor. The actual sunrise point is called the ascendent, and this determines a further classification into twelve houses, equal to the twelve constellations. For example, a man born with Scorpio as his sun sign, and also with his ascendent in Scorpio would be very different in personality from a man born at a similar time but with a different ascendent; in the former case all the characteristics of Scorpio would tend to be emphasized and reinforced.

After these basic influences, astrology looks to the influence of the moon (the second most important 'planet') and the other planets. Not only the positions of the planets at the time of birth, but also their relationships to each other must be taken into account to establish a whole 'plan' of the universe at the moment. Different planets in different positions, and planets in various combinations will give different influences and differing degrees of influence. For such subtle and complex interpretations a fair degree of mathematical skill and accuracy is necessary, and a properly drawn horoscope involves considerable knowledge and ability. The very complexity of such analysis also means that popular accounts of the zodiacal types can never be more than very general statements about a whole category of people all of whom have probably more differences than similarities. All Scorpios are not necessarily alike, since there are important, subtle influences which only a detailed analysis will reveal.

There is quite an amount of modern scientific evidence supporting at least some of the basic assumptions of astrology, and giving a new view of man's place within the universe, and the influence of the universe on man and the world. Investigations into solar and lunar rhythms, the phenomenon of sunspots and the effect of the moon on natural cycles on earth – all these are leading to the possibility that the essential claims of astrology (as distinguished from the exaggerated pretensions of popular astrology) will be validated scientifically.

SOURCEBOOKS

One of the best complete guides to astrology, in a simple, practical form is by Marc Edmund Jones: *Astrology: How and Why it Works*. A classic in its field, this book was first published in 1945, reissued by Routledge & Kegan Paul, 1977. Its author is one of the leading scientific astrologers in the United States.

Paralleling this study is another introduction to the premises behind astrology, giving a detailed background to modern scientific evidence in support of it:

J. A. WEST and J. G. TOONDER: *The Case for Astrology*, Penguin, Harmondsworth, 1973.

A history of astrology and astrologers is given in –

E. HOWE: *Urania's Children: the Strange World of the Astrologers*, Kimber, London, 1967.

C. MCINTOSH: *The Astrologers and Their Creed*, Hutchinson, London, 1969. Both of these books are readable and informative.

R. GLEADOW: *The Origins of the Zodiac*, Cape, London, 1968.
A more detailed study of the origins of astrology.

The range of material on the subject is almost limitless, and includes innumerable books by astrologers and 'do-it-yourself' texts.

Numerology

From earliest times man has been fascinated by the symbolism of numbers, and we find for example the numbers 7 and 12 occurring in many cultures as combinations of sacred significance.

Modern numerology draws much of its inspiration from the sixth-century philosopher Pythagoras, who believed that numbers represent the essence and qualities of things. Hence, an analysis of a person's name will reveal what sort of person he is inherently.

Pythagoras' views on numbers were expanded by the medieval Qabalist Cornelius Agrippa in his book *Occult Philosophy*, first published in 1533. According to Agrippa, numbers have the following qualities:

1 The origin of all things, God. The Central Intelligence in the Universe. The Sun. The Philosopher's Stone.
2 Marriage and communion. Also, alternately, the number of division and evil.
3 Trinity. Fulfilment and sacred wisdom.
4 Solidity, permanence, foundation. There are four elements, four seasons and four cardinal points. Associated with the earth.
5 Justice. In medieval Europe this was interpreted to be Christian justice, there being five wounds in His body; man observed the world also through five senses.
6 Creation. The world was fashioned in six days, God resting on the seventh. According to Agrippa, it also represents labour and service. However, six is the perfect number.
7 Life. Seven is made up of six (perfection) and one (unity and God). In the medieval conception, life is made up of the body (spirit, flesh, bone and humour) and soul (passions, desire and reason) – a total of seven.
8 Fullness. The number eight is remarkably even, for it can be divided twice and still retain the balance of all things. Also associated with infinity (a horizontal 8).

9 The number of the spheres. Cosmic significance.

10 Completeness. One cannot go beyond 10 without including other numbers. Agrippa was a Qabalist and according to this philosophy the world came to be through a divine process of ten stages.

According to modern numerologists, the two most vital aspects of a person's life and character are his birth date and his used name. The latter is said to be the name which most closely defines the identity (or 'essence') of a person.

THE BIRTHDATE

The birthdate is not written as a succession of numbers but is plotted onto a diagram which shows the positions as follows:—

Mind Level	3	6	9
Emotional Level	2	5	8
Physical Level	1	4	7

Numerologists believe that the above represents a three-fold division of man and that the aim of all mystical teachings is perfection. Consequently, the perfect man would have all these numbers in his make-up. The writer was born on 1.10.1947, which would be diagrammatically represented as:

		9
111	4	7

(note: 0 is not included)

This analysis shows a lack of functioning on the emotional level, and this would be an area clearly in need of improvement! Thus, numbers show us to what extent we are unbalanced and what qualities of character are needed for harmonized personality development.

Another method using the birthdate is the concept of the Ruling Number. The numbers in the above diagram total 23, which reduces to 2 + 3 = 5. The fact that 5 is the number of Justice and also that the writer is a Libran (Libra: The Scales = Balance) offers some sort of compensation for the above!

ANALYSIS OF THE NAME

The most popular method used for reducing one's name to a number is to take the name used by a person (this would not normally include the middle name), and then to apply a number value to each letter. A is 1, B is

2 and so on until we arrive at I, which is 9. Since there is no zero, and ten = one, J becomes 1 and K, 2 and so on through the alphabet. The full sequence is as follows:

1	2	3	4	5	6	7	8	9
A	B	C	D	E	F	G	H	I
J	K	L	M	N	O	P	Q	R
S	T	U	V	W	X	Y	Z	

It is usually claimed that the birthdate – the beginning of life – is more important than the name, partly because the name is given by the parents. On the other hand, the birthdate is an inherent quality of the person, and is therefore a more reliable guide. However, it is also recognized that a person grows up, develops and responds, as *one who has a name*, and that in this sense the name comes to symbolize the personality and also in a very limited sense 'predicts' it. Some names are hard and aggressive, others soft and poetic, so that it is little wonder that numerologists stress vibrationary qualities of the name.

A person may find the number value of his name by totalling the sum of its letters. If it comes to a total exceeding 10, it is 'reduced', as with the Ruling Number, above. This number may then be slotted on the birth diagram as a further clue to the personality.

As with astrology, numerology offers an analysis of what a person is, rather than what he may become. During the person's lifetime as his free will comes into play he makes certain decisions as he develops accordingly. Numerology merely offers a framework for what a person may become if he follows a natural tendency; it does not make any claim to prophecy.

SOURCEBOOKS

There are many different approaches and 'schools' in numerology, and hence most books will adopt one approach to the exclusion of others, and, unlike astrology, there are few basic principles which remain consistent throughout all approaches. A good basic introduction is found in the article on 'Numerology' in:

RICHARD CAVENDISH (ed) *An Encyclopedia of the Unexplained*, Routledge & Kegan Paul, London, 1974, and the bibliography refers to other, more detailed, studies.

V. LOPEZ: *Numerology*, Citadel, New York, 1961, is a useful introduction also.

More detailed material will be found in two fairly early volumes, less popular in their approach:

E. T. BELL: *The Magic of Numbers*, McGraw Hill, New York, 1946 and C. W. CHEARLEY: *Numerology*, Rider, London, 1926.

Details on the symbology of numbers can be found in:

C. BUTLER: *Number Symbolism*, Routledge & Kegan Paul, London, 1970.

Palmistry

In its simplest form palmistry is the fortune-telling technique of reading hands popularized by gypsies in side-shows. This, of course, is but a poor imitation of the discipline which today more than ever lays claim to scientific foundations. Palmistry is concerned with the analysis of the hands, not simply the lines on the palms, but their combinations and conjunctions, together with other minute details of the hands and fingers. The features of the hand are, in palmistry, linked with aspects of personality and character and with features of the individual, both physical and psychological. The scientific palmist does not postulate simple correlations between this feature of the hand and that psychological characteristic; rather he looks for significant aspects, their combinations and relationships. He looks for an overall pattern which will be unique in every individual case. The palm of a human being develops its characteristic lines and patterns from the time of birth (and beginning before that time), and these develop and change throughout the years, and may, in their changes, indicate further mutations in the individual's life and personality. But palmistry is not a fatalistic technology; the lines on the palms reflect aspects of personality, they do not cause them. Therefore, palmistry is an analytical science rather than a predictive one – although the skilled palmist, observing tendencies and interrelationships on the hand can postulate likely trends in future.

Palmistry has developed from rather shady origins as a fortune-teller's art to being a realm of legitimate scientific investigation; the side-show gypsy may well be replaced by the laboratory scientist.

The origins of palmistry are extremely ancient, and reference to this method of divination date back some 3000 years in the ancient writings of India and China. Certainly, it was referred to by Aristotle, who, it is said, derived it from ancient Egypt. It was, however, in the sixteenth and seventeenth centuries that palmistry, along with other forms of divination by analysing the body (e.g. phrenology, or reading lumps on the head), became systematized.

It was during this period that the macrocosm/microcosm theory (that is, 'as above so below', meaning that man was linked with the cosmos, and an analysis of his nature revealed the wider universe) was expanded. Textbooks of handreading became popular; most of these were far from scientific, and often worked on the basis of laws of correspondence. In the nineteenth century the first attempts to make palmistry (or 'chirology' as it was often known) respectable were initiated. One of the most important works of this time was *Laws of Scientific Hand Reading* by the American William G. Benham. It was at this time that the famous palmist 'Cheiro' (pseudonym for Count Louis Harmon) brought the study to the height of its popularity.

Gradually the interest in scientific palmistry, as distinct from the more popular fortune-telling, has expanded, and a number of scientists, especially psychologists, have taken an interest in correlations between personality characteristics and lines on the hand. Many psychologists and palmists believe that in statistical correlations such as these some support is being given to the ancient premises of hand reading, especially in relationships between mental disorders and hand characteristics. Certainly, as more serious scientific consideration is being given to the study of the significance of lines on the hand, more information will become available on this ancient technique of character divination.

The traditional palmist, in his analysis of hands, looks for a number of features:

(1) the size and shape of the hands – this includes the size of the palms, the size and shape of the fingers, thickness, width;

(2) the flexibility or stiffness of the hand and the fingers;

(3) the characteristics of the fingers – this includes traditional correlations between the fingers and different aspects of personality;

(4) some palmists also examine the fingerprints;

(5) the mounts – the 'hills' on the hand, with different mounts relating to different aspects of personality;

(6) the lines – traditionally it has been popularly assumed that these were the only things of concern to the palmist, however they are only a part of the whole pattern of the hand, and must be seen in a total context. Different lines are related to different aspects of the individual – the most important being the head, heart and life lines.

Some palmists prefer to read directly from the hand, others prefer to take prints and analyse these in depths; similarly, some palmists state that the hands are merely a point of contact with the person, and say they employ some form of psychic perception for the actual character analysis, while others reject all non-scientific methods of palmistry.

SOURCEBOOKS

FRED GETTINGS: *The Book of the Hand*, Hamlyn, London, 1965.
An excellent introduction to the subject, by one of the world's leading authorities, Gettings explains clearly, and with numerous illustrations, the theory and practice of palmistry. Gettings is also the author of a wide range of more detailed technical books on palmistry.

The 'classic work' in the English language (despite its lack of scientific approach) is by
'CHEIRO' (Count Louis Harmon): *Language of the Hand*, reprinted by Corgi, London, 1967.
Cheiro was probably the most popular and well-known palmist of all time, and his numerous works are still widely consulted.

An important work, showing the scientific uses of palmistry is:
J. SPIER: *The Hands of Children*, Routledge & Kegan Paul, London, 1955, where a German psychologist employs palmistry as a diagnostic technique.

Lost Continents

Throughout history man has tended to look backwards towards an age of perfection, a time when human achievements were greater, human life happier and the world a better place. In religious terms this has usually meant a time when the gods were upon earth; in secular terms it has led to theories of pre-historical civilizations exceeding, or at least equalling modern technology.

Because none of these early civilizations appear to have left visible remains, the theories concerning them have had to explain their almost total disappearance, and have tended to do so by locating them on continents which subsequently sank beneath the oceans, never to be found again. The vastness of the oceans encouraged the idea that such space should not have been wasted, and that, at some time there must have been land occupying it. So the theory of the lost continents runs:

(1) Continents existed in the now empty oceans of the world – the Pacific, the Atlantic and the Indian.

(2) Civilizations developed on these continents, and a high degree of scientific, cultural and technological achievement was attained – perhaps even higher than known today.

(3) Eventually the continents and the civilizations were destroyed – either by natural disasters (earthquakes, movements in the crust of the earth) or by man-made means (e.g. some theories suggest that these civilizations developed nuclear power and were destroyed in a nuclear explosion).

(4) Virtually all trace of the civilizations and the continents were therefore removed from the face of the earth.

(5) However some small traces remain – e.g. alleged similarities in culture between two peoples on different sides of an ocean are cited as evidence that they derive from the same source; the legends of a 'golden age' are cited as racial memories of the lost continents.

Speculation and investigation into the supposed lost continents has ranged from genuine scientific and archæological research, through the whole range of pseudo-sciences into the occult. Many occult traditions claim their origins in the religious traditions of the lost continents. But at present, there is little historic and scientific evidence to give a sound basis to speculation that lost continents did exist; this is not to deny their existence, but merely to place them in the realm of theory, rather than fact. The principal lost continents of the past were:

(1) *Atlantis* – located in the Atlantic Ocean; speculation about this continent developed from the reference by the Greek philosopher Plato to it as an advanced civilization, destroyed for its evil. A number of authors, especially during the Victorian period, wrote extensively on the subject, and it became involved in many religious, occult and anthropological theories. Modern scientific research suggests historical references to Atlantis may have derived from a civilization on the Mediterranean destroyed by a volcanic erruption.

(2) *Lemuria* – was located by some theorists in the Indian Ocean, and by others in the Pacific. Life on Lemuria was generally held to be of a low form and did not reach the advanced civilization of Atlantis.

(3) *Mu* – was located in the Pacific Ocean, and supposedly was the original Garden of Eden, with a highly advanced civilization.

A slightly different set of theories places lost civilizations *inside* the earth, which is said to be hollow, with openings at the ends.

SOURCEBOOKS

The best introduction to the idea of lost continents is by L. Sprague de Camp: *Lost Continents*, Dover, New York, 1970, which covers the whole field in detail. This is also done, in lesser detail by M. Gardner: *Fads and Fallacies in the Name of Science*, Dover, New York, 1957.

The classic work on Atlantis, and the one which originally stimulated most interest in the subject, is by I. Donnelly and E. Sykes: *Atlantis*, revised edn, Steiner, New York, 1970.

This is one in a series of books by Donnelly.

A consideration of the scientific evidence is found in J. V. Luce: *The End of Atlantis*, Thames & Hudson, London, 1969.

Both Atlantis and Lemuria are considered, mainly from an occult viewpoint, in a classic work by W. Scott-Elliot: *The Story of Atlantis and the Lost Lemuria*, TPH, London, reprinted 1962.

And the continent of Mu is dealt with in great detail in a series of books by J. Churchward, the simplest of which is *The Lost Continent of Mu*, Paperback Library, New York, 1968.

Modern interest in these old theories has led to the reprinting of many of the classic works, most of which are now available in paperback.

The hollow earth theory is dealt with in Martin Gardner's book (*op. cit.*).

Inner Space Rock Music

Pop music in the halcyon days of the 1950s was exciting, rhythmic, emotionally naive and structurally rather simplistic. Much of it owed its musical origin to twelve-bar blues, and performers like Little Richard and Jerry Lee Lewis adapted these frameworks in the new frenzy of rock'n roll. Pop then went through its big ballads and strings phase at the hands of Roy Orbison, Elvis Presley, Jim Reeves and Ray Charles, who had converted to orchestrated country and western. And then the gospel side raised its head in the United States, and the first wave of poignant 'soul music' poured forth. Aretha Franklin preached a pentecostal fervour in her songs and Otis Redding had a heart-rending hesitancy in his voice on numbers like 'I've Been Loving You Too Long To Stop Now'.

Around 1967 (and some say, with the Beatles' milestone album *Sergeant Pepper's*) the mainstream suddenly changed. Pop music began to venture inward. The music became more complex, more searching. It had more texture and fewer structural limitations. Electronic techniques were used to give the vocals a surreal, mystic effect, and more and more the lyrics began to speak of the inner journey of the mind.

It was predictable that this change would occur, and it is to their credit that the Beatles foresaw and rode with the change. In the United States – and the Beatles had been playing solidly to American audiences since they first stormed the singles chart in 1964 – there had been some interesting things going on. In particular the drug culture was about to blossom.

At Harvard University, Dr Timothy Leary had been experimenting with hallucinogens, and some opponents in the media were beginning to accuse him of using students as 'human guinea pigs'. In 1963 Leary had told a gathering of psychologists in Philadelphia how in 1960 he had eaten the sacred mushrooms of the Aztecs. For five hours Leary had been whirled through an experience which he said was the 'deepest religious experience' of his life.

Leary soon began to anger the White Anglo-Saxon Protestant authorities by his suggestion that psilocybin and LSD were sacraments which could add a new dimension to one's social existence, and perhaps take one to the core meaning of the inner Universe itself. It was too direct, and suspiciously 'easy' – worse than that, it was potentially a tool of anarchy. Leary attracted a vast following in the counterculture but his days were obviously numbered from the establishment point of view.

While this eventually proved to be so, a new genre of rock music meanwhile sprouted up as a consequence of this new impetus – Moby Grape, Jefferson Airplane and The Grateful Dead all came together when new universes of the mind and sensory experience were being explored.

Suddenly pop lyrics began to reflect spiritual Eastern imagery. Rock discovered the sitar and the sarod. The Beatles had audience with Maharaji Mahesh Yogi and the occult began to filter in.

The Beatles' *Sergeant Pepper's* featured the face of the notorious magician Aleister Crowley. The rock group Steppenwolf took their name from a novel by Hermann Hesse who was being rediscovered as a fine writer of mystical themes. His novel, *Siddhartha*, set in the times of Buddha had an especially strong appeal. Santana named an album *Abraxas* after a deity mentioned in his novel *Demian*.

In the late 1960s this mystical tendency in rock continued to develop, lyrics became even more eclectic and, at the hands of Bob Dylan, apocryphal. The new renaissance pushed forward towards a universal expression of mystical reality. In their song 'Maya' (illusion) The Incredible String Band asked their audience to universalize their vision:

> The great ship of the world,
> Long time sailing . . .
> All . . . in one boat together,
> Troubled voyage in calm weather,
> Maya, Maya,
> All this world is but a play,
> Be thou the joyful player. . . .

The most recent manifestation of the new consciousness in rock music has been in the more complex, electronic-transcendental music popularly known as Cosmic Rock. Much of this music has come from England and Germany. Pink Floyd, Yes, Jade Warrior and King Crimson have been among the most important progressive influences from Britain, and groups like Tangerine Dream, Ash Ra Tempel (who recorded with Timothy Leary) and the solo performer Klaus Schulze have developed the genre in Germany.

Cosmic Rock is elusive – it floats and weaves. It transforms, re-interprets, redefines. Often it has incorporated classical themes alongside a kaleidoscopic collage of moog, keyboards and choral accompaniments. At the end of Pink Floyd's 'Echoes', which is a long, intricate track with a watery, flaccid texture, comes a soaring, uplifting sequence which seems to lead to another dimension of time and space. Tangerine Dream, a remarkable group from Berlin seek similarly to wrap their listeners in the very texture of electronic sound, and their superb album *Phaedra*, with its waves of undulating synthesizer, is a fine example of this.

Cosmic Rock seems always to have an implied occult basis in its formulation as a pathway into the mind. The textures, the sequences, the lyrics, produce a transformation in the listener. Robert Fripp, who plays guitar, mellotron and 'devices' for King Crimson, once stated that the aim of his music was to have a sonic, healing effect as it permeated the fibres of those who listened. He also went on to say: 'It is a very important tool in that if you can bring everybody together on one vibration you can create a oneness and an energy without parallel. Playing before an audience is a magical rite. . . .'

Cosmic Rock is the music of meditation and inner space, and it is not surprising that Fripp's colleague Pete Sinfield began to explore mythology and fantasy legends as a related source of ideas. Magic and yoga both offer man self-realization and the goal of cosmic consciousness.

For Sinfield, it was clear that rock music and mythology both promoted the quest for the super-man:

Still I wonder if I passed some time ago,
As a bird, or stream or a tree?
To mount up high you must first sink down low,
Like the changeable tides of the Caesars and the
Pharaohs, prophets and heroes . . . [from the album *Still*].

Meanwhile in 1973 Bo Hansson, a formerly obscure Swedish keyboards player produced a haunting, reflective interpretation of Tolkien's *Lord of the Rings*. We are reminded again that mythology is an expression of the journey into the fantasy land of the subconscious. Evans-Wentz, the translator of the *Tibetan Book of the Dead*, which had such a profound influence on Timothy Leary and the drug culture, once suggested that the mythology of fairies and goblins was evidence of a continuing psychic ability among 'simple folk' and it is not surprising that Cosmic Rock endeavours to move towards an inner magical reality. In recent years the German groups like Tangerine Dream have gained an ascendancy, perhaps as a result of their newly found simplicity of essence. Albums like T.D.'s

Zeit and *Alpha Centauri*, Schulze's *Black Dance* and Ash Ra Tempel's *Join Inn*, develop variations along a single ethereal, core theme, and their direction is more abstract, towards the edge of time and space.

The following selective discography lists the titles of some of the more mystical albums which could be included in the 'inner space' genre. Since many of them have been issued internationally, specific number references have been excluded. In some instances the titles will appear on alternative labels to those referred to, according to the country of distribution.

England:

Pink Floyd	*Wish You Were Here* (Harvest)
	The Dark Side of the Moon (Harvest)
	Meddle (Harvest)
	Atom Heart Mother (Harvest)
Jade Warrior	*Floating World* (Island)
Pete Sinfield	*Still* (Manticore)
King Crimson	*Larks Tongue in Aspic* (Island)
	Islands (Island)
Yes	*Yessongs* (Atlantic)
	Tales of Topographic Oceans (Atlantic)
Mike Oldfield	*Tubular Bells* (Island)
Hawkwind	*In Search of Space* (United Artists)

Germany:

Tangerine Dream	*Stratospheres* (Virgin)
	Rubyeon (Virgin)
	Phaedra (Virgin)
	Zeit (Ohr)
	Alpha Centauri (Ohr)
Edgar Froese	*Aqua* (Virgin)
	Epsilon in Malaysian Pale (Virgin)
Klaus Schulze	*Blackdance* (Brain Metronome)
	Timewind (Virgin)
	Body Love (Virgin)
	Cyborg (Ohr)
	Irrlicht (Ohr)
Ash Ra Tempel	*Join Inn* (Ohr)
(with Timothy Leary)	*Seven Up* (Ohr)
Walter Wegmuller	*Tarot* (Metronome)
Ashra	*New Age of Earth* (Virgin)

Australia:
    MacKenzie Theory   *Out of the Blue* (Mushroom)

Sweden:
    Bo Hansson   *Lord of the Rings* (Charisma)

Italy:
    Premiata Forneria
    Marconi   *Photos of Ghosts* (Manticore)

USA:

Santana	*Caravanserai* (CBS)
Les McCann	*Layers* (Atlantic)
Paul Horn	*Inside* (Epic)
Chic Corea	*Return to Forever* (ECM/CBS)
Miles Davis	*In A Silent Way* (CBS)
Morton Subotnik	*Silver Apples of the Moon* (Nonesuch)

The American material as a source is the least integrated. Les McCann, Chic Corea and Miles Davis are internationally recognized as jazz artists but the albums specified have a mystical orientation. Paul Horn's *Inside* is an album of flute recorded inside the dome of the Taj Mahal, and has a pantheistic quality which is impossible to categorize. Morton Subotnik's work is experimental electronic music and is included because of its surreal textures.

Occult Art

With the exception of phantasy painters like Hieronymous Bosch, Lucas Cranach and Peter Breughel, art before the 1880s was, in a broad sense, representational. The fashionable incursion of hallucinatory drugs and an interest in dreams and the occult among the Symbolists in Europe saw the emergence of visionary painters like Gustav Moreau, Jean Delville and Richard Dadd, but in effect, what may be termed occult art is very much a phenomenon of the present century.

Of all the major movements of modern art, the most trenchantly occult has been Surrealism, with certain of its members being themselves trance or Satanic occultists. Surrealism developed in Paris between the Wars at a time which saw the total breakdown of society, and a type of mass alienation from all perspectives of 'normality'. In place of rational thinking, which appeared to have failed, the Surrealists proposed a new dimension of phantasy. In the First Surrealist Manifesto, issued by Andre Breton in 1924, he explained why he believed in the omnipotence of the dream. He considered that dreams were not only a reflection of life, but ultimately a valid visual representation of reality, since their structure was unimpeded by rational processes. They thus offered a new freedom. They also constituted a commentary on man's inner being, which was felt increasingly to be more real than his outer social degradation.

The Surrealists are not readily structured, although some preferred to give emphasis to abstract techniques of painting while others painted with the meticulous detail of the living dream.

Wolfgang Paalen, an Austrian who lived for a time in Mexico and who invented a technique known as 'fumage', was one of these. He would hold canvases freshly coated with oil paint above a candle so that the smoke would trace eerie random patterns in the wet paint. He then overlaid these images with surreal, supranormal detail, as in his work 'Conflict of the

Principles of Darkness'. Paalen was very absorbed in the Tarot, and also fused animistic Mayen influences into his paintings.

Max Ernst developed a similarly suggestive technique known as 'frottage'. He would rub lightly with a pencil upon sheets of paper placed on his floorboards, thus allowing the uneven surface to come through on his paper as a texture. When Ernst looked carefully at his frottages he found a mystical process coming into play: 'When gazing at these drawings', he writes, 'I was surprised at the sudden intensification of my visionary faculties and at the hallucinatory succession of contradictory images being superimposed on each other. . . .'

Within the more representational category we find the confessed black magician Felix Labisse, whose painted figures were often a macabre combination of animal, vegetable and human forms. But like all occultists, he knew the power of transformation and that on a subconscious level, anything which the magician could imagine, *could* happen. As an artist, he felt obliged to convey this opinion in his paintings.

Similarly, Salvador Dali and René Magritte, while both employing imagery of a familiar kind, created a strange nightmarish quality by the counterbalancing of objects taken out of their normal context. Magritte overcomes reality by representing images in combinations which defy reality. A mermaid with the head of a fish and the legs of a woman lies hopelessly cast up upon a beach; a succulent green apple fills a room; plants which are also birds grow upon a rocky mountain top.

The Surrealists offered a new means for observing the universe which allowed almost anything to occur. This in itself constituted a potentially occult basis on which ensuing art could build.

Outside the mainstream of modern art, however, there have been some interesting offshoots. In at least three important instances, the relationship of art to trance, mysticism or the occult was even more developed.

The first major English surrealist was Austin Osman Spare (1888–1956) – in fact his work precedes the European School by about a decade. Spare won a scholarship to the Royal College of Art when he was only sixteen, a sign of his remarkable draughtsmanship. His early illustrations, for books like Ethel Wheeler's *Behind the Veil* (1906) and a book on aphorisms entitled *The Starlit Mire* (1911) were fairly orthodox, but Spare meanwhile was training as an occultist as well as an artist. It is thought that around 1910 Spare joined Aleister Crowley's occult Order, the Argentinum Astrum, and he now sought a new mystical direction in his art.

He came to see man as alienated from the cause of all Being, which he called Kia, and he considered that man's role was to learn how to open himself to its creative energies and life processes. In his remarkable work

The Book of Pleasure (Self Love): The Philosophy of Ecstasy (1913) there were some important new concepts. Spare, by now, had developed a theory of sigils which were symbols said to express the human will in a concentrated form. These sigils would express a command which Spare would make, in effect, to his subconscious while in a state of trance or ecstasy. He hoped, then, that he would have enhanced access to the subconscious with all its imagery, and that he would be able to open himself totally to its potential. Spare, like most occultists, believed in reincarnation, and he held that his earlier personalities were also lurking deep in his mind. In the trance state, which he interestingly called 'The Death Posture' he would try to summon these half-man, half-animal forms, and identify with them as earlier facets of his own existence. Spare felt that if he retrogressed far enough, he would rediscover all his personalities, and finally reach the Primal Cause of all.

The work of Austin Spare is a forceful reminder that an occultist who totally surrenders himself tends to become obsessed by the imagery of his subconscious. Many of Spare's paintings contain swirling, atavistic imagery, and there is also an inherent animal sexuality in much of his work. Nevertheless, it does represent a merging of trance occultism and art.

Australia offers two other blendings of art and the occult. The first of these is represented by the work of the self-confessed witch Rosaleen Norton, whose paintings continued the tradition of Norman Lindsay with a marked swing towards black magic imagery. Norton was familiar with the writings of the Surrealist/occultist Kurt Seligmann, and also the magical theories of Dion Fortune (who called herself the Black Isis), Aleister Crowley and Eliphas Lévi. In her work she detailed many of the so-called Qlippoth, the images of the 'black' or negative Tree of Life. Like Spare she appears to have sometimes used a tantric or sexual technique to attain visionary ecstasy for she says in the commentary to her monograph that 'Kundalini, who sometimes assumes the shape of a serpent, is my most powerful familiar . . .' (p. 74). For her, the power of the orgasm was an inroad to occult consciousness.

The other Australian was Victor Angel, who began his career as a commercial artist. Angel had no especial talents and was responsible for some thoroughly mediocre landscapes. However, at the age of twenty-seven, he felt that he was becoming possessed by a spiritual force which urged him to adopt a new approach to his painting. Like Spare, Angel summoned the Presence by means of a sigil, or symbol, which he would hold in his mind. He then became able in a clairvoyant state to perceive remarkable mythological imagery hovering above his blank paper. Spare, who worked in gouache, claimed no credit for these works, for he said that he merely filled in the detail that was made supernaturally available to him. Spare's visionary work resembles William Blake to some extent, although there are also Renaissance influences as well. In his case, the marked contrast between the artist's natural ability and his later occult sensitivity present an interesting and perhaps unique phenomenon. However, in addition, Angel's paintings reveal a pronounced Qabalistic content, and may be accurately correlated with the energies and symbolic colours of the Tree of Life. Angel himself had no knowledge of the Qabalah. One of his works he spontaneously titled *The Tree of Life*, while ignorant of the fact that this title was a central motif in the Jewish mysteries.

More recently in the United States, particularly since the psychedelic phase when hallucinatory drugs provided new access into the occult regions of the mind, a new pattern of cosmic art has emerged. Especially interesting are the mandalas of Jose and Miriam Arguelles, Dion Wright and Roberto Matiello. The work of Abdul Mati Klarwein has also attracted considerable attention, partly because his psychedelic illustrations have appeared on the covers of several of Miles Davis's jazz album covers. His work is vivid and tantric and like that of Spare shows both a Qabalistic leaning, and also a marked sexuality.

SOURCEBOOKS

JOHN MILNER: *Symbolists and Decadents*, Studio Vista, London, 1971.
  A short, concise account of the Symbolist school of art, popular in
  France, Germany, Austria and England in the 1880s. Contains interesting
  references to figures like Sar Péladan, the 'Rosicrucian' writer/art critic/
  occultist, Eliphas Lévi and other fashionables of the period.

General books on Surrealism, and specific artists of the period, include:
SOREN ALEXANDRIAN: *Surrealist Art*, Thames & Hudson, London, 1970.
MAURICE NADEAU: *A History of Surrealism*, Cape, London, 1968 and Penguin,
  1973.
JOHN RUSSELL: *Max Ernst*, Thames & Hudson, London, and Abrams, New
  York, 1967.
PATRICK WALDBERG: *Surrealism*, Thames & Hudson, London, 1965.
DAVID LARKIN (ed.): *The Fantastic Kingdom, Fantastic Art, Salvador Dali*,
  Pan Books, London, and Ballantine, New York 1973-4.
  Larkin's books are strongly recommended as excellent visual surveys of
  the surrealist and phantasy elements in modern art and book illustration.
KENNETH GRANT: *Images and Oracles of Austin Osman Spare*, Muller, London,
  1974.
MULLER, *The Magical Revival*, London, 1972.
  Grant knew Spare personally, and became his literary executor on the
  artist's death in 1956. Grant is himself the head of the OTO in England, a
  tantric group, and he tends to overstress this aspect in his analysis.

Nevertheless, Grant is the undisputed authority on Spare, and has brought together all the diverse strands of Spare's curious genius, in his long-awaited new volume on the artist.

AUSTIN O. SPARE: *A Book of Automatic Drawings*, Catalpa Press, London 1973 (limited edition 1000 copies).

An anthology of Spare's free-form automatic drawings c. 1925. These show macabre occult elements, but already his draughtsmanship had been seriously eroded by his obsessive influences. Spare's best work is contained in his *The Book of Pleasure*, which has been republished by 93 Publishing Co., Montreal, 1975.

NEVILL DRURY and STEPHEN SKINNER: *The Search for Abraxas*, Spearman, London, 1972.

Includes a chapter on Austin Spare and his method of formulating 'sigils'. Also details of the relationship of surrealist painting to the Qabalistic Tree of Life.

WALTER GLOVER: *The Art of Rosaleen Norton*, Sydney 1952 (limited edition 1000 copies).

Scarce, but the only volume of Norton's work, with notes on some of the chief demonic influences, and poems by Gavin Greenlees.

BARRIE NEVILLE: 'The Trance Art of Victor Angel', in N. Drury (ed.), *Frontiers of Consciousness*, Greenhouse Press, Melbourne, 1975.

A major account of Angel's background, and a detailed analysis of the Qabalistic content of his trance paintings.

JOSE AND MIRIAM ARGUELLES: *Mandala*, Shambala, Berkeley and London, 1972.

ABDUL MATI KLARWEIN: *Milk N' Honey*, Harmony Books, New York, 1973.

ABDUL MATI KLARWEIN: *God Jokes*, Harmony Books, New York, 1977.

The above volumes contain some of the most remarkable cosmic and psychedelic art yet to appear.

PAUL WALDO-SCHWARTZ: *Art and the Occult*, Braziller, New York, 1975, Allen & Unwin, London, 1975.

An interesting overview of the fusion between occultism and modern art, including references to occultists like Aleister Crowley. Limited unfortunately by its omission of the contemporary phantasy illustrators and psychedelic artists.

NEVILL DRURY: *The Textures of Vision: Explorations in Magical Consciousness*, Routledge & Kegan Paul, London, forthcoming.

A study of the major surrealists, psychedelic artists and phantasy illustrators including those with major mythological or magical impact such as Ernst, Magritte, Lam, Dali, Satty, Klarwein, Dean, Giger, Vandenberg and Johfra. Also includes a detailed analysis of the mythology of the Tarot.

Part

2

Who's Who in the Occult

Who's Who in the Occult

CORNELIUS AGRIPPA (1486–1535)
Henry Cornelius Agrippa Von Nettesheims was born of noble parentage in Cologne. From an early age he showed that he had a flair for languages and the classics. Agrippa became an attendant to Maximilian I and later entered the German secret service, spying on the French while studying at Paris University. But it was here that he also encountered mystics and Rosicrucians and became vitally interested in the Qabalah and Hermeticism. His famous work *De Occulta Philosopha* was very influential in its day as a key magical text and deals especially with divine names, natural magic and cosmology. Rumour has it that Agrippa possessed a magic mirror in which he could divine future events and his familiar, a large black dog, was said to follow him wherever he went.

ROLLO AHMED
An Egyptian magician and author living in England, associated with Aleister Crowley (qv) and Dennis Wheatley (qv), he was raised in Guiana (West Indies) and became involved in black magic in England, eventually rejecting it and establishing himself as an authority on the occult. He is the author of *The Black Art* (John Long, London, 1936), which has been reprinted several times, and remains of considerable interest. Ahmed, who is especially interested in Raja Yoga, has travelled widely throughout Europe, Africa, Asia and South America studying religion and the occult.

ALBERTUS MAGNUS (1205–80)
Albertus was born in the town of Larvigen on the Danube. Regarded by his contemporaries as a major alchemist and theologian, he attributed much of his vitality to visionary inspiration from the Virgin Mary. He became Bishop of Ratisbon, but was not an orthodox cleric. Some of his colleagues whispered among themselves that he communicated with the devil, and he

himself claimed to have magic control over the weather. He is best known as an adept who discovered the Philosopher's Stone, and states in his work *De Rebus Metallis et Mineralibus* that he had conducted tests on alchemical gold. Several other books on magic, love philtres and curious superstitions have been wrongly ascribed to him.

KENNETH ANGER

An American underground film-maker who was involved in the occult in the United States, and was inspired by his involvement to make the film *Lord Shiva's Dream*, an occult psychedelic spectacular, the initials of which form LSD. He was also involved in the original magical group run by Anton La Vey which eventually developed into the Church of Satan. Anger's films are bizarre, difficult to understand and embody a wide range of elements of sexuality, violence, magic and the occult, drugs, rock culture and all manner of obsessive images. At one stage Anger proclaimed himself a member of Crowley's Thelema cult. His films have included: *Invocation for my Brother Demon, Inauguration of the Pleasure Dome, Fireworks, Heatwave or Devil in Disguise.* Anger was in part responsible for the uncovering of the erotic paintings in the Abbey of Thelema, in Sicily, remaining from the time of Crowley's occupation.

GEORGE ARUNDALE (1878–1945)

An English theosophist and associate of Annie Besant (qv) and Charles Leadbeater (qv), Arundale joined the Theosophical Society in 1895, and in 1903 went to India as Professor of History at the Central Hindu College, being elected Principal in 1909. He resigned in 1913 to become tutor to Krishnamurti (qv). He returned to India in 1917 and supported Mrs Besant in her campaign for home rule. He rapidly rose in the ranks of the TS and eventually became President in 1934.

SRI AUROBINDO (1872–1950)

An Indian mystic, philosopher and poet. His philosophy, known as 'integral yoga' is being followed by many converts throughout the world, and is said to be the beginning of a new world religion. He began his career with a classics degree from Cambridge, and returning to India became the leader of the extremist faction of the nationalists, advocating armed revolt, and was eventually jailed. Turning from politics to mysticism, he studied the traditional forms of yoga, and eventually synthesized them into his new philosophy of *purna* (integral) yoga. He developed a community of his disciples at Pondicherry, and after his death the community built a new city, Auroville, on the Bay of Bengal, which is intended to be a self-sufficient city state based entirely on his principles. Mira Richard, the wife of a French diplomat who met Aurobindo in 1914, took over the leadership after his death, supervising the building of Auroville, and founding the Sri Aurobindo Society in 1960. She died in 1974 at the age of ninety-five, but the community has continued to grow.

MARCUS BACH

An American psychic researcher and author, and authority on comparative religion. He heads the Foundation for Spiritual Understanding and is a leader of the Spiritual Frontiers Fellowship. He was previously a professor of comparative religion at the University of Iowa. He has written numerous books, including *They Found a Faith*, *Will to Believe*, *Strange Altars* and *The Inner Ecstasy*.

ALICE BAILEY (1880–1949)

An English writer on theosophy and mysticism, who founded the 'Arcane School'. After a period of activity in the Theosophical Society, she left to pursue an independent course. Believing she had contacted several 'Masters' on the inner planes, Mrs Bailey was a prolific author, many of her books deriving their ideas, so she said, from these Masters. After her death in 1949 her organization was carried on by her husband. Today the twenty-four volumes of her writings are published by the Lucis Publishing Companies in the United States, England and Switzerland, and her teachings are perpetuated by The Arcane School which she founded in 1923, and which is conducted throughout the world by correspondence. Several other organizations – including 'Triangles' and 'World Goodwill' – exist to carry on various aspects of her work. Her *Unfinished Autobiography* was published in 1951.

FRANZ BARDON

Little known outside specialist occult circles, Austrian writer and magician, Franz Bardon has authored three important books *Initiation into Hermetics*, *The Practice of Magical Evocation*, and *The Key to the True Quabalah*. Bardon's work has the same pragmatic stamp as Aleister Crowley's, and his second book contains the magical sigils and descriptions of the entire pantheon of spirits and elementals of the astral world.

FRANCIS BARRETT

Apart from the possibility that Francis Barrett may have been connected with Bulwer-Lytton, who was himself an initiate and occultist, little is known of Barrett's life and magical interests. In 1801 he published *The*

Magus, complete with illustrations of devils like Theulus and Asmodeus, which was described as 'The Celestial Intelligencer', being a complete system of occult philosophy. His work encompasses the symbolism of magical stones, numerology, alchemy and Qabalistic magic.

ALAN BENNETT (1872–1923)

Bennett, known in the Hermetic Order of the Golden Dawn as Frater Iehi Aour, was none other than Aleister Crowley's tutor in the magical arts. Bennett was originally absorbed in ceremonial magic, and wrote the powerful evocation of Taphthartharath, used for manifesting a spirit of Mercury into visible appearance. He also compiled part of the exhaustive magical reference system *777* which was later published by Crowley.

Eventually Bennett tired of magic, and in 1900 he left England for Ceylon where he became a worshipper of Shiva, and assumed the title Bhikku Ananda Metteya. Later he joined a Buddhist monastery in Burma.

PIERRE BERNARD

Known as 'Oom the Omnipotent', Bernard was probably the first person to introduce the teachings of Tantric sex magic to the West publicly. He began teaching Hatha Yoga in the USA in 1909 at his own 'New York Sanskrit College', where the first of a series of sexual charges was made against him by young girls under his tuition. After marrying a vaudeville dancer, he developed a system combining Hatha Yoga, dancing and Tantra Yoga, which he called a 'Tantric health system'. Bernard acquired a number of very wealthy disciples, founded the Sacred Order of Tantriks, and opened the 'Brae Burn Club', an occult college in New Jersey, where he performed a variety of strange rituals.

ANNIE BESANT (1847–1933)

An English Theosophist and social reformer, who became the second President of the Theosophical Society in 1891. She was actively involved in various social movements throughout her life, ranging from feminist causes and the advocacy of birth control, to the Fabian Society, Home Rule for India and the Boy Scout movement. Having been an outspoken atheist, she was converted to the Theosophical view by Madame Blavatsky (qv) in 1889, and rapidly rose in the Society, achieving a widespread reputation as a lecturer and author. She was closely associated with Charles Leadbeater (qv) in the sponsoring of Jiddu Krishnamurti (qv) as the new world teacher, and was involved in the Order of the Star in the East which propagated that claim. Dr Besant was also a leader of the Co-Masonic movement, a group of Freemasons originating in France and admitting

WHO'S WHO IN THE OCCULT

women as well as men. She wrote prolifically, her most important Theoso-phical work being *The Ancient Wisdom* (1897), a summary of Theosophy. She also wrote widely on other subjects, and published her *Autobiography* in 1893. Cf. *The First Five Lives of Annie Besant* and *The Last Four Lives of Annie Besant*, both by A. H. Nethercott.

ALGERNON BLACKWOOD (1869–1959)
Blackwood grew up in the Black Forest and later attended Edinburgh University. A one-time member of the Order of the Golden Dawn, Blackwood was a journalist for the *New York Times*, and later wrote occult and mystical short stories with an authentic flair. Among his most signifi-cant magical anthologies are *John Silence* (1922); *Selected Tales* (1943) and *Pan's Garden* (1914).

HELENA PETROVNA BLAVATSKY (1831–91)
A Russian mystic and adventuress, who founded the Theosophical Society in 1875. After a life of adventure and travel, she claimed to have been contacted by 'Mahatmas', or 'Masters', who inspired her to found the Society, and to write several books laying the foundations of Theosophy. She also claimed these Masters helped her to perform supernatural events; others claimed these were the result of trickery. Her main works were *Isis Unveiled* (1877) and *The Secret Doctrine* (1888), and she also wrote a series of smaller books. Probably more than any other figure, this enigmatical and mysterious woman has influenced contemporary occultism, albeit in indirect ways; there is no doubt that she was a powerful medium, and possessed psychic powers. She sought to synthesize Eastern and Western philosophy and religion, and science and religion, but her rather ponderous style and the incredible detail of her two main books makes their analysis extremely difficult. Madame Blavatsky was involved in a number of other occult movements, including an unorthodox branch of Freemasonry. Cf. *Madame Blavatsky: Medium and Magician* by John Symonds.

ELEANOR BONE
Together with Patricia Crowther (qv) and Monique Wilson, Mrs Bone was one of the heirs to the estate of Gerald Gardner (qv). She has obtained a considerable amount of press publicity, and claimed to be a spokesman for the witchcraft movement. Her husband, Raymond Bone, shares her witchcraft interests.

ISAAC BONEWITS
Awarded a degree in magic from UCLA, Bonewits claims to be the first

201

'academically accredited magician'. He is the author of *Real Magic*, and the founder of the Aquarian Anti-Defamation League in the USA. He is currently the associate editor of the American occult magazine *Gnostica News*.

RAYMOND BUCKLAND

An American witch, who operates a coven in Long Island with his wife, having joined the Gardnerian tradition of witchcraft after corresponding with Gerald Gardner (qv) and joining one of his covens. They now claim the leadership of eighteen American covens and operate a witchcraft museum. Buckland claims a degree of Doctor of Philosophy, and is often stated to be an anthropologist, although he reportedly works as a travel brochure editor for an airline. He is the author of a number of books on witchcraft, including *Witchcraft from the Inside* and *Practical Candle Burning*.

EDWARD BULWER-LYTTON (1803–73)

Best known for his book *The Last Days of Pompeii*, the once popular Bulwer-Lytton considered his most significant books to be those with a strong occult theme. These included *Zanoni*, a novel modelled on the Comte de Saint Germain, and *A Strange Story*. He studied at Cambridge, and on several occasions entertained the French magician Eliphas Lévi at Knebworth, his family residence. Bulwer-Lytton was at one time the honorary Grand Patron of the Societies Rosicruciana in Anglia, a predecessor of the Golden Dawn. It is said that he and Lévi exchanged magical secrets, and Bishop Wedgwood of the Liberal Catholic Church believed that Bulwer-Lytton was one of a long line of Rosicrucian initiates.

W. E. BUTLER

A leading English authority on magic and the occult, who trained as a member of Dion Fortune's (qv) 'Fraternity of the Inner Light', and also under the English psychic, Robert King. Butler has written extensively on the Western magical tradition, and acquired a reputation as a highly skilled lecturer and teacher. His books include: *Magic, its ritual, purpose and power*, *The Magician, his training and work*, *Apprenticed to Magic*, *Magic and the Qabalah*. He has established a magical school, 'The Servants of the Light' which offers an extremely good correspondence course in magic and the Qabalah.

ALESSANDRO DI CAGLIOSTRO (1743–95)

Regarded by Carlyle as 'The Prince of Quacks', Cagliostro, whose real name was Guiseppe Balsamo, was a traveller and something of an occult poseur. One of Cagliostro's early trickeries was to dupe a superstitious goldsmith named Marano over some hidden treasures which could be located by ceremonial magic. He escaped to Messina, where he met a mysterious, eccentric occultist named Althotas, who claimed to be a magician of natural law and an alchemist. They travelled together to Alexandria and Rhodes and later pursued further alchemical experiments with Grand-master Pinto on Malta. Pinto's sponsorship allowed the Count Cagliostro, as he was now known, to live in wealth and, returning to Italy, he married Lorenza Feliciani, whose father was dazzled by Cagliostro's opulence. Their stormy marriage took them to Madrid, Lisbon, London, and eventually Paris. Cagliostro gained something of a reputation as an alchemist in the courts of Europe at a time when princes and kings were keen to keep extra gold in their coffers. He later returned to London and was initiated into Freemasonry, subsequently making the acquaintance of the legendary Comte de Saint Germain. Cagliostro was infatuated with the Egyptian origins of Freemasonry, however, and he continued travelling around Europe as an occultist and resident magician-cum-faith healer. He was quite often paid as much as 100 louis for his consultations.

Subsequently Cagliostro became involved in the famous Diamond Necklace affair, and was eventually charged by Mme de Lamotte of conspiring to steal the necklace. He succeeded in enticing the judges with his eloquence and was discharged. But his luck ran out in Rome when he was arrested on the grounds that Masonry was a heresy. His life sentence was commuted to life imprisonment by the Pope in 1791, and Cagliostro spent the rest of his years in the Castle of San Leo near Montefeltro.

ALEXANDER CANNON
A highly qualified physician and scientist who developed an interest in magic, the occult and psychic phenomena whilst travelling in India, and became an author and student of psychiatry and hypnosis. He produced a number of odd inventions, including a high power 400,000 volt static electricity machine for de-possessing people, a psychograph or thought-reading machine and a 'Hypnoscope'. His books include *The Invisible Influence* and *Powers that Be*.

PAUL FOSTER CASE (d. 1954)
An American occultist and magician who founded the 'Builders of the Adytum', centred in California and deriving from the traditions of the Order of the Golden Dawn, and which was centred largely on the Tarot Cards. Case was the author of several books on this subject including

Highlights of the Tarot, The Tarot and *The Book of Tokens*. He claimed to have been the head of the Order of the Golden Dawn for the United States and to have received personal revelations from the Masters who constituted the 'Inner School' of that Order. The BOTA has its Temple in Los Angeles and operates largely by correspondence lessons. Its present Head is Dr Ann Davies, who succeeded Case when, so the BOTA says, he 'graduated to the Inner School'.

CARLOS CASTANEDA (1925–   )
While studying at the University of California, Carlos Castaneda made the acquaintance of an old Yaqui Indian named Don Juan Matus. Don Juan allowed Castaneda to become his pupil in shamanism and sorcery, and Castaneda's books are a remarkably lucid account of Don Juan's ritual practices and philosophy of perception. Castaneda's first book *The Teachings of Don Juan* (*1968*) attracted considerable attention among the American sub-culture, partly because of its vivid descriptions of hallucinogenic states of awareness. Castaneda describes how he transformed into a crow and flew through the air, in a manner reminiscent of the classical Greek shaman Aristeas of Proconnesus. Castaneda now regards his apprenticeship in sorcery as most significantly providing a new vision for perceiving the ordinary world. His other books include *A Separate Reality*, *Journey to Ixtlan*, *Tales of Power* and *The Second Ring of Power*. They represent perhaps one of the most significant encounters of alien intellects in the history of anthropology.

RICHARD CAVENDISH (1930–   )
A leading authority on magic and witchcraft, Cavendish was educated at Oxford, and has written and lectured extensively. He is the author of *The Black Arts*, a study of black magic, and the editor of the encyclopedia *Man, Myth and Magic*.

EDGAR CAYCE (1877–1945)
An American psychic and healer, born in Kentucky and the son of a farmer, Cayce received a limited education, but found later in his life he could go into a trance and diagnose other people's illness, and prescribe treatment. He also claimed to be able to describe former incarnations, and thus came to hold, contrary to his religious upbringing, the theory of reincarnation. His readings, given while in a trance, have been recorded and kept, and in 1931 the Association for Research and Enlightenment was formed to collate and utilize them. Although Cayce wrote comparatively little himself, numerous volumes have been written about him, and compiled from his readings. Cf. J. Millard, *Edgar Cayce, Man of Miracles* and J. Stearn, *Edgar Cayce – The Sleeping Prophet*.

'CHEIRO'

Count Louis Harmon, one of the world's most famous palmists and occultists, who achieved a reputation amongst the rich and the notable who flocked to him for readings. His reputation was enhanced by his prolific writing, and his books include: *You and Your Hand, Language of the Hand*, and his memoirs, *Confessions of a Modern Seer*.

R. SWINBURNE CLYMER

An American occultist who claimed to have succeeded P. B. Randolph (qv), and operated a number of allegedly Rosicrucian organizations in the USA. He headed a range of groups including 'The Sons of Isis and Osiris', 'The College of the Holy Grail', 'The Church of the Illumination' and 'The Rosicrucian Fraternity'. Clymer had a puritanical attitude towards sexual matters and fervently denied all claims that Randolph had taught sexual magic. His main books are *The Philosophy of Fire, A Compendium of Occult Laws, Ancient Mystical Oriental Masonry* and *Mysteries of Osiris*.

ALEISTER CROWLEY (1875–1947)

Probably the most famous occultist of the twentieth century, self-styled 'The Great Beast'. He was the author of numerous key works on magic, including *Magick in Theory and Practice* (1929) and *The Book of Thoth* (1944). See also pp. 82–7.

PATRICIA CROWTHER

An English witch, who with Eleanor Bone (qv) and Monique Wilson, was heir to the estate of Gerald Gardner (qv). She has received a considerable amount of publicity as the result of her witchcraft activity. She published her autobiography, *Witchblood* in 1974.

LOUIS T. CULLING

An American magician, who was originally a member of the GBG (said to stand for various titles, including the 'Great Brotherhood of God'), led by C. F. Russell, a disciple of Crowley (qv), but who eventually left that body, of which he had become 'Neighbourhood Primate', for the San Diego Lodge (1937). Until his recent death. Culling continued to operate at least one lodge in the traditions of the GBG, practising a variety of sexual magic, somewhat in accordance with the traditions of the Ordo Templi Orientis and Crowley's own teachings. Culling has published a number of books, including *The Complete Magickal Curriculum of the Secret Order G.B.G.* (1969), *The Incredible I Ching* and *A Manual of Sex Magick*.

SIR FRANCIS DASHWOOD (1708–81)

Dashwood, one time Chancellor of the Exchequer, is best known for his notorious 'Hell-Fire' club, at Medmenham Abbey in Buckinghamshire. His monks and nuns travelled by boat to the abbey and made use of a series of underground passages beneath the Abbey that were supposed to imitate the entrance to Hell.

Mostly the rituals were a sexual orgy combining drunken revelry with a parody of the Mass. Dashwood's 'Hell-Fire' caverns still exist and are open to the public.

ANDREW JACKSON DAVIS (1826–1910)

Known as the 'seer of Poughkeepsie' Davis was an American psychic and healer. He was heavily influenced both by Swedenborg and Mesmerism (qv), and wrote extensively on the basis of his clairvoyant visions, becoming one of the leading theorists of the young American spiritualist movement. His main work was *The Principles of Nature* (1847) in which he presented his peculiar cosmology, mixed with mysticism and socialist politics.

DR JOHN DEE (1527–1608)

Classical scholar, philosopher, mathematician and astrologer, John Dee began his career as an academic at Cambridge and travelled widely in Europe. Following a meeting with one Jerome Cardan in England in 1552, he became interested in the conjuration of spirits, and when Elizabeth I came to the throne, he was invited to calculate the most beneficial astrological date for her coronation. Dee again travelled extensively on the Continent – visiting Antwerp, Zurich and Venice. His magical career really begins however, in 1581, when he met Edward Kelley, who was both a medium and a 'skryer', that is, one who can communicate with angels and spirits. Kelley, who is said to have had his ears cropped on account of committing forgery, possessed an alchemical manuscript and Dee was especially interested in Kelley's alchemical secrets.

Dee and Kelley made use of wax tablets (called 'almadels') engraved with magical symbols and the sacred names of God. The tablet for a given invocation was to be laid between four candles, and it was then that an angel would appear. Eventually the angels began to dictate the types of magical equipment to be used, and in 1582 Edward Kelley began to receive messages in a new angelic language called Enochian. These Enochian communications were calls from the angels of the Thirty Aethyrs, and were later tested ceremonially by Aleister Crowley and Victor Neuburg with surprising results.

A dictionary of Enochian was recently published in the United States by Israel Regardie.

JEANE DIXON

An American psychic who has achieved a great deal of publicity for her predictions regarding national and international events, she is a practising Catholic and a regular church attender. She claims to have predicted the assassinations of President Kennedy, Martin Luther King and Senator Robert Kennedy. While she has accurately predicted a number of world-wide events, and even more of importance in the United States she has made an even larger number of predictions which have simply never been fulfilled. In addition to simply 'feeling' events will occur, Mrs Dixon uses cards, a crystal ball, astrology and numerology as methods of divination. She has written of her own history in *My Life and Prophecies* (1970) and Ruth Montgomery has published a study of her, *A Gift of Prophecy* (1966).

HARRY EDWARDS (1893–)

A British Spiritualist and healer who has acquired world-wide fame in the course of many years healing work, beginning in the 1930s. He has claimed to cure even 'incurable' diseases, both through direct and absent healing, centred in his 'Sanctuary' at Shere, Surrey, England. He said this healing was accomplished through the controls of several Red Indians, Pasteur and Lord Lister. He has published a number of books on spiritualist healing, including *Spirit Healing* (1960) and *The Power of Spiritual Healing* (1963).

FLORENCE FARR

Actress and mistress to George Bernard Shaw, Florence Farr was introduced to magic in the Isis-Urania Temple, by W. B. Yeats. She tired of MacGregor Mathers' autocratic tendencies with the Order of the Golden Dawn, and eventually formed her own group, 'The Sphere'. Her most significant contribution to magic was perhaps a volume entitled *Egyptian Magic*, which relates several key Egyptian texts and invocations to the modern magical tradition.

J. ARTHUR FINDLAY (1883–1964)

An English spiritualist and author, founder of the Glasgow Society for Psychic Research, and co-founder of Psychic Press Ltd, which publishes *Psychic News*. He spent many years investigating spiritualist phenomena and wrote widely on the subject. His best known book was *On the Edge of the Etheric*, which ran into sixty editions.

ARTHUR FORD (d. 1971)

A well-known American spiritualist and medium, member of the American Society for Psychical Research and an ordained minister of the Disciples of

Christ since 1923. His psychic experiences began during World War I. Although he began his career through a meeting with Sir Arthur Conan Doyle, it was for his association with the controversial Episcopalian clergyman, Bishop Pike, that he attained much of his fame. The Bishop consulted Ford after the death of his son, Jim, and believed Ford made contact with the young man's spirit. Pike wrote a book, *The Other Side*, recounting his experiences with Ford. Ford was also involved in the notable 'Houdini case' in which he claimed to have contacted the conjurer's spirit and broken the secret code which Houdini had left to test proofs of survival. Charges of fraud were levelled against him as a result, and the whole matter eventually subsided after a great deal of unpleasant publicity. Ill-health forced Ford to retire, and he died in 1971. With M. H. Bro he wrote *Nothing so Strange*.

DION FORTUNE (1891–1946)

Dion Fortune, whose real name was Violet Firth, was born in England and grew up in a household where the teachings of Christian Science were rigorously practised. When she was twenty, she suffered a serious nervous breakdown, and as she recovered she found herself motivated to study psychology and also the occult. She joined the Theosophical Society and meanwhile took courses in psychoanalysis at London University. In 1919 she became a member of the Order of the Golden Dawn and began to write occult fiction based on her understanding of magic and the astral world. Dion Fortune came into conflict with Mrs Mathers, wife of one of the co-founders of the Order, and claims that she was subject to 'magical attack'. In 1924 she established the Society of the Inner Light with her husband Penry Evans, himself both a doctor and an occultist.

In her later years, Dion Fortune was flamboyant and exotic. Kenneth Grant recalls that she 'wore rich jewels beneath a flowing cloak, and on rare occasions when she went out, a broad-rimmed hat from which her sun-glinting hair sometimes strayed and fluffed about like a golden numbus.' She died shortly after World War II, leaving behind a legacy of writings, most of which present a clear common-sense approach to the occult. Her book *The Mystical Qabalah* is regarded by many occultists as one of the best textbooks on magic ever written.

OLIVER FOX

Oliver Fox was one of the first pioneers in the area of controlled out-of-the-body experiences, or 'astral projection'. He considered one of the best methods of projection to be the 'Dream of Knowledge', by which he meant acquiring consciousness in the dream state. His personal account of these practices was published in the *English Occult Review* in 1920, and in popular book form by University Books, New York, in 1962. Dr Hereward Carrington, one of the foremost experts in this occult field considered Fox's account to be 'the only detailed, scientific and first-hand account of a series of conscious and voluntarily controlled astral projections which I have ever come across . . .'. Fox's work on out-of-the-body experiences has done much to shape the current research of parapsychologists like Dr Charles Tart (qv) of UCLA, and Celia Green (qv) of Oxford.

FULCANELLI

A mysterious and semi-legendary alchemist, Fulcanelli is said to be one of the only serious researchers to pursue the *magnum opus*, or Philosopher's Stone, this century. In the early 1920s a French student of alchemy named Eugene Canseliet was given a manuscript by his mentor, a man now referred to as Fulcanelli. The book, *The Mystery of the Cathedrals* caused a sensation in esoteric circles when it was first published in Paris in 1926. Basically it expounded the alchemical symbolism carved in the decorative motifs on the Gothic cathedrals in Bourges, Amiens and Paris.

Fulcanelli suddenly disappeared and for many years appeared to have vanished without any trace whatever. Canseliet claims however that years later he saw him briefly when he should have been around 110 years old and 'he looked not older than I was myself' (around 50).

Some consider that Fulcanelli found the great alchemical secret of eternal youth, and that like Comte de Saint Germain, age appeared to be no barrier to him.

GERALD BROUSSEAU GARDNER (1884–1964)

An Englishman who has become known as the 'Father of modern witch-craft', Gardner spent much of his life in the Far East as a rubber planter and customs official. He was especially interested in primitive religion, magic and mythology, and on his return to England claimed to have con-tacted a surviving witchcraft coven in the New Forest, which he joined, and for which he subsequently became a sort of public relations officer. His first book was *High Magick's Aid*, a novel about witchcraft, and this was followed by two non-fiction works, *Witchcraft Today* (1954) and *The Meaning of Witchcraft* (1959), in which he claims to have revealed many of the teachings of traditional witchcraft as continued in its modern succes-sors. Gardner was characterized by his interest in the naked body, a taste for sado-masochism and marked voyeuristic tendencies; these also characterize the witchcraft groups which derive from him. He was also involved in the Ordo Templi Orientis, and is said to have employed

Crowley (qv) to write rituals for his witchcraft movement. Gardner laid claim to several academic degrees, and spoke of himself as an anthropologist. However there is no evidence to substantiate this. Cf. *Gerald Gardner: Witch* by Jack Bracelin (1960).

URI GELLER

Uri Geller, the young Israeli psychic, has recently become famous for his strange faculty for bending forks and stopping watches under will. Scientists at the Max Planck Institute in Germany, and Stanford in the United States have found his apparently magnetic faculties difficult to account for. Geller is able to produce his effects both in the laboratory and in front of large TV audiences. Geller is not merely another psychic however; he claims that his power derives from an extraterrestrial source. According to Andrija Puharich, who compiled the first biography on Geller, the ESP power comes from nine UFO entities 'whose souls have transformed into computers'. These computer beings are said to be using him as a mouthpiece until they commence an invasion of the planet, and to select him they undertook a computer analysis of the whole of mankind.

The case of Uri Geller appears to contain elements of both fact and fantasy. Geller's extrasensory abilities appear to be beyond reproach, but his extraterrestrial allies seem often to reflect Geller's own nationalistic fervour and wishful thinking. This part of his account at least, seems open to question. Cf. *Uri* by Andrija Puharich (1974).

KARL GERMER (1885–1962)

German-born Karl Germer became the head of the sex magic Ordo Templi Orientis following the death of Aleister Crowley in 1947. Germer was very much a follower of Crowley and accepted his mentor's claim to be the Lord of the New Aeon. He was responsible for the publication of some of Crowley's obscure works like *Magick Without Tears*. While in the OTO he took the magical name of Frater Saturnus.

JOAN GRANT (1907–)

An English authoress and writer on the subject of reincarnation, who claims to be able to recall her former incarnations, an ability she refers to as 'far memory'.

She has written a series of semi-fictional works recounting in detail individual previous incarnations, from the Egyptian period through to the Middle Ages, and pre-Columban America. In conjunction with Dennis Kelsey, a psychiatrist, she developed techniques of employing 'far memory' as a psychiatric technique for the diagnosis and treatment of various psychological disorders. They also developed various theories to explain these techniques and summarized them in their joint book *Many Lifetimes* (1968), a study of reincarnation and the origins of mental illness. Mrs Grant has written extensively, her best known works being: *Winged Pharaoh, Life as Carola, Eyes of Horus, Lord of the Horizon, Return to Elysium* and *So Moses was Born* – all being accounts of previous incarnations. Her autobiographical works include *Time out of Mind* and *A Lot to Remember*.

KENNETH GRANT (1924–   )

Following the death of Aleister Crowley, Kenneth Grant continued as a practising devotee of Crowley's Law of Thelema and in 1955 set up his own Isis Lodge in England. Grant follows the form of magic pursued by Crowley after the latter's Egyptian initiation in 1904. Crowley claimed to be the divine offspring of the Egyptian gods Nu and Hadit, and the successor to Jesus Christ.

Much of Grant's interest has its focus in sex magic – the ritual union of opposites. He is also an authority on the great trance artist-magician Austin Spare and is the author of a definitive treatise on him titled *Images and Oracles of Austin Osman Spare* (1975).

WILLIAM G. GRAY

A modern ritual magician and author, whose works include *The Ladder of Lights, Inner Traditions of Magic* and *Seasonal Occult Rituals*. He is considered by Israel Regardie (qv) to be the best modern author on occult matters.

CELIA GREEN

The present Director of the Institute of Psychophysical Research, Oxford, Celia Green has been largely responsible for the revival of interest among British psychologists in out-of-the-body states of consciousness, and 'lucid dreams'. The documented evidence in her book *Out of the Body Experiences* continued the view of pioneers like Oliver Fox and Sylvan Muldoon, that 'astral projection' was a natural function of the mind, and could be achieved at will.

STANISLAS DE GUAITA (1861–97)

De Guaita, born of a distinguished Lombardy family, was one of the main figures behind the fashionable Rosicrucian revival in the salons of Paris in the 1890s. Together with Sar Peladan he founded the 'Ordre de la Rose-Croix Kaballistique'. De Guaita was a published poet and a student of law, but after reading the works of Eliphas Lévi he devoted himself completely to ritual and the occult.

MANLY PALMER HALL

An American author and student of the occult, he founded the Philosophical Research Society in Los Angeles in 1936. He is a prolific author on virtually all aspects of occultism and the esoteric tradition. His books include: *The Secret Teachings of All Ages, Man, the Grand Symbol of the Mysteries, Codex Rosae Crucis* and *Twelve World Teachers*. In all he has written thirty-five books, hundreds of articles and delivered thousands of lectures.

FRANZ HARTMANN (1838–1912)

A German occultist, theosophist and physician who spent many years in the United States. His books include: *Magic Black and White, Occult Science and Medicine, Life of Paracelsus, Life of Jehoshua*.

Hartmann was the founder of the 'Order of the Esoteric Rose Croix' and was connected with Engel's 'Order of the Illuminati', and with John Yarker's masonic group. He was also involved with Reuss (qv) and another German named Klein in an occult group which eventually developed into the Ordo Templi Orientis.

MAX HEINDEL (d. 1919)

The name under which Max Grashof wrote. He was a member of that group of Theosophists in the United States led by Katherine Tingley, and was heavily influenced by Rudolf Steiner (qv) (whose personal student he had been). Heindel claimed he had been initiated into the traditional Rosicrucian Order in Germany, and as a result founded the Rosicrucian Fellowship in California, and published numerous books on Rosicrucian teachings, including *The Rosicrucian Cosmo-conception*. He was especially interested in astrology. After his death the Fellowship, in part torn by internal quarrels, was led by his wife, Augusta Foss Heindel, who died in 1938.

ADOLPH HITLER (1889–1945)

It is claimed by many theorists that Hitler was deeply involved in the occult, and could have been a 'front man' for an inner occult group which actually controlled the Nazi Party. Various authors have also suggested that Hitler's power over the German people was based at least in part on his possession of occult gifts and being capable of predicting the future.

There were a number of occult and magical groups operating in Germany at the time – the Order of the New Templars, the Germanen Order, the Vril Society, the Thule Group – and links with Hitler and other high-ranking officials of the Party have been established. Even the use of the swastika, traditionally the sign of the power of light, but reversed, as in Nazi usage, to symbolize the power of darkness, suggests an occult link. Cf. *Occult Reich* by J. H. Brennan (1974). Also *The Spear of Destiny* by T. Ravenscroft (1972) and *Gods and Beasts* by D. Sklar (1977).

HANS HOLZER
An American author and psychic researcher who has written extensively on a wide range of occult and psychic phenomena and groups. Trained as a journalist, and educated at the Universities of Vienna and Columbia, he subsequently specialized in investigating and writing about psychic subjects, ESP and healing. Additionally, he has narrated several film documentaries. His best known books include *ESP and You*, *The Truth about Witchcraft*, *Psychic Photography : Threshold of a New Science* and *The New Pagans*.

HARRY HOUDINI (1874–1926)
The famous stage magician and escape artist who, being highly critical of spiritualism, took part in a number of investigations of alleged 'phenomena'.

Prior to his death he made a secret pact with his wife to try to return and communicate a message to her in code; she attended a number of seances in the hope of receiving the appropriate message, and in 1929 it was claimed she had received it via the mediumship of Arthur Ford (qv). This was followed by claims and counter-claims of fraud, and the matter was never satisfactorily resolved. It has been suggested that Houdini was unconsciously possessed of psychic powers and that some of the more difficult feats he managed on stage were thereby made possible. He, needless to say, fervently denied this. He wrote extensively on his exposures of spiritualists; see his *Miracle Mongers and their Methods* (1920). Cf. *Houdini: The Untold Story* by M. Christopher (1969).

LAFAYETTE RONALD HUBBARD (1911–)
The founder and leader of the Scientology movement and author of numerous books on that subject. Hubbard began his career as a science fiction author, but eventually discovered a technique which he called 'Dianetics', later developing an additional philosophy called 'Scientology', and establishing a movement, which eventually spread throughout the world, to propagate both.

Hubbard claims to possess a wide range of extrasensory powers and through these says he gained the information used in dianetics and scientology, including details of the reincarnational history of man, the nature of mental illness, its causes and treatment, and the development of vastly increased intellectual powers. Hubbard now says he has relinquished the leadership of scientology, and continues his research cruising the world on his ship. Hubbard was involved with the Ordo Templi Orientis, and worked with one of Crowley's (qv) disciples, named Parsons, in 1945, and many of his techniques derive from those influences. Hubbard's books include: *Dianetics: The Modern Science of Mental Health*, *History of Man*, *Creation of Human Ability*, *Axioms and Logic*, *Introduction to Scientology Ethics*. For an inside, and critical view of Hubbard and scientology, see *The Mind Benders* by C. Vosper (1971).

LOUISE HUEBNER

An American witch who achieved widespread publicity as 'The Official Witch of Los Angeles County', a title she was given as part of a publicity campaign in which she cast a spell to increase the sexual vitality of Los Angeles. She claims to possess her witchcraft as an inheritance of six generations of witches. She does radio programmes on the subject, writes a weekly column for numerous newspapers, casts horoscopes and does psychic readings. Mrs Huebner has published a book *Power through Witchcraft*, and has made a long-playing record, *Seduction through Witchcraft*.

J.-K. HUYSMANS

Decadent French novelist J.-K. Huysmans acquired an immediate reputation in Paris for his indulgent *A Rebours*, but he is best known in the occult for his later work *La Bas*, which contains a detailed account of a Black Mass. Huysmans was fascinated by the career of the French satanist Gilles de Rais who prior to his involvement in the black arts had been Marshal of France. De Rais committed some hideous crimes under satanic influence and much of Huysmans' novel is built around these events. Dr Johannes, another figure in *La Bas*, was based on Abbe Boullan, an unorthodox exorcist of evil spirits, who was at one time accused of child sacrifice. Huysmans came to know Boullan during a magical feud between the Abbé and Stanislas de Guaita. Consequently his writing is highly authentic in its description of the occult developments of the period.

ALLEN KARDEK (1804–69)

The pseudonym of Hyppolyte Leon Denizard Rivail, a French spiritualist and physician, who has had great influence on the spiritualist movement (generally known as 'spiritism') in South America, where his books are used as textbooks for mediumistic and healing work. In Europe they have generally been ignored. Rivail chose the name 'Kardek' after being informed by a spirit messenger that in a previous incarnation he had been a Druid of that name. His books are: *The Book of Mediums*, *The Book of the Spirits* and *The Gospels According to Spiritism*. An account of his teachings and his influence on modern spiritism is given in *Drum and Candle* by D. St Clair (1971).

KARL KELLNER

While travelling through India and the Middle East in 1896 Karl Kellner, a German business man, claimed to come into contact with three adepts, two of whom were Arabs and the other a Hindu. It was on the basis of the sexual-yogic techniques that he learnt from them, that he decided to establish an occult society. Kellner believed that the Knights Templar had been the guardians of secret sexual rights, and so he named his new society, the Order of the Oriental Templars, now known as the OTO. Later members of the OTO included Aleister Crowley and Kenneth Grant.

FRANCIS KING

In recent years Francis King has taken over A. E. Waite's role of fifty years ago, namely to document the growth and development of the occult traditions in modern society. Whereas Waite dealt mostly with the Qabalistic, Rosicrucian and Masonic influences leading up to the Golden Dawn, King has specialized in the more contemporary groups like the OTO, the Order of the Cubical Stone and the Stella Matutina. His books include *Ritual Magic in England*, *Crowley on Christ* and *The Secret Rituals of the O.T.O.*

SEMYON DAVIDOVICH KIRLIAN

A Russian electrical technician who has developed the techniques now known as 'Kirlian photography' for photographing aura and energy fields, which are now being investigated at some of the Soviet Union's most advanced research centres. Kirlian is assisted by his wife, Valentina. Their researches confirm much of the traditional teaching of occultism concerning the aura. Cf. *Psychic Discoveries Behind the Iron Curtain* by S. Ostrander and L. Schroder (1973).

GARETH KNIGHT

The pseudonym of an English author and magician, whose works include *A Practical Guide to Qabalistic Symbolism* (2 volumes), *Occult Exercises and Practices* and *The Practice of Ritual Magic*. He was previously associated with W. E. Butler (qv) who was responsible for operating a correspondence course on the practical Qabalah, administered by the Helios Book Service in England. He now operates a course of his own, entitled 'The Gareth Knight Course on Christian Qabalistic Magic'. Like Butler, he received his own training in the Fraternity of the Inner Light Operated by Dion Fortune (qv).

JIDDU KRISHNAMURTI (1895–)

An Indian mystic, philosopher and author, who first came into prominence when he was claimed to be the vehicle for the manifestation of a World Teacher by a number of Theosophists, including Annie Besant (qv) and Charles Leadbeater (qv). Dr Besant gained guardianship of the boy and his brother and they were both educated by Leadbeater, Arundale (qv) and herself. Krishnamurti's father launched an unsuccessful legal attempt to regain custody of his son, claiming that, because of alleged homosexual offences, Leadbeater was unfit to have guardianship. An organization, The Order of the Star in the East, was established to prepare for the forthcoming manifestation of the Christ in Krishnamurti. However, he eventually renounced such claims in 1929, and the Order was disbanded. The Theosophists lost thousands of members as a result of the failure of the manifestation to occur. Krishnamurti established himself as a philosopher and author in his own right, and has spent the rest of his career touring the world lecturing. He has published numerous books, and the texts of most of his addresses have been published verbatim. A Krishnamurti Foundation exists to administer his work. His books include: *Commentaries on Living*, *The First and Last Freedom*, *The Impossible Question*, *You are the World* and *The Urgency of Change*.

ANTON SZANDOR LA VEY

The founder and leader of the Church of Satan in the United States, which now has some 9,000 members throughout the world. After a varied career, which included playing in an orchestra, working with a circus, assisting in hypnotism shows and being a police photographer, La Vey began holding an occult study group, which included Kenneth Anger (qv), the underground film-maker, amongst its members, and eventually began the Church of Satan in 1966. In addition to writing for the press, La Vey has been a technical adviser on several occult films, including *Rosemary's Baby* and *The Mephisto Waltz*, and appeared on screen as the Devil, whose child Rosemary eventually bore. The Church of Satan being incorporated in California as a religion, carries out regular services of worship, in addition to marriages, funerals and a form of baptism. La Vey is the author of *The Satanic Bible* and the *Satanic Rituals*.

CHARLES WEBSTER LEADBEATER

An English Theosophist and author, who left the Church of England, in which he was a minister, to follow Madam Blavatsky (qv) in her Theosophical work, and eventually became the leading colleague of Annie Besant (qv), and one of the major influences on Krishnamurti (qv). He lectured and wrote extensively on Theosophy, and divided his time largely between Adyar, the TS Headquarters and Sydney, Australia, where he headed a commune of students of Theosophy. He became a Bishop in the Liberal Catholic Church, which he helped to found, and was its second Presiding Bishop. He also attained high rank in the Co-Masonic Order. Leadbeater was the subject of several scandals, and at one stage resigned from the TS for a time as the result of accusations of homosexual activities with young students. Although never formally charged by the police, he was the subject of a police investigation in Australia, and it has been alleged that the accusations were in general true. He appears to have been a paedophile, gaining sexual gratification from the company of young boys. There is no doubt that he possessed considerable psychic gifts, and wrote extensively on the basis of clairvoyant investigations. His numerous books include: *The Masters and the Path, Man Visible and Invisible, The Hidden Side of Things, The Science of the Sacraments.* He also co-authored several books with Annie Besant.

SYBIL LEEK

Probably the best known modern witch in America, Mrs Leek came to the USA from England in 1964, and claims to trace her witchcraft ancestry back to the twelfth century. She claims to have been initiated into the craft in France by her paternal aunt. In the USA Mrs Leek has achieved a widespread notoriety through press, radio and television publicity, has opened a restaurant ('Sybil Leek's Cauldron') and does a regular radio programme on witchcraft. Her books include *Diary of a Witch, The Sybil Leek Book of Fortune Telling* and *Cast Your Own Spell.*

ELIPHAS LEVI (1810–75)

Baptized Alphonse-Louis Constant, Eliphas Lévi was born in Paris, the son of a poor shoemaker. He studied for the seminary but was obliged to leave because of his sexual permissiveness, and his revolutionary political tendencies. Despite his limited abilities as a graphic artist, he contributed some political caricatures and moved for a time in select literary company. His marriage to Noemi Cadiot in 1846 when she was eighteen did not prove successful although it was not nullified for another nine years.

Lévi turned to magical philosophy and produced a succession of works during his literary career, the most important being *Le Dogme et Ritual de la Haute Magie, Histoire de la Magie* and *La Cle des Grandes Mysteres*.

A. E. Waite, the occult authority who translated the first two of these, considered Levi's work to be historically important, but fraught with errors. Aleister Crowley, who produced the English edition of *La Cle des Grandes Mysteres*, however, considered himself to be Lévi's reincarnation and admired him unreservedly.

Lévi's main contribution to modern occultism was his discovery that the twenty-two Major Tarot Trumps correlated exactly with the paths on the Tree of Life. They were thus an important key to magical consciousness.

HOWARD PHILLIPS LOVECRAFT (1890–1917)
An American author of some fifty-three stories and assorted fragments and collaborations, all of which are based upon a bizarre and terrifying occult mythology. They were originally written for the cheap pulp horror magazines of his time, but have subsequently acquired a reputation for their powerful occult quality, and have resulted in Lovecraft becoming something of a cult figure. He developed a mythology centring on 'the dread Cthulu', concentrated evil and powers of darkness struggling to break through and control the world, knowledge of which is contained in a variety of evil books, especially the 'Necronomicon' – an imaginary book created by Lovecraft, but one which, after his invention of it, was spoken of as really existing by some subsequent authors. Lovecraft's life was an unhappy one, and he was plagued by frightening dreams and the presence of his own mythology. Kenneth Grant has drawn an interesting, and significant comparison between Lovecraft's mythology, and the occult teachings of Crowley (qv) in one chapter of his book, *The Magical Revival*. Lovecraft's stories have been collected into a number of volumes, including *The Tomb, At the Mountains of Madness, The Case of Charles Dexter Ward, The Haunter of the Dark, The Lurker at the Threshold* and *The Shuttered Room*. His *Collected Letters* have also been published.

ARTHUR MACHEN (1863–1947)
Regarded as one of the finest Welsh mystical writers of the century, Arthur Machen grew up in Caerleon-On-Usk, a town with a legendary association with King Arthur. He studied to be a surgeon, and then worked for a publisher, George Redway, who was producing some notable books on the occult tradition at that time. Machen was a friend of Oscar Wilde, and W. B. Yeats, with whom he shared a love of Celtic lore and the Grail legends. In 1900 he joined the Order of the Golden Dawn – Yeats was at that time in command. But Machen was never a major figure in the world of ceremonial magic.

Most of his best stories have a hint of pantheistic mystery about them, and are far away from the theatre of ritual. His best books include *The Great God Pan* (1890), *The Hill of Dreams* (1895) and *The Shining Pyramid* (1923).

CHARLES MANSON (1934–   )

Currently serving out a life-sentence for his part in the Sharon Tate murders in August 1969, Charles Manson was a self-proclaimed messiah figure for his cult. He proclaimed himself to be 'both God and Satan', and called his gang 'The Family'. In California at that time occultism was beginning to entrench itself as a major philosophy of the subculture and Manson's commune existed side by side with groups like the Process and the O.T.O. Solar Lodge. These and Manson share one common attribute: the ascendency of a spiritual leader over his followers. Manson came through the works of Aleister Crowley and L. Ron Hubbard with an expectancy that the time of the end of the world was near. He began to look for portents relating to Operation Helter Skelter, and found several on the Beatles' double album. 'Piggies' was a song about police, 'Blackbird' a warning about the negroes. Towards the date of the multiple murders Manson increased his Satanic desire to kill. Another song on the album was called 'Happiness is a warm gun'. Today, in San Quentin Prison, Manson's claim to messianic supremacy seems remote, and the immortality he hoped to gain through Scientology is a sour hope. For detailed studies of the gang and the murder see *The Family* by E. Sanders (1972) and *Five to Die* by Le Blanc and Barnes (1970).

LEO LOUIS MARTELLO

An American witch and author, and Director of Witches International Craft Association (WICA), leader of the Witches Liberation Movement and founder of the Witches Encounter Bureau, Martello is also a hypnotist and graphologist. He writes extensively as a freelance author, contributing to many magazines and newspapers, and has published an extensive range of books of his own. He usually refers to himself as 'Dr' and says he is an ordained minister, and while it is not stated of what denomination, he has been a pastor of the Temple of Spiritual Guidance. Martello's books include: *Weird Ways of Witchcraft*, *It's in the Stars*, *It's in the Cards* and *How to Prevent Psychic Blackmail*.

SAMUEL LIDDELL MACGREGOR MATHERS (1854–1918)

Samuel Mathers was undoubtedly one of the key figures in the realm of ritual magic and ceremonial, although he has not become a popular cult like his rival Aleister Crowley. Nevertheless, he helped to found the Hermetic Order of the Golden Dawn which Crowley later aspired to lead.

In 1887 Dr Wynn Westcott (qv), who was a London coroner and Freemason, as well as a delver into the occult arts, showed some Rosicrucian papers to Mathers. Though written in cipher they could be interpreted, and they turned out to be a series of rituals. Westcott asked Mathers to modify and embellish these so that they could be the basis of a new magical Order. Mathers had a flair for this, and the rituals of the Golden Dawn, and the more esoteric Order of the Red Rose and Cross of Gold, have great poetic beauty.

Soon, however, Mathers claimed to be obtaining his inspiration from exclusive, Secret Chiefs, and he began to wield autocratic authority over his fellow Order members. In particular he demanded financial support while translating key occult texts in Paris. It was here that he located and translated a medieval grimoire, *The Sacred Magic of Abra-melin the Mage*, regarded by some as the most powerful magical document in the entire Western Tradition. Mathers loved ancient mythology and occult lore, and among his other translations are the alchemical book *Splendor Solis* by Solomon Trismosin, and *The Kabbalah Unveiled*. He also wrote a short book on the Tarot.

ANTON MESMER (1734–1815)

Mesmer was at first headed for a career in the Church, but he had a strong inclination for mathematics and philosophy. He entered the School of Medicine at the University of Vienna and obtained his medical degree in 1875. Best known for his theory of natural magnetism, Mesmer believed that a magnetic fluid pervaded the Universe and also could be made to exercise a healing power on the mind and constitution of man. The 'force' could be transmitted to patients by touch. In one experiment, Mesmer established a type of group therapy. Patients sat around a tub of water containing iron filings. They were themselves linked together with ropes, and had access to the tub through metal rods. Mesmer would make gestures, and stroke each patient until one of them was overcome by convulsions. This was alleged to indicate a cure.

Mesmer also experimented with cures for blindness and paralysis, and created considerable controversy among the medical profession in Vienna. Eventually a Commission found that his practices were fraudulent, and Mesmer left his country to experiment elsewhere. Some writers have compared his natural magnetic fluids with the force fields at play in acupuncture and in Kundalini Yoga.

VICTOR NEUBURG (1883–1940)
Victor Neuburg was a poet, author, editor and magician. A literary inspiration to Pamela Hansford Johnson and Dylan Thomas, he was also a follower of Aleister Crowley in the days when the 'Great Beast' practised an obscure form of homosexual sex-magic.

Neuburg accepted Crowley's claim that the perfect symbolic form of man was the heavenly androgyne – a figure containing both sexes – and he took part in the rites of the Argentinum Astrum as Crowley's magical partner. He also went with him to a mountain in Algeria, where Crowley wanted to summon the spirits of the thirty Aethyrs – a series of invocations based on the findings of Dr John Dee and Edward Kelley, the Elizabethan magicians. Choronzon, the demon of Chaos was summoned to appear, and during the events which followed, Crowley became possessed and, for a tense moment, Neuburg was in danger of losing his life.

Neuburg avoided Crowley later in life, and moved away from the occult. Nevertheless, he is better known for his magic than his poetry, and was a key figure in some of ritual magic's more fascinating episodes.

ROSALEEN NORTON (1917–)
Probably Australia's most sensational occult artist, Rosaleen Norton worked as an artist's model, a nightclub assistant and a banana plantation-hand while evolving a curious, demonic form of art. For many years she carried on private research into psychic phenomena, magic and psychology, while maintaining a somewhat misleading public image as Australia's leading witch.

Her pictures bear some resemblance to Austin Spare's trance art and Norman Lindsay's exuberant nudes, but are said to have been inspired by The Qlippoth – the dark forces of the Qabalah. In 1949 she was acquitted of an obscenity charge, but her work continued to find its way into private collections rather than public galleries. A collection of some of her drawings was produced in book form in Sydney in 1952.

NOSTRADAMUS (1503–66)
Nostradamus' real name was Michel de Nostre Dame, and he became Catherine de Medici's favourite astrologer. Conversant with French, Latin and Provençal, he dabbled in magic while maintaining that he was inspired by God alone. His book The Centuries, which has appeared in numerous editions since 1555, when it was first published, purports to include prophecies for the world up to its 'end' in 1999. Some writers have been impressed by the apparent references in The Centuries to the French Revolution, which Nostradamus is said to have predicted some two

hundred years in advance. The main difficulty with Nostradamus is that his prophecies are heavily disguised beneath a veil of symbols in quatrains of poetry whose sequence is unclear.

SAR PELADAN (1858–1918)

Astrologer, magician, art critic and novelist, Joséphin Péladan became a fashionable dandy and aesthete in the Rosicrucian salons of Paris in the 1890s. Péladan took the title 'La Sar Merodack' after the King of Babylon, and he himself sported a full, Assyrian styled beard. He was fascinated by the symbol of the androgyne, and also contrived to establish decadence as a major art form. He produced a cycle of novels entitled *La Decadence Latine*, which he hoped would counter the materialistic tendencies of France in his day. Influenced by de Sade, he was also a good friend and tutor in the magical arts, to Stanislas de Guaita, with whom he revived the Rosicrucian Mysteries in the gaudiest way possible.

PAPUS (1865–1916)

Papus was the nom de plume of Gerard Encausse, a Spanish-born occult writer, who trained originally for medicine. Influenced by Theosophy, he was impressed by the idea that all elements of the universe – mineral, vegetable and animal – evolve towards perfection in a sequence of struggles and sacrifice. He delved into hermetic and alchemical texts and found there a chemistry of the soul. Papus acquired a reputation as a necromancer, and was summoned to the Russian Imperial Palace, where it is said he evoked the ghost of Czar Alexander III into visible appearance.

Papus wrote a large number of books on the occult and, like Eliphas Lévi, was fascinated by the symbolic connections between the Tarot and Qabalah. His best known work is *The Tarot of the Bohemians*.

PARACELSUS (1493–1541)

One of the most illustrious physicians and alchemists who ever sought the *prima materia*, the source of all life and virtue, Paracelsus was born Theophrast Bombast von Hohenheim, in Einsiedeln, Switzerland. He pursued medical studies under his father, who was a physician in Basle, and also delved into alchemy and occultism under the watchful care of Trimethius of Spanheim. Paracelsus travelled widely in Europe, seeking primarily a working basis on which to improve the poor medical standards of his day. While merciless in his criticism of errant chemists and doctors, he had faults himself, including a bad temper and a continuing state of drunkenness. His writings, however, reveal a deep love of Christian mysticism, tinged with the pantheistic spirit common in alchemy.

Paracelsus stressed the parallel between man, the *microcosm*, and the universe, or *macrocosm*, and considered that illness was a symptom of imbalance, nothing more. The three great principles of manifestation were sulphur (male), mercury (female) and salt (neutral), and the healthy man would combine these elements in harmony. For example he attributed the cause of fever to an excess of sulphur. He also believed in the magical creation of artificial creatures – *Homunculi* – a medieval precursor of test-tube babies.

Included in his alchemical and hermetic tracts are discourses on the planets, the elements and metals, and the relationship of alchemy to mysticism. His work marks the transition from alchemy as a crudely con-ceived pre-science for the transmutation of lead into gold, into a spiritual science of man. Paracelsus makes it quite clear that alchemy, the 'true' chemistry, relates to the inner man, and not to the workings of the laboratory.

BISHOP JAMES PIKE (1913–69)

An Episcopalian Bishop in California who was the subject of accusations of heresy and resigned from his office to continue his writing career. He became involved in the occult when, after the death of his son by suicide, he endeavoured to contact him through various mediums, and eventually believed he had done so through the mediumship of Arthur Ford (qv). The Bishop wrote an account of this quest, and its outcome, in *The Other Side*. He eventually died in the desert in Israel while travelling.

HARRY PRICE (1881–1948)

A famous British psychic researcher, and one of the first people to establish the investigation of such phenomena on a scientific basis. From his back-ground in stage conjuring, Price became an expert on detecting fraud, although in later years some of his own investigations came under criticism. He established a massive library of works on the occult, spiritual-ism and psychic phenomena, which eventually became the National Library of Psychical Research. He was the author of *Fifty Years of Psychical Research* (1939), *Poltergeist Over England* (1945) and two studies of the famous Borley Rectory haunting which he investigated, *The Most Haunted House in England* (1940) and *The End of Borley Rectory* (1945).

TUESDAY LOBSANG RAMPA

The pseudonym of Cyril Henry Hoskins, an Englishman and author of numerous books allegedly written by a Tibetan lama of high degree. The books range from *The Third Eye*, a basically factual account of the

WHO'S WHO IN THE OCCULT

childhood and training of a Tibetan lama, through a series of philosophical works claiming to convey the esoteric teachings of Tibetan Buddhism and its occult techniques. Hoskins claims that he is really a genuine lama, occupying the body of an Englishman, and despite several 'exposures', he continues to attract a wide readership, and now runs a business in the United States on the basis of his claims.

PASCAL BEVERLEY RANDOLPH (1825–71)

An American occultist and the founder of numerous occult groups, few of them of any significance. He had been a member of the Societas Rosicruciania in Anglia (a Masonic order), and claimed to have been initiated into a secret Syrian Order. He began his occult involvement as a medium in America, and eventually developed an especial interest in sexual magic, on which he published several books, some of which led to charges in court. He committed suicide in 1871. It is generally believed that he had taught Kellner (qv) the theory and techniques of sexual magic which were later to be expressed in the Ordo Templi Orientis, although his successor, Clymer (qv) denied all knowledge of such teachings. A French magical group continues to carry on Randolph's teachings. His principal works were: *Ravalatte: The Rosicrucians' Story, Dealing with the Dead, Eulis: The History of Love.*

ISRAEL REGARDIE (1907–)

Israel Regardie was born in England, but has lived most of his life in America where he practises as a Reichian psychotherapist. He is best known however as one of the major occult writers on magic, mythology and the rituals of the Golden Dawn. In 1928 he became Aleister Crowley's personal secretary, and in 1937 he published the first of four volumes providing full details of the magical rituals of the Golden Dawn and Stella Matutina occult societies. Many occultists felt that Regardie had broken an oath of secrecy but it is undoubtedly true that the collected 4-volumes of *The Golden Dawn* are a major source work, and are of great value.

Regardie's best writing is probably that contained in *The Tree of Life*, which includes details of the mythology underlying modern magic, with special emphasis on Egyptian gods and the Hindu *tattvas* (elements) which are used for meditation.

Among Regardie's other key books are *The Middle Pillar*, which relates magic to Kundalini Yoga, *The Philosopher's Stone*, a study of alchemy and psychology, with a commentary on the *Coelum Terrae* of Thomas Vaughan, and *Roll Away The Stone*, which relates drugs to magic.

As one of the last of a line of genuine occultists, Regardie has become much sought after by the new-consciousness converts to the counter culture. He is one of the greatest living authorities on the Qabalah and ceremonial magic.

THEODOR REUSS (d. 1924)
Reuss succeeded Karl Kellner as head of the tantric magic group the *Ordo Templi Orientis* in 1905. It was he who invited Aleister Crowley to join their organization – accelerating The Great Beast's direction away from ceremonial ritual into the shady areas of sexual magic. Crowley in fact set up his own variant on the OTO in England, calling it the *Mysteria Mystica Maxima*. Eventually, after a stroke, Reuss resigned from his post as head of the OTO in 1922 and handed over to Crowley, who endeavoured to incorporate his own brand of occult lore. The OTO was suppressed by the Nazis in 1947 although key Lodges still operate in England and California.

JOSEPH B. RHINE (1895–)
Dr Rhine and his wife Louisa have dominated the scientific research programmes into ESP for the last forty years. Rhine contacted William McDougall, professor of psychology at Harvard, after hearing a lecture on psychical research by Sir Arthur Conan Doyle. Both Rhine and McDougall later moved to Duke University, which has since become synonymous with research into telepathy, clairvoyance and psychokinesis. Rhine endeavoured in the 1930s to give ESP scientific respectability by producing laboratory reports of subjects who appeared to show ESP ability far greater than chance. Rhine worked in collaboration with the well-known psychologists K. E. Zener (famous for his 'Zener cards') and Dr J. G. Pratt, and produced evidence which he now regards as conclusive of an ESP function in man. Rhine's approach has been mostly statistical and his laboratory safeguards against fraudulence and error have been criticized by writers like Professor C. E. M. Hansel.

While it is true that Rhine paved the way for serious academic study into ESP, it is probably also true to say that the more exciting breakthroughs have occurred since his heyday, especially with regard to the modern research into dream telepathy (Montague Ullman *et al.*) which eliminates laboratory error altogether.

MOUNI SADHU
An occultist and author who, although deriving much of his background from French occult schools, was a follower of the Indian teacher, Sri Ramana Maharishi. He conducted an occult group in Melbourne, Australia, where he spent much of his life, but was in contact with similar

groups throughout the world. His books include: *The Tarot* (1962), *Concentration* (1959), *Theurgy* (1965), *Ways of Self-Realization* (1962), *In Days of Great Peace*, and *Samadhi*.

COMTE DE SAINT-GERMAIN (1710–80)

Popularly known as an aristocratic Freemason and Rosicrucian 'who did not die', the Comte was said to be the son of Prince Rakoczy of Transylvania. He grew up under the care of the last of the Medici, Gian Gastone, and was educated at the University of Siena. The Comte seems to have had a desire to masquerade under grandiose titles and during his mysterious and elusive career passed under the names of Comte Bellamarre, the Marquis de Montferrat and Chevalier Schoening among others. A welcome visitor in many European Courts, the Comte was said to have spoken Italian, German, English, Spanish, French, Greek, Sanskrit, Arabic and Chinese. Madame de Pompadour writes that he 'had travelled the whole world over and the king lent a willing ear to the narratives of his voyages over Asia and Africa, and to his tales about the courts of Russia, Turkey and Austria.'

The Comte enticed his audience with his extravagant claims, including the tale that he had received the magical wand of Moses from King Cyrus in Babylon, thus intimating that he was one of the ageless *illuminati*. But he was also a political envoy of great reputation, and held discourses with figures as diverse as the Shah of Persia, Horace Walpole, Clive of India and Frederick the Great.

It is said that Saint-Germain acquired his wealth and immortality from his discovery of the *Philosopher's Stone*, and that he demonstrated his alchemical prowess to The Marquis de Valbelle by transforming a silver coin into gold.

Whatever the source of his knowledge and opulence, there is no doubt that Saint-Germain produced one of the most remarkable occult manuscripts ever in his *Most Holy Trinosophia*, a collection of alchemical/mystical visions. This work has recently been reissued by Manly Palmer Hall in the United States and constitutes a complete framework for initiation.

ALEX SANDERS

A contemporary English witch and leader of a worldwide movement in witchcraft, Sanders has received considerable publicity, in the press, on radio and television, especially for his claim that he is the 'king of the witches'. He has been the subject of several full length books and one film. Sanders claims he comes from a family in which witchcraft has been traditional for generations, and that he was initiated at the age of seven when he accidentally stumbled onto his grandmother performing rituals in her living room. Sanders says his grandmother trained him for several years before her death, and that after this he turned to black magic, through which he acquired a considerable fortune. He turned away from the 'left hand path' after the death of his sister and thereafter established himself as a teacher of witchcraft, heading a number of covens throughout England. He married (according to the rituals of witchcraft) his present wife, Maxine, who assists him as his High Priestess. Sanders lives in London and conducts courses, both personally and by correspondence. He lays claim to a variety of titles and degrees. Cf. *King of the Witches* by June Johns, and also *What Witches Do* by Stewart Farrar, a study of the 'Alexandrian' school of witchcraft.

KURT SELIGMANN (1901–62)
An evocative artist, and interested also in heraldic and esoteric symbolism, Kurt Seligmann was a key member of the Surrealist movement between 1934 and 1944. Like Wolfgang Paalen, André Breton and Max Ernst, he was absorbed by the relationship of magic to surrealist/dream conscious-ness, and published an important book *The Mirror of Magic* in 1956. It has recently been republished by Allen Lane, London.

AUSTIN SPARE (1888–1956)
One of the most extraordinary artist/occultists who ever lived, Austin Osman Spare was hailed as a prodigy and won a scholarship to the Royal College of Art when he was only sixteen. Soon he came into contact with magic, Egyptian mythology and the teachings of Aleister Crowley, and he began to incorporate his mystical philosophy into his art. Spare believed in reincarnation, and claimed that all of his former lives, whether as a human or animal, were deeply embedded in the subconscious. The mystical purpose of man was to retrace those existences back to their source, which he called Kia. Spare considered that this could be done in a state of trance, whereby one allowed oneself to be possessed by the atavisms of former lives. Spare developed an interesting system of magical 'sigils', which were symbols of meditation used for unleashing the potencies of the subconscious mind. He employed various techniques for supplement-ing this method of mind-focusing, including the so-called 'death posture' (or trance) and the sexual orgasm. He became fascinated by witchcraft, and his paintings took on an increasingly menacing air.

Spare was undoubtedly one of England's finest illustrators, and some of his best work is contained in his *Book of Pleasure*, conceived when the artist was only twenty-two. This book has been republished in Canada alongside a definitive study of Spare by his friend Kenneth Grant. Other details of the artist's work are contained in *The Search for Abraxas* by Nevill Drury and Stephen Skinner (1972).

LEWIS SPENCE

An English scholar of the occult and author of a number of books on various of its aspects, including *The History of Atlantis, An Encyclopedia of Occultism, Myths of Mexico and Peru, The Problem of Atlantis, Atlantis in America* and *Will Europe Follow Atlantis?*

RUDOLPH STEINER (1861–1925)

The German occultist, Theosophist and scholar who founded the Anthroposophical Society after breaking away from the Theosophical Society, largely over the issue of Krishnamurti (qv). Steiner acquired his Ph.D. for work on the German author Goethe, on whom he became an authority. Throughout his life he remained a scholar, as the rather academic tone of his writings attests. Steiner was a clairvoyant who built up a complex philosophy and cosmology on the basis of his clairvoyant investigations, developing theories about subjects as diverse as farming and organic gardening, Atlantis and Lemuria, the treatment of syphilis and cancer and the inner truths of Christianity. The Anthroposophical Society eventually spread throughout the world and eventually developed a sub-group known as the Christian Community, in which members, who sought a specifically Christian tradition could worship. Steiner's theories on education led to the development of 'Steiner schools' throughout the world, where particular success has been achieved in the education of retarded children.

Steiner was also connected with several other occult movements, including the Ordo Templi Orientis, Engel's 'Order of the Illuminati' and a group of Rosicrucians. An incredibly prolific author and lecturer (many of his books are lecture notes), he published an astonishing amount of literature, including *Occult Science ; an outline, Christianity as Mystical Fact, Knowledge of the Higher Worlds and its attainment.* His autobiography is titled *The Course of my Life.* Cf. *A Scientist of the Invisible* by A. Shepherd and *The Life and Work of Rudolf Steiner* by G. Wachsmuth.

MONTAGUE SUMMERS (1880–1948)

An English author of numerous books on satanism, demonology, witchcraft and black magic, the value of which is a matter of dispute. He also translated a number of the 'classics' in the field, including the *Malleus Maleficarum*. He was a believer, almost to the point of fanaticism, in the reality of the powers of evil, and openly advocated the reintroduction of the death penalty for witchcraft. He was also an authority on the history of theatre. His books include: *The History of Witchcraft and Demonology*, *The Physical Phenomenon of Mysticism*, *The Vampire in Europe*, *The Werewolf*, *The Geography of Witchcraft*. Summers was generally known as 'The Reverend' or even 'Father' and usually dressed in elaborate clerical attire, although precisely what Holy Orders he possessed, or from where, remains a matter of conjecture. He also had an elaborately furnished chapel in his home, although the nature of ceremonies held there has been the subject of some speculation – not all of it charitable. He was an acquaintance of Aleister Crowley (qv) and various other eccentrics in the occult world of the time.

JOHN SYMONDS

John Symonds is best known for his illuminating study of Aleister Crowley, *The Great Beast*, and his edited productions of several other books by the Master Therion, 666, as Crowley called himself. These include *The Confessions of Aleister Crowley*, *Moonchild*, *White Stains* and *The Magical Record of the Beast*. Symonds is also an author of note, and besides his novels, has written a lucid account of the life of Madame Blavatsky, *In the Astral Light*, and a work on the Shaker communes of America.

CHARLES TART (1937–   )

Professor Tart has become well-known for his scientific research into trance, dreams, out-of-the-body experiences and ESP. At present he is continuing laboratory tests on the astral-projection state, with subjects like Ingo Swann and Robert Monroe, who claim to be able to produce it at will. Tart is a researcher in Experimental Psychology at UCLA, Davis, and is one of a new line of scientists (which also includes Claudio Naranjo Paul Ornstein and John Lilly) who are endeavouring to close the gulf between science and mysticism. Professor Tart's key work is his *Altered States of Consciousness* (1969).

PAUL TWITCHELL

The American founder of the 'Eckankar' movements, which he led until his death. Twitchell claimed to have been taught the techniques of Eckankar by various masters, including the Tibetan 'Rebazar Tarzs', and to teach the techniques of out-of-the-body travelling. His books give details of his own astral travelling, and his disciples frequently reported seeing him while his physical body was elsewhere. Twitchell's biography, *In My Soul I am Free*, was written by Brad Steiger (1968). Twitchell's own books include *The Far Country* and *Introduction to Eckankar*.

ARTHUR EDWARD WAITE (1857–c.1940)

Towards the end of its day, the Golden Dawn magical society was headed by the learned Christian occult scholar, A. E. Waite. A reactionary against Theosophy, he detested the anti-Christian aspects of ritual magic and rewrote the ceremonial grades of the Order. His own view was that occult science could possibly provide an esoteric, mystery teaching which the orthodox Christian church had either forgotten or had never possessed.

Waite could not read Hebrew but he produced three notable volumes on the Jewish Qabalah at a time when Jewish scholars themselves were neglecting this aspect of their tradition. The best of these was *The Holy Kabbalah*, which has since been republished. He wrote on nearly every aspect of the occult, and produced, with Pamela Coleman-Smith, a famous Tarot pack, now known as the 'Waite' or 'Rider' pack. His other works include *The Occult Sciences*, *The Brotherhood of the Rosy Cross*, *The Mysteries of Magic* (a digest of Eliphas Lévi's teachings) and a fine mystical tract called *Azoth*. Waite also edited numerous alchemical and masonic works including the hermetic writings of Paracelsus. He was, however, surprisingly ignored by Carl Jung, whose researches into the visionary areas of the mind in many ways paralleled Waite's own endeavours.

Waite was undoubtedly a scholar of genius but he took so much care to obliterate lesser writers when in error, that his own works tend to be long and heavy. Aleister Crowley referred to him scornfully as 'Dead-Waite'. These criticisms notwithstanding, Waite was the finest occult historian of his day, and many of his books are still standard references.

WYNN WESTCOTT (1848–1925)

Dr Westcott was a leading Freemason and coroner in London when a Rosicrucian manuscript in cipher came into his possession. MacGregor Mathers used the Rosicrucian rituals to form the basis of the Golden Dawn. After this, Westcott gradually lost significance in the Order, which he had hoped would rival the esoteric section of the Theosophical Society in London. Westcott installed himself as a spiritual master of the Order but his influence was only slight. He contributed a small volume on Qabalistic symbolism and edited an occult series for the Theosophical Publishing House in the 1890s.

DENNIS WHEATLEY

An English author who has written both novels with occult plots and also non-fiction books on magic and the occult. His books include *The Devil and all his Works* (a study of magic and the occult), *The Devil Rides Out*, *The Gates of Hell*, *To the Devil – a Daughter*, *They Used Dark Powers* and *The Haunting of Toby Jugg*. Wheatley emphasizes in his introduction to most of his books that he has never taken part in any black magic or occult ceremonies, although he has investigated the subject extensively, and has been acquainted with many leading individuals in the occult world.

COLIN WILSON (1931–)

When *The Outsider* was first published in 1956, it attracted widespread acclaim in literary circles as a treatment of the existential 'loneliness' of visionaries, artists and creators. Wilson's view that such people have access to varying levels of inspiration and consciousness led him to compare two broad types of people: *murderers and criminals*, who have a type of negative intensity, and *mystics*, who could integrate these powerful, and sometimes transcendental, energies. Wilson's book *The Occult* was well received as an encyclopaedic treatment of the influences underlying modern magic: alchemists, magicians, adepts and imposters, freemasons and witches – all were included. Wilson also advanced the view that man has an innate 'magical capacity' which he called *Faculty X*. He argued that primitive man respected and applied this natural ability but that civilized man gradually repressed and lost it. Only now is he becoming aware of it again, as science probes the mysteries of ESP, and the occult emerges popularly as an 'alternative' to science, technology and orthodox religion. Wilson believes that man needs to rediscover Faculty X as part of the next phase of his evolution. His other books, on an occult theme, include the novels *The Philosopher's Stone*, *The Mind Parasites* and *The God of the Labyrinth*. He followed *The Occult* with *Strange Powers*, a volume which discussed the findings of Arthur Guirdham and other modern mystics.

W. B. YEATS (1865–1939)

As a disciple and follower of the Celtic mystery tradition, Yeats naturally gravitated towards the occult, and founded a small group in Dublin called the Hermetic Students. A friend of 'A.E.' the Irish mystic, Arthur Machen and MacGregor Mathers, he joined the Golden Dawn, and eventually became its leader at the turn of the century, after Mathers retired to Paris to translate occult manuscripts. Aleister Crowley, who was jealous of Yeats's poetic gifts, attempted to unseat Yeats as head of the

Order, and visited him at midnight with a cloak and dagger, after being granted assurances by Mathers. Yeats became disillusioned with the Golden Dawn and left it, but magic continued to exercise an important influence on his poetry, and he often incorporated Tarot imagery from his visions into his verse.

C. C. ZAIN

The pseudonym of Elbert Benjamin, the founder of the First Temple of Astrology in America. This eventually became the Church of Light, which conducts services and offers courses in a variety of occult subjects. Zain claims he was contacted by 'The Brotherhood of Light' in 1909, and became a member of that secret society, and was told to prepare a complete occult system for teaching the religion of astrology. This he did in a series of twenty-one volumes of lessons, which are still being sold throughout the world.

Index

For Product Safety Concerns and Information please contact our EU
representative GPSR@taylorandfrancis.com
Taylor & Francis Verlag GmbH, Kaufingerstraße 24, 80331 München, Germany

www.ingramcontent.com/pod-product-compliance
Lightning Source LLC
Chambersburg PA
CBHW070402270326
41926CB00014B/2659